This book is a gift to

My Wife, Jan

Message

From

Mark

Date

25th December 2009

Musk

Intimate Moments with GOD

366 Devotions

Strength for each day of the year

Solly Ozrovech

CHRISTIAN ART PUBLISHERS

Originally published by Christelike Uitgewersmaatskappy
under the title *Uit die Skatkamer van God*

© 1990

English edition © 1993
Published by Christian Art Publishers
PO Box 1599, Vereeniging, 1930, RSA

First edition 1993
Second edition 1999
Third edition 2005

Cover designed by Christian Art Publishers

Translated by Suné Kannemeyer

Scripture quotations are taken from the *Holy Bible*, New International Version® NIV®
Copyright © 1973, 1978, 1984 by International Bible Society.
Used by permission of Zondervan Publishing House. All rights reserved.

Set in 11 on 13pt Palatino by Christian Art Publishers

Printed in China

ISBN 978-1-86920-566-9

© All rights reserved. No part of this book may be reproduced in
any form without permission in writing from the publisher, except
in the case of brief quotations in critical articles or reviews.

09 10 11 12 13 14 15 16 17 18 – 12 11 10 9 8 7 6 5 4 3

My soul finds rest in God alone; my salvation
comes from Him. He alone is my rock and my salvation;
He is my fortress, I will never be shaken.

– PSALM 62:1-2 –

JANUARY

January 1

Read: Revelation 1:7-20

The important first step

"I am the Alpha and the Omega," says the Lord God, "who is, and who was, and who is to come, the Almighty." "Do not be afraid. I am the First and the Last. I am the Living One."

– REVELATION 1:8, 17-18 –

This verse offers great comfort and hope to all God's children as we enter a new year with new challenges. It is not the language of overconfident and impulsive youth; neither is it the self-conceit of megalomania: it is a joyous confession of faith in an eternal and almighty God who holds the destiny of every person in His loving hand.

We can hold God's hand as we enter the year, live through it to His honor and glory, and still holding His hand, we can end the year joyously … because He is the Alpha and the Omega, the first and the last!

God first! This is our salvation. There are many things in which man can place his trust to cope with the challenges of the new road: wealth; possessions; honor and prestige; achievement and expertise. However, if God is not at the center of it all, everything is in vain.

With God in the center in our personal and spiritual lives, in our family lives, in our community lives and in our national lives, the future holds rich blessings and also the promise of God's much needed assistance.

The new year, with its difficult challenges and dark secrets, cannot break us. With God, who is omniscient and eternal, we have the courage to go the distance.

That is why we can walk out into the darkness courageously today because we know for certain: "The Lord is my light and my salvation – whom shall I fear? The Lord is the stronghold of my life – of whom shall I be afraid?" (Ps. 27:1).

Eternal and unchangeable God, I trust You unconditionally and faithfully. In Your almighty name I take the first uncertain step with the knowledge that You are the Conqueror. Amen.

Read: 2 Corinthians 5:11-21　　　　　　　　January 2

The art of starting again

Therefore, if anyone is in Christ, he is a new creation; the old has gone, the new has come!

— 2 CORINTHIANS 5:17 —

We often end the year on a spiritual mountain top. Then a brand-new year dawns and we unearth all our old New Year resolutions. For a short while we are determined to be "better" people. Unfortunately, these high ideals disappear quickly and before January has passed, we are back in the old, soul-destroying and monotonous ruts from which we would very much like to be saved.

For many people, to fluctuate from the spiritual heights to the depths of despair is so common that it causes a soul-destroying depression. Then people start to wonder whether it's worth it to even try.

Do not trust in yourself and your own observations when you look to the future. Do not rely on your own strength to become a better person. The future is vast and unknown and if the road becomes too difficult, you will be overwhelmed by your own insignificance and inability. Despondently you will fall back on old habits and thought patterns. Good intentions then die a bitter death. Habits are more powerful than intentions, however good the intentions may be.

The secret to a victorious life is not to make long-term promises to yourself or to the Master. You need His living presence every single moment: He does not make a better person out of you, He changes you into a new person! Therefore, look to Jesus in prayer every day and say, "Master, this is Your day and I want to spend it as You want me to." Then you will be at the Source of Power that renews and you will learn the fine art of starting anew.

Victory will follow on victory, from day to God-given day!

Redeemer and Master, I again confirm my love for You and my dependency on You, so that I can meaningfully start again on the path of growth and victory. Amen.

January 3

Read: Psalm 25:1-22

When mirages become real

Show me your ways, O LORD, teach me your paths.
— PSALM 25:4 —

It is so easy to get lost on your way to a new place. Your greatest need in such a time is a road map or a trusted friend who can give you directions.

Sometimes you find yourself on the wrong path in life. Or you have to make an important decision but you are unable to do so because your judgment has become clouded. Possibly there are forces and opinions outside yourself that carry a lot of weight and affect your judgment.

Isaiah has a comforting word for exactly such a situation, "Whether you turn to the right or to the left, your ears will hear a voice behind you, saying, 'This is the way; walk in it'" (Is. 30:21). The Christian who constantly follows the path that God shows him will become sensitive to the voice of God through the Holy Spirit.

Subject every decision you have to make this year to the approval of God. Wait on Him in silence and in prayer. He will guide you. When you then go out to face life in faith, you will know that you are not doing it alone, because the living Christ is ready to guide and lead you on the right path.

A personal relationship with Christ is a primary condition for this. It is your road map. It has to apply to all fields of life. Teach yourself to be aware of the Savior's continuous presence in your life. Then the danger of mistaking mirages for something real will disappear. Then you will be walking in the Light of the world on the path of life!

Redeemer and Guide, fill my life to such a degree that I will clearly understand Your will for my life, and that I will walk Your path in obedience. Amen.

Read: Hebrews 11:1-10   January 4

Faith in the invisible

Now faith is being sure of what we hope for and certain of what we do not see.

— HEBREWS 11:1–

To many people, faith is a mystic and almost supernatural phenomenon which seems far removed from the hard and practical realities of everyday life. Although they wish to have more faith, they are deeply conscious of their ignorance about what faith really is. "If I could just have faith," they sigh.

Others are continually pleading with God for more faith, but in spite of their efforts, their faith is still ineffective.

What we must realize is that faith is an integral part of human nature. Most people use their faith negatively and therefore incorrectly. People believe in their inability to attain a high goal; they believe the endless fears that obstruct their view; they believe in failure rather than success. It is not a question of receiving more faith, but of putting the faith we already have to positive use.

When Christ says, "You must have faith in God!" He is commanding His followers to live in a constructive and positive way. Anyone can believe in "someone" or "something" but without faith in the victorious Christ, no one can be saved.

Faith is necessary in our spiritual lives. Without it, it is impossible to live in true fellowship with God. Faith is complete, unconditional trust in God.

The glorious result of Christian faith is the definite certainty of God's living presence. When faith gives you the certainty that God loves you, all other things in your life fall into place.

I thank You, Spirit of God, for making me sure of my faith. Let me see the invisible every day, to the glory of God the Father. Amen.

January 5

Read: Joshua 1:1-9

Conquer your fear

"Have I not commanded you? Be strong and courageous. Do not be terrified; do not be discouraged, for the LORD your God will be with you wherever you go."

— JOSHUA 1:9 —

Just like Joshua, we are at the beginning of a new, unknown road, filled with hesitation and anxious fears. The unknown, linked to our insignificance and incompetence, robs us of our self-confidence.

Many great plans have miscarried or were not fulfilled because the people concerned lacked courage to tackle them with conviction. Or, once they had started, they did not persevere.

This attitude is equally true of our spiritual and secular lives. Even your work for the Lord becomes handicapped by paralyzing fear. One of the ground rules of life is that you won't attain anything of permanent value, or make any task worth your while unless you tackle it in His strength and carry it out to His honor and glorification. You may experience a degree of enjoyment, but permanent satisfaction and the certainty of the inherent value of your achievements depend on God's place in your plans.

Very few things of worth are obtained easily and without effort. You will always encounter stumbling blocks, temptations and problems that could compel you to give up your plans. You will always be confronted with compromises, which if accepted could lead to a lowering of your standards.

In such cases it is important to realize and accept that you should always make Jesus Christ a partner in your dreams, plans and ideals. Let Him prescribe the standards according to which you are supposed to act.

In the knowledge that you are experiencing His loving guidance and approval, fear will not paralyze you and success will not evade you.

Guide and Perfecter of my faith, my eyes remain fixed on You, convinced that fear cannot overwhelm me. Amen.

Read: Revelation 21:1-8 January 6

Failure need not be permanent

He who was seated on the throne said, "I am making everything new!"

– REVELATION 21:5 –

Failure in any respect whatsoever, is a very depressing experience. Ideals are shattered, hope dies and dreams turn into nightmares. At the same time your self-image receives a blow and it appears as if nothing worthwhile remains. A nagging feeling of guilt about your own inability is all you have left.

It is of the utmost importance not to overreact in times of failure. You probably feel as though your world has collapsed like a house of cards. The future appears dark and bleak. Then self-pity becomes a very real danger. You easily start blaming other people or circumstances.

It is much more rewarding to do some honest soul-searching. Evaluate your own life with sincerity, objectivity and honesty. Confront the truths that caused your failures and deal with them decisively.

One thing is essential: you must realize that, however big your failure, you should never regard it as final. It may be necessary to admit that you have made a mistake and to confess because you may need forgiveness. You possibly need a new outlook and renewed determination. However, remember that whatever your need may be at the moment, you only remain a failure as long as you accept yourself as such.

We have all experienced failure at one time or another. You are not a unique exception at all. If you are a disciple of Christ, you have His unparalleled power for renewal at your disposal. He makes everything new!

Risen Lord and Savior, with You in my life, I can triumph over every failure and disappointment. Make me into a new person every day. Amen.

January 7

Read: Romans 12:1-8

Positive thinking ... plus!

Do not conform any longer to the pattern of this world, but be transformed by the renewing of your mind. Then you will be able to test and approve what God's will is – his good, pleasing and perfect will.

– ROMANS 12:2 –

Many people are able to lead fuller and richer lives through the practice of positive thinking. There are more positive thinkers in this decade than at any other time in the history of mankind. Many people utilize this practice to achieve their highest objectives.

While we acknowledge the importance of positive thinking, we should also remember that one does not necessarily have to be a Christian to think positively. There are many unbelievers, agnostics and even atheists who use this form of thinking successfully.

The doctrine of our Master, Jesus Christ, incorporates positive thinking, but goes even further and touches the hidden possibilities of the soul. When we are confronted with the reality of a situation, positive thinking can assist us up to a point, but the living Christ enables us to achieve so much more.

Positive thinking by itself won't help you. You should be able to move past pure thought and show steadfast and unshakable trust in the working of Christ in your life. All things are possible through Him.

Through the power of the Holy Spirit we are able to conquer those forces that could weaken us intellectually and spiritually. Positive thinking, together with unshakable trust in the almighty Christ, is a creative force which enables you to live as God intended: victoriously and abundantly.

Do not tackle life without the power of the Holy Spirit. He is available to you, if you only just ask Him. He will bring sparkle and joy back into your life so you can live abundantly.

Holy Spirit of God, fill my thoughts with the courage of faith so that I will know what is good, acceptable and perfect to You. Amen.

Read: Ephesians 4:17-24

January 8

The good old days

You were taught, with regard to your former way of life, to put off your old self, which is being corrupted by its deceitful desires; to be made new in the attitude of your minds; and to put on the new self, created to be like God in true righteousness and holiness.

— EPHESIANS 4:22-24 —

Man is marching forward on the path of progress in a time when knowledge is on the increase. Yet millions of people all over the world nostalgically long for the past.

You often hear remarks such as: "In my day ..." or "Life was much better then". Everyone joins in and reminisces about "the good old days". This is a very natural human inclination. We have difficulty in accepting change because we become comfortable with the existing state of affairs.

However, we should accept that change is taking place all the time and that it is often irreversible. Whether we accept the computer age or not; whether we accept new songs in the place of old hymns – the facts of change are real and we will have to learn to live with them.

The important thing is how we approach change. If we refuse to change, there is little doubt that we will become lonely, unhappy and even embittered people. If we approach change more openly, if we investigate and weigh up the advantages and disadvantages, we may perhaps discover many good things in the new methods and ways.

Even if we do not agree, the tolerance and goodwill we receive from a daily walk with Jesus Christ will enable us to understand change in a mature and sympathetic way. Our own spiritual growth is in fact nothing but continuous change and renewal. Then we live with the best from the "good old days" as well as the best from the time of rapid change we live in.

Loving Father, when I see everything changing around me, help me to accept it with wisdom and maturity. Keep me from stubborn stagnation through the renewing power of Your Holy Spirit. Amen.

January 9

Read: Isaiah 43:14-21

Inner healing

Forget the former things: do not dwell on the past. See, I am doing a new thing!

— Isaiah 43:18-19 —

We cannot begin a new year with emotional wounds. They need attention and healing. Tender fingers are needed to touch those raw wounds. Only Christ can do that.

Every one of us has things we would rather forget. It may be a thoughtless mistake we made in the distant past. But the memory of it appears over and over at the most inconvenient moments to torture and humiliate us. To many it brings fear of discovery, and this robs the present of its beauty and drives promise and peace from our lives.

The memory of sins from the past can cause great dismay and pain. When these appear, you should not try to suppress them or wish them away. Bring them to God in repentance and in confession. His wisdom and forgiveness will erase them completely.

If you have harmed anyone and it is still possible to reconcile with that person, do so without hesitation. Remedy, as far as it is humanly possible, all the wrong things you have done. Then you can claim the forgiveness through the reconciliation brought about by Christ. Experiencing His forgiveness is one of the most enriching experiences of life.

Are you being tortured by memories of disappointments or failures from the past; unfriendly or inconsiderate words you have said; insults and reproaches you have foolishly uttered? They have just as much power over your life as you allow them to have. As long as you aimlessly brood over them, they keep you in their iron grip and they cause unnecessary dismay in your life.

The healing power of confession and repentance can ban these memories from your life. For this you have to trust and obey Christ completely. He is the Great Healer!

I thank You, merciful God and Father, that You also cure the painful memories in my innermost being and give me peace in Jesus Christ, my Lord and Master. Amen.

Read: 1 Peter 2:1-12

January 10

Feelings of guilt

Like newborn babies, crave pure spiritual milk, so that by it you may grow up in your salvation.

– 1 PETER 2:2 –

In refurbishing our spiritual house for the new year, a clean-up beforehand is essential. Many Christians have a fundamental guilt complex. They blame themselves because their commitment to the Master is half-hearted; their prayer life is insufficient; their study of God's Word is fragmentary and their practice of fellowship with believers is changeable and ineffective.

Often this feeling of guilt can be ascribed to a spiritual laziness or indifference. This in turn causes the depressing feeling of spiritual inadequacy. Another reason for feelings of guilt among Christians is the fact that they have stopped growing spiritually. When Christ's love shone on their lives for the first time; when His presence enriched and inspired their thoughts and deeds, they were filled with joy and a quiet determination to learn even more about their newly found Lord.

For a certain time their love for Christ was their most precious possession. But slowly the practice of their belief and faith became mere routine and other things started claiming their interest and loyalty. Although they still respect and admire Jesus, they lack the fervor which they once had in their love for Him.

Without growth, the most beautiful spiritual experiences die. When you accepted Jesus Christ as Lord and Redeemer, He occupied the center of your life. If you have relegated Him to second place, you will necessarily experience intense feelings of guilt.

It is not necessary to overburden your life with guilty feelings of this nature. Renew your relationship with Christ every day and practice your loving loyalty to Him. Through prayer, Bible study and an application of His holy will in your life, you will regain the glory of faith and peace in your heart.

Lord my God, I long for solid spiritual food so that I may grow to complete salvation, delivered from all feelings of guilt. Amen.

January 11

Read: Romans 6:1-14

Forgiveness is final

For sin shall not be your master, because you are not under law, but under grace.

— ROMANS 6:14 —

True Christlikeness is characterized by a life of victory in Jesus. He delivers His followers from the bondage of negative thinking and bad habits. The Spirit of the living Christ becomes a motivating force in our lives. Sin is erased by the omnipotence of the indwelling Christ.

Unfortunately, many Christians say that their sins have been forgiven, yet they cling desperately to their feelings of guilt. They often speak so emotionally about their past sins that they create the impression of being sorry for renouncing them.

If you believe that God has forgiven you, be assured that He will not recall your sins and remind you of them. "As far as the east is from the west, so far has He removed our transgressions from us" (Ps. 103:12). As He has forgiven you, you must forgive yourself.

You may argue that you recall your sins so that you may thank Him for delivering you from all of them. Then you are like the man who was walking to town with half a bag of wheat on his back. A man with a horse-drawn cart picked him up, but on the cart he kept the bag of wheat on his sweaty back. When the cart driver asked him why he did not put the wheat down, he answered, "No, Sir, it was very good of you to offer me a lift. I cannot expect you to take my wheat along as well!"

Christ's forgiveness is complete and final! You need not cling to your bag of renounced sins. You should look ahead in faith. The Master has called you to a life of sanctification: a life completely free from sin and the memory of sin. Therefore, stop worrying about sins that have been forgiven and concentrate on the mercy and love of your Savior and Redeemer. Then you will have more time available to grow spiritually.

I praise You, loving Master, that I may enter the future delivered from the sins of the past. Let Your Holy Spirit lead me in all Your truth. Amen.

Read: Hebrews 12:1-13   January 12

Determining a goal

Let us fix our eyes on Jesus, the author and perfecter of our faith.
— HEBREWS 12:2 —

In our spiritual lives, it is so easy to become bogged down by trivialities and to lose sight of the most important matters. You may place a high premium on noble traditions, or enjoy theological debate. You may devote all your time to your church or community service; you may be anxiously concerned with rendering a specific type of Christian service and with a good task that demands all your spare time. Nevertheless, you will experience those quiet moments of contemplation and meditation when incisive questions will prey on your mind and call for answers.

What practical value, except for temporary inspiration, does tradition really have? Theological debate can be an escape from spiritual challenges, and is often used as such. The things which should actually deliver you spiritually, bind you because they have become meaningless. They have only become pleasant habits that flatter your conscience. Many "good" things can burden your life to such an extent that there is no room for the best of all and the most supreme.

Whichever part of the treasure of the gospel you have made your own, and whatever you may call yourself, the portion of the truth you possess will darken and become uninspiring unless it focuses completely and totally on Christ.

Only Jesus Christ can give true, pulsating life. Only He can give dynamic power and meaning to your faith. Everything that leads you away from this truth, however noble it might appear to be, is doing you an injustice.

In your spiritual conversations and in rendering of service, you never dare lose contact with the dynamic and motivating love of Jesus Christ. Purposefully and continuously fix your eyes on Him so that you can achieve your spiritual ideals and your Christian calling.

You are the center of my entire existence, Lord Jesus. I thank You for the inspiration that You alone can give. Amen.

January 13

Read: Hebrews 10:32-39

Trust in God is essential

So do not throw away your confidence; it will be richly rewarded.
– Hebrews 10:35 –

To lose your self-confidence is devastating. It robs your life of all joy and you are constantly tormented by the innocent or indifferent remarks of your friends. You may instinctively know that you can finish something successfully, but just when you are on the point of enthusiastically carrying it out, you start doubting your ability. You draw back into yourself and mutter excuses about your inability.

At such times, you treat yourself cruelly. You create bitter dissatisfaction, pain and depression in your own heart. In addition, you rob yourself of the spiritual and mental growth God wants you to obtain from every experience: whether it is successful or not.

So many potential spiritual giants unfortunately remain dwarfs and never fulfill their God-given calling because they lack the confidence to push forward and do what God expects them to do. Every time you deny yourself, the paralyzing forces in your life get bigger. There are many effective and sound psychological methods you can use to regain, develop and rebuild your self-confidence.

To reform and reshape your thoughts is very important and by thinking positively and constructively you are filling your life with renewed self-confidence. The most important thing is to believe that Jesus Christ has confidence in you. If He has called you to a task which you think is beyond your abilities, you should remember that He would do this only if He had confidence in your ability to carry it through.

God does not necessarily call the qualified, but He qualifies those He calls! The only condition is that they should unconditionally trust in Him.

My Lord and God, I trust You with all my heart; that is why I have the confidence to do Your work to Your glory through the strength of Your Spirit. Amen.

Read: 1 John 3:11-24   January 14

Let your love be alive

Let us not love with words or tongue but with actions and in truth.
— 1 JOHN 3:18 —

True love is almost unfathomable to humankind's mind. It cannot be defined quite satisfactorily either. Yet, of all human emotions, it is the strongest and most noble.

Due to the unique quality of love and humankind's inability to express it in understandable terms, words are inadequate to explain it. Sympathy, tenderness, compassion and many other such words do not express the power and force of love completely. There is also a tendency to confuse love with sentimentality and then this dynamic force becomes weak and ineffective.

The foundation of true love is total identification with the loved one. You experience the same joys, sorrows, temptations and defeats. True love embraces sacrifice and often shares pain. Love's qualities go much deeper than sympathy and sentiment, and are revealed in loyalty and faithfulness – even if the whole world were to turn against the one you love.

Love in action is more than doing good deeds, although such deeds can be an expression of love. True love is steadfast, sincere and unselfish, and embraces the qualities of trust, loyalty and integrity. Such values enrich the thoughts and the spirit of man. It cannot be bought, begged or borrowed; that is why true love is so infinitely precious. It does not carry the price tag of idle words or pious lip service but is proved in sincerity and in action.

In this, God Himself was the perfect example: He proved His love for us by a reverberating act of which the echoes still sound across the plains of time! Out of love, God gave His best, His most precious, His Son, to show His love through a deed.

God of love, I thank You for the example of Jesus Christ who has shown me how to express my love in a tangible way in my everyday life. Through Your Spirit my love lives. Amen.

January 15

Read: Hebrews 13:7-19

Unchangeable Rock of Ages

Jesus Christ is the same yesterday and today and forever.
— HEBREWS 13:8 —

Change and decay are the characteristics of everything that surrounds us on earth. That is why we pray: "O unchangeable God, abide with me!"

It is only natural that our image of Jesus Christ would be of someone with a Palestinian background from the Roman golden age. It was at that time that God chose to reveal Himself to the world and ever since, people have thought of Christ in terms of the idiom, costume and customs of that time. Because we imagine Him in that time, we easily lose sight of the eternal and unchanging Christ.

He can only enter your life effectively if you experience Him in the context of modern times and within the frame of reference of your own existence. Because He is eternal He lives today! He is forcefully present in your life and waiting to guide you.

As He taught, guided and blessed His first disciples, He wants to do the same for you. Unfortunately our perspective on His ability to help and to bless us is clouded by the problems and confusion of our modern society.

You may think that you are living in a unique period of time, and in a certain sense it is obviously true. But the basic problems of the world today are still the same as when Jesus was on earth.

Greed, lust, self-centeredness, pettiness, hatred and bitterness are still powerful influences in man's existence.

The living Christ can deal with these deviations and illnesses of man's spirit and intellect, just as He could centuries ago, because He is eternal and unchanging. On this steadfast Rock we can build our lives.

Holy Master, I gain peace of mind from knowing that You are eternal and steadfast in this fast-changing world. Thank You that I may firmly ground my life on You. Amen.

Read: 2 Thessalonians 3:1-5   January 16

Peace or fear?

The Lord is faithful and he will strengthen and protect you from the evil one.

— 2 THESSALONIANS 3:3 —

We enter the year with a thousand nameless fears which lurk in every dark corner of the path ahead. We fear for our health, we fear the past and the future, we fear for our children, for our possessions, for our lives ... and we fear death! We fear the dark omens which the evil one sends to flit about in our hearts. We become so ensnared in the grip of fear that life becomes unbearable.

Perhaps you have forgotten: "The Lord is faithful!" You may even theoretically accept and believe this, yet you find it extremely difficult to apply it in practice to your daily life. If you truly believe it in theory and in practice, fear will no longer have a paralyzing hold over your life.

It is imperative that your faith in God should be greater than your fear of the unknown. God gives you faith as a gift of grace, but it is your responsibility to develop it through meditation, contemplation of the Scriptures, prayer and the continuous cultivating of His holy presence in your life from moment to moment.

Your faith must be practically expressed if you want to find peace. It is meaningless to talk about faith unless it is revealed and expressed in your thoughts and deeds.

Faith and fear cannot live together. If you are one of those people who fluctuate between faith and fear you should concentrate all your mind's power on trusting God unconditionally. In this way, the continuous cultivating of your faith will become a dynamic reality and the strongest power in your life.

You should immediately decide whether faith or fear will dominate your life. With Christ at the center of your life, you will triumph and know true peace.

I thank You, my risen Redeemer, for the peace of God which surpasses all understanding. I trust You with all my heart, mind and spirit. I thank You that my love for You drives out all fear from my life. Amen.

January 17

Read: Philippians 4:10-20

Linked to the Source of power

I can do everything through him who gives me strength.
— PHILIPPIANS 4:13 —

As a child of God you have infinite spiritual reserves available. Since they cannot be seen or calculated, they are often not appreciated or rated according their true worth. Instead of rejoicing in the power of your faith, you have a struggle against defeat and frustration. You try to keep up the appearance of Christlikeness, but you are deeply conscious of your own inability. Admitting your spiritual need is the first step on the road to recovery and strength.

It is only possible to live a Christian life if the strength of the risen Redeemer is present in your life. This knowledge of complete dependence drives you on in your search for a power source. Unless the indwelling Spirit of Christ possesses you completely, all your efforts will be doomed to failure.

A successful Christian life does not involve a struggle for victory, but a claiming of the victory that is ours through Jesus Christ. Your victory has already been secured by Jesus Christ. You only have to claim and accept it in faith.

When this glorious truth becomes part of your thinking and your deeds, your attitude towards life will change radically. You will no longer expect defeat and failure, but you will live with the conviction that you can be victorious through the omnipotence of your living Redeemer.

Christlikeness is not what you can do for Christ, but what you allow Christ to do in you through the unlimited power of the Holy Spirit. Then there are no limits to the possibilities in your life.

I confess, Lord Jesus, that I often want to conquer life in my own strength. Thank You for Your patience with me. Once again I confess my total dependency on You. Use me as You wish, and to Your glory alone. Amen.

Read: Psalm 32:1-11   **January 18**

God's will for my life

I will instruct you and teach you in the way you should go; I will counsel you and watch over you.

                                        – PSALM 32:8 –

It is not always easy to recognize the will of God for your life. A few special people may know without any doubt what God expects of them, but most of us often hesitate and involuntarily ask, "What is God's will for me in this situation?" Naturally all of us know that God expects us to obey the Ten Commandments and live the Golden Rule. But it is when you face the personal complexities in your life that it is not so easy to recognize the will of God.

To experience God's guidance so that you can do His will requires a special relationship with your Redeemer. Within this fellowship you develop a sensitivity to obedience. Every time you want to do something that is contrary to His will, a feeling of discomfort and guilt arises in your heart. Then you know without any doubt that you are acting in disobedience.

Living close to God so that you can clearly distinguish His will means that you should love His Word and study it, since in it you will find His revealed will for your life. It contains God's answers to your deepest human problems. An intimate knowledge of the holy Scriptures makes it easier to understand the principles of God's Kingdom as they apply to your personal life.

Continuously living in fellowship with Christ and in obedience to His Word ensures that you will be guided by the prompting of the Holy Spirit. Then you achieve that ideal situation to which a child of God aspires and longs for – that everything you are and do will be acceptable to God. Then you live within the framework of His advice and under His loving eye.

Loving Teacher, through fellowship with You and the knowledge of Your Word, I am deeply aware of Your will for my life and Your merciful guidance from day to day. Amen.

January 19

Read: 2 Corinthians 4:16-5:10

Vital values

So we fix our eyes not on what is seen, but on what is unseen. For what is seen is temporary, but what is unseen is eternal.
– 2 CORINTHIANS 4:18 –

It is easy to develop a false sense of values. You are part of the world and make a living among different types of people. It is inevitable that the determining norm accepted by society will have a profound effect on you.

Before becoming a follower of Christ, you strived for the things you could see, evaluate and deal with. These things became your aim and goal, but most often they brought no satisfaction or peace.

After surrendering yourself to Christ you underwent a transformation, and it became possible for you to see the true meaning of old values which had carried a false sense of security into your life. You discover that the values of the world can never satisfy the soul.

The most important things in life are invisible and intangible and are often difficult to define. The unconditional love of a happily married couple cannot be explained by cold logic. The breathtaking beauty of the sun rising and setting which enriches the spirit and the soul, cannot easily be put in words. Appreciating music and poetry, sacrifice that does not count the costs – these things reach past the earthly, into the elevated sphere of the spirit.

These are qualities that have eternal value. They give a new dimension to life and a greater appreciation of the cardinal and intrinsic values of our existence. They reveal to us what can be achieved if we live according to spiritual standards. Then we are living by the grace of God, not in vain or without purpose.

Lord Jesus, grant me a still greater appreciation of You so that I can have a pure appreciation of the invisible things of cardinal value. I ask this in gratitude and in praise of Your holy Name. Amen.

Read: 1 Corinthians 13:1-13   January 20

The horror of envy

Love is patient, love is kind. It does not envy.
*   – 1 Corinthians 13:4 –*

Envy and jealousy are two soul-destroying diseases of our time. They are revealed in many ways, but always inevitably end in frustration and bitterness. You react negatively because your neighbor has something that you cannot afford. A colleague is promoted but you do not get promoted; envy and jealousy well up in your heart. You allow your emotions to rule your life. You lose your joy in life because you are constantly under the pressure of personal grievances. You are caught up in negative thinking. Envy takes hold of the better you, to your detriment.

Fortunate is the person who does not envy anyone else. He sees the successes and possessions of other people without a trace of envy and rejoices in the prosperity and happiness of his fellow man. Such a person has in his heart a spirit of acquiescence, and jealousy has no room in his thoughts.

One of the positive results of the Christian life is possessing exactly such an attitude. If you have accepted Jesus Christ as Lord and Master of your life, if you have opened yourself to the influence of His Holy Spirit, you have an entirely new set of values.

The standards of the world now become subordinate to God's standards. Your life is now ruled by the latter. As your values change for the better, the reasons for your envy vanish.

It is impossible to experience the reality of the indwelling Spirit of Christ and still be plagued by the awful disease of envy. It is a God-given deliverance and a great mercy to learn the secret of this love that allows others their space and does not make you poorer for it. On the contrary, we are enriched by our joy in God's good gifts to others.

God of mercy, through Your indwelling Holy Spirit, I will, in the Name of Jesus, conquer the weakness of envy. Make me satisfied with the richness of Your grace and mercy in my life. Amen.

January 21

Read: Colossians 2:6-15

Intellectual word game or faith

So then, just as you received Christ Jesus as Lord, continue to live in him, rooted and built up in him, strengthened in the faith as you were taught, and overflowing with thankfulness.
– COLOSSIANS 2:6-7 –

Many sincere people have intellectual problems regarding Jesus Christ and His gospel. They cannot accept His Divinity and they find a virgin birth impossible and unnecessary and therefore treat it as unimportant. Since the resurrection has never been repeated, they reject that too. In fact, anything which they cannot understand or explain is written off as impossible. In this way they rob Christ of His uniqueness and His Divinity.

The truth of the matter is that Christ holds a quality of life and a depth of spirit that the human mind can never fathom. Understanding the living Christ completely is understanding God. Who can presume to have such knowledge?

The crucial question is whether you have the courage to live according to your knowledge of Him. Your intellectual problems could possibly just be a smoke-screen to indemnify you against a full surrender to His will and the calling to a holy life. It is easier to debate on one or other topic of faith than to subject yourself in childlike faith to the will of God.

In your act of commitment and obedience, your intellectual doubt will not just disappear. But if you long for a still deeper experience of the love of God in Jesus Christ, you will, through fellowship with Him, increasingly develop an understanding of His mysteries. You will gradually realize that personal dedication far exceeds any intellectual word game. You'll discover that faith does not adhere to strict scientific formulae or rules. Then you will live with faith in God and His peace will descend on your soul.

Incomprehensible God, You revealed Yourself to me in Christ. Through Your Holy Spirit, my daily relationship with Him drives out all doubt and fear. I praise Your great Name for this. Amen.

Read: Deuteronomy 31:1-13   **January 22**

Take courage!

"Be strong and courageous. Do not be afraid or terrified because of them, for the LORD your God goes with you; he will never leave you nor forsake you."

— DEUTERONOMY 31:6 —

We dare not let the first month of the year pass without impressing on one another that as Christians we should be courageous.

Courage takes on many forms. Every battlefield has its heroes. In hospital wards and sickrooms there are brave fighters who, with heroic effort still retain their courage. Our towns and cities are full of people who quietly struggle for a dignified human existence day after day; there are those who maintain honesty and self-respect in the face of apparently insurmountable problems. Courage is often found where it's least expected and recognized.

Courage comes into play when everything seems lost and all hope seems gone. Even when this happens the courageous person will stand upright and still persevere while others despair.

Where does this type of courage come from? Great love and trust, which are expressed in unshakable loyalty, can inspire one to a hero's courage. Think of the scenes that unfold on a sinking ship or a mother who saves her child from a burning building. It is the determination to conquer which calls forth a very special type of perseverance in the moment of trial.

One thing is certain: even if circumstances create the situations in which a hero's courage is displayed, real courage originates deep in man's innermost being. The true quality of man's courage is determined by what is buried in the depths of his heart.

When your spirit is in harmony with the Holy Spirit you are filled with a holy power that enables you to face life with courage and confidence. If you have the indwelling presence of the victorious Christ, no fear can paralyze you. Go out and meet the year with the courage of faith that only God can give to you.

I praise Your Name, almighty God, as I face the future with courage because Your Spirit dwells in me. Amen.

January 23

Read: Philippians 4:10-20

What you need – not what you desire

My God will meet all your needs according to his glorious riches in Christ Jesus.

– PHILIPPIANS 4:19 –

One of the big reasons why many people are unhappy with life is because people of our generation want more than they can afford. They see the advertisement of an item that is not essential, but because it will contribute to their social prestige and because it is available on "easy terms" they are determined to have it. Soon their expenses exceed their income and all kinds of problems arise.

God has promised to provide for our every need, but He did not say that He would give us everything we desire. This brings us to a basic truth: we should rid ourselves of all unnecessary baggage that handicaps our clear thinking and prayers. Then we will be able to understand the true goal and meaning of life.

When you have determined your needs, those things which are essential for your well-being, you can confidently and boldly place them before God, with the assurance that He will lovingly provide.

True knowledge of what you really need and like to have, will keep you from superficial requests for artificial things that are just the by-products of pride and greed. So many things that you desire – but do not really need – are unnecessary for your spiritual growth and progress. Your happiness does not depend on those things either.

If God provides in your daily needs and you thank Him for it, you will discover that life is less complicated and that your relationship with your heavenly Father will become more meaningful.

Then you will have a good understanding of Jesus' words, "Seek first His kingdom and His righteousness, and all these things will be given to you as well" (Mt. 6:33).

Provider God, teach me through Your Holy Spirit to distinguish between the things I really need and the things I desire. I thank You in Jesus' name. Amen.

Read: John 6:1-15 January 24

He does so much with so little!

"Here is a boy with five small barley loaves and two small fish, but how far will they go among so many?"

— JOHN 6:9 —

The Christian sometimes feels insignificant and inadequate. What you are trying to do for the Master in all earnestness, appears to be so trivial. In such times you are inclined to feel depressed. You lose your awareness of Christ's living presence. Temptation, in its variety of forms, then becomes overwhelmingly strong.

Although you may have a poor self-image in times like this, remember that you are very important to Christ. You are aware of the smallness of your offering. However, he does not only see the offering, but also the spirit in which it is given. When you are disappointed about the smallness of your contribution, remember how He used five barley loaves and two small fish to feed a great crowd of people.

If you give to the Master what you have, and stop finding reasons why you cannot be an efficient servant in His Kingdom, you will be surprised about what God can do through you.

There is work for everyone in the kingdom of God and no one needs to feel redundant or inadequate because he does not have particular gifts or abilities. The qualification that God requires is a spirit which is in harmony with Him, which loves Christ and others and is willing to serve Him unconditionally and follow Him obediently on the path that He indicates.

The omnipotent Christ can work miracles with the most humble disciple. Your heart should only be filled with love for your Redeemer and your hands should be stretched out in service to others. Then there are no limits to what God can do through you as a committed and obedient instrument!

Redeemer and Savior, everything I am and everything I have I commit to You and Your service. Use me as You will, only to Your glory and honor. Amen.

January 25

Read: John 16:25-33

In the world, but not of the world

"In this world you will have trouble. But take heart! I have overcome the world."

$-$ JOHN 16:33 $-$

The mystery of Jesus Christ becoming flesh is that the Redeemer became one with all people of all times. He mingled with all types of people and called them His friends. He was never exclusive in His relationships with people.

Many of His followers form selective or closed groups. They isolate themselves from those who do not believe and direct their thinking exclusively to Christ. On the surface, this may sound praiseworthy, but if the exclusiveness becomes too strict, these groups are in danger of even excluding Christ.

The meaning of Christ's incarnation is that God became human in Christ and came to live among people. He came to share in their experiences and understood their problems. He wanted to guide them in this way to a meaningful relationship with God the Father.

Strange as it may appear, the Christian needs the world in order for his faith to be fully revealed. Jesus knows everything about the world and its temptations, fears and ugliness: all the sinful factors. He does not withdraw from them into peaceful isolation.

Do not fear the problems and difficulties of the world. Even if we are not of this world, we are inevitably in the world. Jesus states unequivocally that His followers will experience difficult times during their earthly pilgrimage. However, He has also promised never to leave or forsake us. That is why we can persevere courageously to give our testimony in a corrupt world – Christ has already gained the victory. In the strength He gives you, you will be able to confirm that through Christ's influence you can be victorious.

Christ does not call His disciples to a solitary life protected from the onslaught of the evil world. He does promise us that we, as His faithful witnesses in the world, will gain the victory.

I praise and glorify Your Name, my Lord and God, that I may gain victory over sin and corruption through the power of Your Holy Spirit in me, although I am in this world. Amen.

Read: John 13:31-35

January 26

Love that inspires

"By this all men will know that you are my disciples."
— JOHN 13:35 —

There is a wide variety of active Christians and each of them is attached to his own discipline or belief. This is important, since we will merely drift about and never find a safe harbor if we do not have anchors.

The biggest shortcoming of our approach becomes evident since every church or society has the conviction that they are the only ones who are right and that all the others are wrong. Then antagonism results in our discipleship becoming weak and ineffective.

The Christian belief should center on the living and risen Christ. Accepting Him as your personal Redeemer and Savior, declaring faithfulness to Him and obeying His commands, form the core of our discipleship. This covers every aspect of your daily life and requires a high degree of commitment.

Christ demands that love should be the dynamic driving force in your life. All other things may be important, but are secondary. Love is the genuine mark of discipleship and without it no one can be a follower of Christ. The true test for discipleship is therefore not the doctrine that you support and preach, but a life in which Christian love is continuously revealed.

The contemplation of this truth may cause some people to hesitate before accepting the challenge of discipleship. Indeed, which one of us can love truly while we are surrounded by the bitterness and sorrow caused by the sin of hatred in its many disguises?

The great and all-encompassing commandment of Jesus Christ to show love to others is perhaps, seen in the human sense, impossible to obey completely. But if the Holy Spirit fills your life, the impossible becomes possible. Gradually, love becomes part of your life and enables you to be a true disciple of the Master. The world will undeniably see this in your life.

Source of all true love, let Your Holy Spirit saturate me to such an extent that love will become the inspiring force of my entire life. Amen.

January 27

Read: Proverbs 23:1-16

Tried and tested values

Do not move an ancient boundary stone.

– PROVERBS 23:10 –

There are certain things in life that we should rather forget: harsh words spoken thoughtlessly; arrogant attitudes; envy or other destructive emotions. Continuing to harbor and nurture them in our hearts will poison our thinking and weaken our spirits. It creates a barrier between yourself and God.

Since the future demands so much from you, it is foolish to become ensnared by the ghosts from the past, or even to continue to nostalgically contemplate the good old days.

But when the pilgrimage becomes taxing, when the shadows of doubt overshadow your faith and a feeling of loneliness and depression settles around you, then recall the times and circumstances when you were filled with self-confidence and when God was a glorious reality in your life. These are essential markers on your path of life.

An honest evaluation of your spiritual condition will probably reveal to you that the devil wants to diminish or lower the high standards that you previously maintained. The process of decline was probably so gradual that you hardly noticed it, until you were suddenly threatened by a total spiritual collapse. All at once you may discover that you no longer have a living and sparkling faith.

There are standards which are eternal and apply at all times. They are as credible today as they were yesterday and the day before. To relinquish these principles is to lose the basics and fundamentals of your faith.

Of all these principles, Jesus Christ is the most important. He is the criterion for a living faith. He is the foundation on which you should build to obtain strength and inspiration for the future.

Lord Jesus, I thank You for the inspiration that I obtain from Your living presence. Strengthen me and help me to remain faithful, to Your great glory. Amen.

Read: Hebrews 12:14-29

January 28

How great You are!

Therefore, since we are receiving a kingdom that cannot be shaken, let us be thankful, and so worship God acceptably with reverence and awe.

– HEBREWS 12:28 –

As Christians, one of the dangers we face is that the Most High becomes so familiar to us that we lose our sense of amazement, worship and awe. This causes a superficial and meaningless relationship.

It is true that God became flesh in Jesus Christ and came to live among us. During His earthly stay He called God His Father and He invited His followers to do the same. This intimacy is one of His children's most glorious privileges.

Nevertheless, our approach and attitude should maintain the respect and worship that is due to God. To lose your sense of worship or to attenuate it when you think of Him or speak about Him, is to lose something invaluable.

It is possible to form an image of God and personalize Him to such an extent that you lose your sense of His majesty and holiness. When this happens, you limit God to the imperfect ideas of man and you obstruct His working in your life by familiarizing and disrespecting Him.

We dare never lower the standard of God's greatness and majesty, not even when we approach Him as "our Father". The realization of His Greatness rejects the idea of a "genial" Divinity who possesses the more noble qualities of man and who just ignores sin and human failure. We may never play off God's love against His holiness.

When you enter God's presence, you are on hallowed ground. You must glorify and worship Him with reverence and wonder. This element should never disappear from our worship.

Holy, holy, holy are You, O God whom I worship. I praise Your holy Name as King of glory while I love You eternally. Amen.

January 29

Read: Exodus 3:1-14

You can! ... with God

But Moses said to God, "Who am I that I should go to Pharaoh and bring the Israelites out of Egypt?"

– Exodus 3:11 –

God never calls anyone for a specific task unless He knows that the person is able to carry it out. God does not necessarily call the competent people either, but He enables those whom He calls. A person who has been called by God may question his own abilities and he may offer all kinds of excuses: I do not have any influence; I have no social standing; intellectually I am inferior and many other reasons why you supposedly cannot obey God.

If God calls you for a specific task, He sees qualities in you of which you may be unaware. He knows that once your hidden talents have been discovered, your service to Him will be more effective. At the same time you will experience more satisfaction and fulfillment in life. If you refuse to do what you intuitively know God wants you to do, you reveal a lack of trust in God. He equips His children fully for every task to which He calls them.

If you try to evade the challenge, or if you offer weak excuses for not being able to do it; if you even ask God to use someone else for the task, it is an indication of an unwilling spirit or incomplete surrender to Him.

When God honors you with a particular task, He will give you the guidance of His Holy Spirit to inspire you and to equip you for the task. When you accept a task to which God has appointed you joyfully and carry it out in obedience, you enrich your own spiritual life and you grow towards God. When Jonah abandoned his excuses and obediently went to Nineveh to carry out God's task, God did miracles of salvation through him. Such obedience eventually results in hearing God's encouraging promise, "I will be with you." You and God are a majority!

Enabling and merciful God, I praise Your name in deep gratitude because You want to use me in Your great divine plan. I promise anew that I am willing to do any task to which You may call me. Amen.

Read: Colossians 1:9-14

January 30

Live fully!

We pray this in order that you may live a life worthy of the Lord and may please him in every way: bearing fruit in every good work, growing in the knowledge of God.

– COLOSSIANS 1:10 –

One often hears the moans and groans of people who say that it is senseless to live or that there is nothing to live for. It appears as though man is becoming more dissatisfied and bored as his life becomes more sophisticated. If this is how you think, it is time for honest introspection.

God's promise to you in Jesus Christ has always been and still is that He will give you true life, and that in abundance! There are no limitations to the quality of the life that Christ offers you. He was resolved to do the will of His Father and to extend the honor of God while He was on earth.

By the grace of God and the power of the Holy Spirit, this is the type of life Christ expects you to lead, here and now.

Refresh your thinking while studying the eternal Word of God; renew your spirit through spending time in prayer and meditation. Come into His holy presence often, with wonder and expectation. Live within the sphere of the work of the Holy Spirit. Then you will suddenly discover a new aim, a new sparkle and effervescence and a new joyous energy in your actions.

Above all, enrich your own life and the lives of those you come into contact with, every moment of every day, by showing the same loving nature as Jesus Christ. Then He will guide your thoughts through the work of the Holy Spirit and give purpose and direction to your life. You will start living to His glory and obediently do what He expects. The rich harvest of spiritual fruit will become noticeable in your life. You will seize every day as a gift from God's hand and utilize it optimally. Your life will contribute to the glory of God.

Perfect Example and Redeemer, through You I rejoice in the blessed knowledge that I can experience true life in all its richness and fullness. Amen.

January 31

Read: Psalm 31:1-13

Christ opens doors

Since you are my rock and my fortress, for the sake of your name lead and guide me.

— PSALM 31:3 —

The moment you commit yourself unconditionally to Christ, it becomes the most significant decision of your entire life. You may be guided onto strange and exciting paths, since God undoubtedly guides those who swear obedience and faithfulness to Him. When you subject yourself to His guidance, wonderful things will start happening in your life. Where life probably seemed like a dead end before, doors now open in remarkable ways. Problems which you feared previously, now shrink to trivialities and you become aware that you are not alone on the path.

The experience and perception of Christ's guidance elevates it beyond the world of theological speculation. It finds practical application in the harsh realities of our daily lives. This is faith in action!

There will be times when doors slam shut or close quietly and it would be wise not to try to force them open. When Christ wants you to walk a certain path and you are sensitive to what He expects from you, you will always get a clear indication of the direction you must follow.

Experiencing the presence of the great Guide is an exciting and satisfying event. You will know no greater joy on your entire pilgrimage. It will lead you to "green pastures" and to "quiet waters".

It is only when you are guided by Christ that you learn to understand the true wealth and deep satisfaction of your partnership with Him. Then your heart sings, "Jesus, Source of all my joy!"

Guide and Perfecter, guide me simply and in a practical way on my path of life so that the quality of my life will reflect whose follower I am and will contribute to Your glorification. Amen.

FEBRUARY

February 1

Read: John 15:1-8

The condition for Christian growth

"Remain in me, and I will remain in you."

– JOHN 15:4 –

Come, let us enter the new month with a spiritual challenge on the banner of our lives. Perhaps your spiritual life has started to become an unbearable burden to you. You are possibly not experiencing the enthusiasm and dynamism you enjoyed previously. Then it is time that you stop for a while and prayerfully seek the reason for this.

It is undoubtedly true that when your faith loses its splendor, when the reality of it starts fading, it is because you have turned your eyes away from Christ. Possibly you may be focusing on something which may be good in itself, but ultimately appears to be inadequate in satisfying your deepest longing and need.

Faith that has Jesus at the center is alive and sparkling. Jesus does not ask you to be faithful to a dogma or a specific religious code in the first place, but to be primarily devoted to Him. He places an important premium on His relationship with you and your personal relationship with Him. The miracle of His mercy is that He has given His Holy Spirit to us to fill our lives so that He can manifest Himself through us. If we place Him first, all other things will fall into place.

The uninformed would perhaps think that such unconditional surrender speaks only of an overdose of piety, which will rob life of its energy and excitement. Such people have only a vague concept of the Master. He has come to give life, abundantly and richly at that! This is the inheritance of those in whom He lives, and who in turn remain in Him.

Indwelling Lord Jesus, come and live in me through Your Holy Spirit. May my life reflect You. Amen.

Read: Ephesians 4:25-32

February 2

The glory of compassion

Be kind and compassionate to one another, forgiving each other, just as in Christ God forgave you.

— EPHESIANS 4:32 —

Being a Christian has its own relentless social requirements. It is so easy to become immune to these requirements that you become indifferent to the distress of your fellow man. Perhaps there used to be a time when the poverty or destitution of the underprivileged really touched you. Perhaps you did something about it or gave them something to alleviate their distress. Now you are no longer touched and the only thing you ever do is blame the government for not doing more for such people.

If you have allowed your conscience to become numbed by the generality of such occurrences, you have allowed an important part of your spiritual make-up to be stripped away.

To move through life untouched by the distress of your fellow man means that you make it increasingly difficult for the Holy Spirit to work through you. It is through sensitive people that God does His work on earth.

It is not easy to live with a sensitive conscience since you then identify yourself intimately with the pain and distress of others. However, it makes you a more understanding person. A guilty conscience can be a hard taskmaster to live with. It accuses you and challenges you. It reminds you of things you would rather forget.

A clear conscience is one of life's most precious treasures. It is the channel by which God's mercy streams into your life; it is the road on which He leads you; it keeps you in harmony with Christ and your fellow man. It reminds you time and again of how mercifully and compassionately God acts towards you in your own need. In this way you constantly reveal more of the attitude of Jesus Christ and you become filled with compassion for other people.

Lord, my God, let me remain sensitive and understanding and give me a compassionate attitude. Do this through the work of Your Holy Spirit, following the example of Jesus Christ. Amen.

February 3

Read: Romans 8:1-17

Undoubtable certainty

The Spirit himself testifies with our Spirit that we are God's children.
— ROMANS 8:16 –

True religion is a wonderful experience. It is a pity that to many people it has become just a subject of debate that often only requires mental exertion and deprives the spiritual needs of the soul.

It is a strange phenomenon that one can have a religion without the Spirit. You can know every possible fact about God without knowing Him. Theory is not enough.

On the other hand, your theological knowledge may not be that much, but you can be gloriously aware of Christ's living presence that inspires you to reach unparalleled spiritual heights.

It is when the Spirit of Christ has descended on your soul that you become aware of your unity with the Most High and that your religion undergoes an essential and exciting change.

To have this indwelling Spirit requires that you believe He can be yours. On the basis of this certainty we open our entire lives to Him. It is an act of simple, childlike faith.

Before you doubt this possibility, rather try it. If you do this, you may perhaps have great emotional experiences, but whether this is the case or not, you will experience a new life inspired by Christ.

According to this new standard of life, hatred and bitterness will be cleansed by the purifying power of the Holy Spirit; your weakness will be converted into an ability by Christ who gives you strength. His disposition will bring all pettiness and lack of faith to an end, and your life will be filled and enriched by the glorious certainty: I know for sure that I am His child!

I praise You, Lord God Almighty, that it has become possible for me to know for certain, through Christ my Savior, that I am Your child. Amen.

Read: Colossians 3:8-4:1 February 4

Are you happy in your job?

Whatever you do, work at it with all your heart, as working for the Lord, not for men.

— COLOSSIANS 3:23 —

There are few people who can truthfully say that the work they do does not at times become boring or even a burden they have to carry. It is especially true of our daily, routine tasks. This attitude is often seen in the lazy, unwilling attitude of many workers and in the untidy way in which they do their daily jobs.

To gain the most from your job and, in fact, from life itself, you should change your attitude about it. Whatever work you do, this is a prerequisite.

The mere fact that your work is simply routine, or is possibly uninteresting, is not sufficient reason to be unmotivated. You should see your contribution as part of the larger totality and measure it according to the end result.

For instance, thorough attention to the apparently unimportant task of keeping an operating room clean is essential for the well-being of the patients, since germs and dirt can cause death if the patient becomes infected during an operation.

When you are called to do a task, make sure that you dedicate yourself and your work to God in prayer. This is the point of departure for experiencing joy and pride in your work. Ask Him to equip you for the task and allow His Spirit to lead your thoughts. In this way you will become more and more aware of the fact that you are executing a God-given task.

Once you do this, it will become a holy calling and not just a way to make a living. In His power you will do it well, to His honor, as if you are doing it for God. Then one joyous and exciting work day will follow another.

Heavenly Master, I want to do everything I undertake as though I am doing it for You, through Your power and to Your honor. Amen.

February 5

Read: Psalm 27:1-10

Trust in God

"Though an army besiege me, my heart will not fear; though war break out against me, even then will I be confident."

— PSALM 27:3 —

This trust in God can only be possible if we can also make this foregoing pronouncement: "The LORD is my light and my salvation – whom shall I fear? The LORD is the stronghold of my life – of whom shall I be afraid?" (Ps. 27:1).

An essential concern about the future has infiltrated every aspect of society. People are concerned about what the future holds for us and our children.

In times like these it is essential that people will have a spiritual foundation on which they can base their hope and expectations. Trust in the material things of life has failed and unless you have a positive faith in a force greater than yourself, the future is extremely uncertain.

Faith in God must be intimate and personal if it is to contribute to hope for the future. The omnipotent Creator God has not surrendered this world to its fate, despite the fact that the contrary appears to be true. His master plan for humankind will still be carried out.

This is the truth which a living Christ brings to a despairing world. In an ever darkening world, He proclaims, "But take heart! I have overcome the world" (Jn. 16:33).

If you put all your trust in Him, you will be able to meet the future with an internal peace and calmness, and this will also inspire trust in those who surround you.

A Christian, who is permeated by the Holy Spirit, will have a stabilizing effect on his society, since he knows irrefutably that the future is in God's almighty hand.

Savior and Lord, I live from day to day in the undeniable reality of Your presence and omnipotence in this world. Therefore, I do not fear, since You are my refuge. Amen.

Read: John 4:27-42

February 6

Vocation and loyalty

"My food," said Jesus, "is to do the will of him who sent me and to finish his work."

– JOHN 4:34 –

People without purpose or aim achieve little. To constructively pursue a particular purpose is the secret of a successful life, but only if the purpose is true to the most noble ideals of your heart.

Many people have great clarity about what they expect from life. They know that they will experience the joy of fulfillment and success only in the realization of that aim. Nevertheless, because this pursuit requires commitment and hard work, discipline and possibly also great sacrifice, they satisfy themselves with second best. This does not happen because they are incompetent, but because they are lethargic and lazy to fulfill their calling in faithfulness.

In whichever part of society you move and work, you have a responsibility to God and to yourself to give only your best, and this at all times. You dare not be satisfied with a second-rate life, but you should live with decisiveness to the maximum of your God-given abilities. This means that you will have an aim that is noble and large enough to lift you from mediocrity; an aim that will inspire and impel you to be and to do that which God has intended.

Your calling and duty to God are not foreign to the reality of life, but consists of a way of life that includes God in every thought and deed of your existence. Then He becomes your holy inspiration through Jesus Christ, and His will becomes your calling and mission in life. It guarantees a fulfillment and inner satisfaction that cannot be put into words.

Master, knowing and doing Your will gives me a positive calling and mission in life, and this gives sense and meaning to my life. Amen.

February 7

Read: Matthew 11:2-19

Do you try to satisfy everyone?

To what can I compare this generation? They are like children sitting in the marketplaces and calling out to others: "We played the flute for you, and you did not dance; we sang a dirge, and you did not mourn."

– MATTHEW 11:16-17 –

If you try to satisfy everyone, you will ultimately satisfy no-one. There comes a time when you should take a stand on account of a principle and disagree with others.

To small-minded and immature people, a difference of opinion necessarily means conflict and estrangement. Many people cannot be in the company of someone who holds an opposing view without becoming angry. If you do not agree with them and underwrite their opinion they won't be friends with you.

The fact of the matter is that you will experience clashes of opinion with others if you are true to your principles. This is inevitable.

A wise person regards two things of primary importance: the principles that he supports through study, meditation and prayer; and the right of the other person to have his own point of view. You do not have the right to force anyone to accept your viewpoint purely and simply for the sake of friendship. Trying to do this only creates a spirit of hostility where there would otherwise be love and understanding.

The fact that you cannot agree with everyone should not influence your relationship with others negatively. As a disciple of Christ, with His love in your heart and mind, you should love, even where there is a difference of opinion. It is impossible to agree with everyone, but it should not keep you from loving them.

Help me, Lord, to show respect and love to those from whom I differ. Amen.

Read: 1 Samuel 17:40-47

February 8

Never underestimate God

All those gathered here will know that it is not by sword or spear that the LORD saves.

– 1 SAMUEL 17:47 –

People are inclined to put God on their own intellectual level. If they encounter an aspect of the Deity which they cannot understand, they reject the existence of such an aspect or try to reason it away. They find it unacceptable to recognize the creating influence of someone who is greater than their intellectual capacity.

The fact is that God is so great that, however much you may know about Him in your opinion, your knowledge is always like the light of a candle in comparison to the afternoon sun. To come to a deeper and more complete knowledge of the eternal Creator God requires more than intellectual ability. God requires a firm and unshakable faith in His existence and that He be a reality in your life.

Such faith dares to believe, even when explanations seem to be inadequate. To hold on to the reality of God leads one into a new human experience. It enlarges your image of God in a way you would never have been able to do in a purely intellectual way.

It is a strange thought that God does not need your understanding to do His work. As you put your complete faith in Him He leads you increasingly in such a way that you are ultimately unaware of the fact that He is leading you. Until, like a clear revelation, you suddenly realize that He has actually always led you, and that He has brought you to the place where He wants you to be.

Then you profess with humility and wonder: "O LORD, our Lord, how majestic is Your name in all the earth!" (Ps. 8:9).

Mercifully grant me the faith, O Lord, that will help me to see and appreciate Your work in my life! Amen.

February 9

Read: 2 Corinthians 4:7-15

For days of affliction

We are hard pressed on every side, but not crushed; perplexed, but not in despair.

— 2 CORINTHIANS 4:8 —

No human being is without problems. At some time the smooth passage of our lives is cruelly disturbed. Upsetting influences drive away our inward peace and calm. Yet suffering can serve a purpose.

If you have traveled selfishly along the highway of life for a long period, and have become self-centered, if you have perhaps become insensitive to the distress of those who are less privileged than you are, suffering can suddenly make you aware of their distress.

God can use trials to motivate you to serve Him with greater commitment and to serve Him and your fellow man with more understanding.

When you are tested, wait on the Lord and try to find out whether He is not teaching you something. Never allow problems and trials to conquer and govern your spirit. Whatever happens, remain in control of the situation and do not become upset, however great the temptation may be.

Every form of suffering has its own method of attack. It may overpower you suddenly and unexpectedly or it may stealthily creep into your thoughts and life. The ordeal will undoubtedly assert itself and you will need a powerful antidote to oppose it.

A tried way of triumphing over problems and trials is to have faith of such quality that it will enable you to conquer fear. Faith in the goodness of God, and the certainty that He has a purpose with everything in your life, will enable you to face the future confidently, instead of sinking into depression. This will strengthen the conviction that nothing can separate you from the love of God which is in Jesus Christ!

Heavenly Father, grant me the mercy to learn from my tribulations and to change problems into tokens of mercy. Do this through the Holy Spirit for Jesus' sake. Amen.

Read: Luke 24:36-49   February 10

Peace in the eye of the storm

While they were still talking about this, Jesus himself stood among them and said to them, "Peace be with you."

– Luke 24:36 –

Life is full of frightening and horrifying experiences for all of us at times. These experiences charge at you from many different directions. Before you realize it, they cause you to stress and build up inner conflict. You become moody and discontented and your health begins to suffer. Your loved ones observe this with concern. And all of this, just because your peace has vanished.

Since you are continuously under pressure, it is imperative that you develop inner reserves from which you can obtain strength in situations fraught with stress. Only in this way will you be able to withstand storms.

The most important source of power in such a time is the peace that Jesus Christ offers to everyone who loves Him, lives close to Him and serves Him in obedience. To possess His particular peace and to live according to it every day is liberating and enriching. It is available to everyone who is willing to maintain Christian discipline in spirit and thought.

When stress develops and things start going wrong, you should purposefully refuse to be swept along. Guard against bad temper and irritability. Do not share the breakneck pace of the masses surrounding you. Stop, calm down and spend a few minutes alone with Christ. Once again, just confirm your dependence on Him and believe that His peace is available to you.

Very soon your tired, rushed spirit will become calm and His peace will revive your life like refreshing rain. Nothing and no one can take this peace from you, since it is God Himself who whispers to you, "Peace be with you!"

Eternal God who gives me peace in Jesus Christ, lead me to quiet waters where there is peace, in the midst of the hustle and bustle and unrest of life. Amen.

February 11

Read: Acts 12:6-19

Be ready for answered prayers

Peter knocked at the outer entrance, and a servant girl named Rhoda came to answer the door. When she recognized Peter's voice, she was so overjoyed she ran back without opening it and exclaimed, "Peter is at the door!" "You're out of your mind," they told her.
— ACTS 12:13-15 —

The early church was in a crisis. Their leader was in prison and the authorities were involved in an act of cruel persecution. The majority of the believers were scattered over Asia Minor. Then they did the very best they could do under those circumstances: they prayed!

John Wesley said, "God does not do anything unless it is in answer to prayer." When Peter was in prison, they gathered in Mary's house, "where many people had gathered and were praying" (Acts 12:12). When he knocked on the door and Rhoda heard his voice, she excitedly ran to convey the good news. Their reaction was one of boundless astonishment and disbelief.

How slow we are to acknowledge answered prayers. We are quick to seek all kinds of different explanations rather than to praise God and thank Him for answering our prayers.

When God is slow to answer our prayers we become impatient or we complain that He is not listening to us. We do not wait in excitement for the revelation of His omnipotence.

When we pray, we should also beg God for the ability to recognize His answers when they are given. We sometimes continue praying for things which God has already given us. Because it is sometimes not exactly as we expected it, we fail to recognize it as God's answer to our prayers.

God always knows what is best for us. We should, however, develop a sensitivity to recognize our answered prayers with joy, and without sceptical surprise.

Lord, help me to wait with excitement on Your answers and to know when my prayers are answered. Thank You for listening and answering, through Christ who is our Advocate and the Holy Spirit who teaches us to pray. Amen.

Read: Job 5:8-19 February 12

Can correction bring happiness?

Blessed is the man whom God corrects; so do not despise the discipline of the Almighty.

– Job 5:17–

Sometimes an idea may appear to be a contradiction that contains an untruth or impossibility. Yet, when we examine it carefully and test it against life, we find it to be true indeed.

Some people are an affliction to themselves. They complain about their plight continuously and can only see the faults and shortcomings in their fellow man. The smallest illness or problem is exaggerated beyond all proportion and the theme of all their conversations is their own disappointments, struggles and missed opportunities.

To avoid this crippling sickness of the spirit, you should make peace with yourself and remember that your attitude towards life is of the utmost importance. It may be that you are experiencing difficult times and that you feel that you are on your own, that even God has forgotten you.

If however, you shake off your self-pity and ask what God wants to teach you in these circumstances, you will find perspective in the chaos.

Believe with conviction that God has a plan for your life and that everything that befalls you is part of this plan. When God corrects you, it always results in healing if it is accepted with the right attitude.

Trust Him step by step and it will bring a feeling of safety and peace to you. In this way you become a co-worker of God in facilitating your own happiness in life. Then even when you are reprimanded and corrected, you can still experience joy.

Holy Guide, even though I do not understand Your ways, help me through Your Holy Spirit to be a joyful person because I follow in obedience wherever You may guide me. Amen.

February 13   Read: Deuteronomy 10:10-20

"I love you with all my heart, O Lord"

And now, O Israel, what does the Lord *your God ask of you but to fear the* Lord *your God ... to love him, to serve the* Lord *your God with all your heart and with all your soul and to observe the* Lord's *commands and decrees that I am giving you today for your own good?*

— Deuteronomy 10:12-13 —

Have you ever asked yourself seriously and truthfully: "What do I give to God?" It enriches the spirit and often shames one to ask yourself this question and to answer it honestly. This you can only do if the Holy Spirit guides you in truth.

We often unthinkingly sing in church:

> *Take my life, and let it be*
> *Consecrated, Lord, to Thee.*
> *Take my moments and my days;*
> *Let them flow in ceaseless praise.*

But then we proceed to live our selfish and self-centered lives. It is disturbing to discover that the sum of what we give to God is often so shamefully little.

It is impossible to commit your possessions to God without first giving yourself to Him. Though you may confess that everything you have does belong to God there is something that is yours to give or to refuse. That is the sacrifice of your love.

Whatever you give God is not hallowed or of any lasting value if it is not accompanied by your pure love. It is the gift of your love which makes everything else acceptable to God.

Love holds back nothing. As God gave His most precious, His Son, to you in love, you should also in love give everything to Him. More than your sincere love He does not expect, but neither anything less.

O, God of love, with all my love I commit to You my spirit, my body and my soul. Hallow my gift through the love which is in Jesus Christ, my Savior. Amen.

Read: Psalm 71:1-24　　　　　　　　　February 14

Nevertheless I shall rejoice

Though you have made me see troubles, many and bitter, you will restore my life again. I will praise you with the harp for your faithfulness, O my God.

— PSALM 71:20, 22 —

We need not be overcome by depression or collapse under the load of our adversity. For all who are depressed by life, there is liberating advice. Praise is one of the most remarkable forces in your spiritual life.

The Holy Spirit leads us to the discovery of this dynamic power. In the book of Psalms we find proof of the strength that arises from praise time and again.

You can try this remedy with confidence. When you go through dark and difficult days; when your spirit has reached a new low and you start doubting the wisdom and goodness of God, it is time for you to start exchanging your doubt, self-pity and complaints for praise and thanksgiving.

In your depression, such advice may sound ridiculous, even cruel, but this constitutes God's method of picking you up from the dark depths and revealing to you the glory of His living presence. Gratitude and praise are not spiritual luxuries, but doors which lead to His holy presence.

Do not in your depression delude yourself into believing that there is nothing you can thank God for. God is still there, He has not rejected you, His love still shines upon your life. When you realize this anew, you will discover God in nature, in the Scriptures and in your fellow man. Life will smile on you once again and you will discover that faith in God is a prerequisite. With Habakkuk you will confess, "Yet I will rejoice in the LORD, I will be joyful in God my Savior" (Hab. 3:18).

Give me in my inner being, O Lord, a grateful heart, so that I can triumph over depression in the name of Jesus Christ. I praise You, heavenly Father, and I will not forget Your mercies. Amen.

February 15

Read: 2 Corinthians 4:7-15

"In imitation of Christ"

*For we who are alive are always being given over to death for Jesus'
sake, so that his life may be revealed in our mortal body.*
— 2 Corinthians 4:11 —

Regarding certain questions of doctrine, Christianity is unyielding even though there may be widely divergent theological points of view and various forms of worship.

Such differences are unavoidable since people are so complex and different. But despite differences in Christian thinking, the final aim of all Christian doctrine is to cultivate lives which are, as far as possible, expressions of the example of our Lord and Master.

Such a goal may intimidate those people who refuse to surrender their lives to Him completely. They admire the doctrine of Christ and find joy in His calling to discipleship, but they never answer His calling as though it is a holy calling, because they think that He expects more of them than they can give.

If it is your sincere desire to lead a life that follows in the footsteps of Jesus, then there are certain unavoidable requirements which are put to you. Since you have accepted Christ as your Deliverer and Savior and have pledged your loyalty to Him, you will welcome His Holy Spirit into your life in faith.

To have the gift of the Holy Spirit and to allow Him to reveal Himself in you, is such a privilege. It does not only bring peace, a sense of purpose and spiritual power, but you will joyously become aware of the presence of the living Christ in your life. Then you are living in imitation of Christ.

*Perfect Lord, the recognition of Your kingship in my life means
that I am inspired daily by the power of the Holy Spirit. Amen.*

Read: 2 Timothy 4:9-18

February 16

Friendship under strain

For Demas, because he loved this world, has deserted me and has gone to Thessalonica. Crescens has gone to Galatia, and Titus to Dalmatia.

$-$ 2 TIMOTHY 4:10 $-$

Nobody knows why Demas, Crescens and Titus left Paul. Neither do we know whether the separation was temporary or permanent. Friendship is such a precious possession that a breach always means sorrow and loss.

Even among Christians it is possible for friendship to be severely tested. If there is strain, it should not be ignored or left to continue because it can destroy the spirit of unity in a community of believers.

In the most intimate of human relationships it is essential that personal privacy be respected. Moments when one wants to be alone with God should never be encroached upon or be disparaged. It does not matter how firm or intimate the friendship may be. It is only through respect for the individuality of the other person that friendship can thrive and grow in strength and beauty.

Prayer, love and openness are positive mechanisms to relieve the tension in a strained relationship. Pray for God's blessing in the life of the person from whom you have become estranged. While praying, you may discover something in your own life that has caused the tension. The Holy Spirit will provide you with the wisdom on how to handle it. With His help you can possibly correct the misunderstanding.

Prayer can rekindle the flame of friendship and love. When it is necessary to talk the problem through, remember to be honest, but also sensitive.

Teach me, Savior and Friend, the value of true friendship and grant me the mercy through Your Holy Spirit to value my friends and do what I can to nurture our friendship. Amen.

February 17

Read: Proverbs 3:1-18

Advice for difficult times

In all your ways acknowledge him, and he will make your paths straight.

– PROVERBS 3:6 –

It is an irrefutable fact that God wants to help you with your problems and that He can help you. This He tells us emphatically in His infallible Word.

Life is full of problems; this need not be argued. Some are undeserved and unexpected; others are the product of your own foolish behavior. Whatever the cause may be, if you do not find a solution, your problems will govern your life and thought.

If you speak to a trusted and sympathetic friend about your problems, they are placed in perspective and become less intimidating. There are, however, people who revel in their problems and secretly hope that no solution will ever be found. They live on the sympathy of others and degenerate into painful self-pity.

If you have a problem for which you honestly seek a solution, lay it before your heavenly Father. Focus on Him and not on your problem. A vague awareness of God and enormous concentration on your problem make a solution difficult, if not impossible. Trust God with your problem. Confirm His sovereignty in your heart and mind and allow Him to create order from your confusion.

In His time and according to His plan He will provide a solution to your problem. There is no problem that He cannot solve. He cares for you and He can do far more than you think possible. You will experience a feeling of complete peace and new spiritual strength because you have given God His rightful place in your life.

Even if I encounter dark afflictions, almighty Father, I will not fear, since You are with me. Always make me remember that You are greater and more powerful than any problem I might face. I praise Your Name in Jesus Christ. Amen.

Read: Psalm 32:1-11

February 18

The way out of my distress

Then I acknowledged my sin to you and did not cover up my iniquity. I said, "I will confess my transgressions to the LORD" – and you forgave the guilt of my sin.

– PSALM 32:5 –

We are not generalizing when we say that we are living in a world broken and torn apart by sin. There are so many menaces surrounding us, so many sinister temptations charging at us with thundering hooves and so many enslaving bonds binding us.

Time and again we are forced into gloom and we sit trapped within the cold prison walls in which sin has incarcerated us. There is a way out of this misery. It is the way leading to Jesus Christ. It is the way in which we have to confess our sins in sincere repentance as David of old. The lost son also did it when he returned from a distant country to his father's house and his father's heart, where life became a celebration of liberation.

If you have come to Christ with your spoilt and bound life and have confessed your sins, then forget the failures and disappointments of the past and reach out for a new life in Jesus Christ. Forget your disgrace and shame and accept that you are a child of the King. Forget your defeats and follow Christ on the road to victory. Keep your eyes fixed upon Him as the Perfecter and Finisher of your faith with the expressed conviction: "You are my hiding place; You will protect me from trouble and surround me with songs of deliverance" (Ps. 32:7).

Our Merciful and Eternally Strong God is adequate in all circumstances. If you faithfully fight sin in His powerful name you will taste victory. Then you walk into the future with daring and with a song of deliverance in your heart and on your lips.

How wonderful is the deliverance You provide, my Lord and Savior. I thank You that I can bring my sin and distress to You and sing songs of deliverance. Amen.

February 19

Read: Ephesians 4:17-24

When faith has lost its lustre

You were taught, with regard to your former way of life, to put off your old self, which is being corrupted by its deceitful desires; to be made new in the attitude of your minds; and to put on the new self, created to be like God in true righteousness and holiness.
— EPHESIANS 4:22-24 —

It is true, unfortunately, that there are many Christians who have lost their sparkle. Disciples who were once enthusiastic workers, now rest on the laurels of their past performance. This lusterless existence does not come about suddenly. It is the result of long-standing neglect of those essential elements which are vital and dynamic.

When your faith is burning low, you may have become indifferent about your spiritual discipline. Faith that is dead or dying is an indication of a waning life of prayer and neglected Scriptures. A critical or restless spirit will find excuses why communal worship is unnecessary. You feel uncomfortable when spiritual values are discussed. These are all indications that your faith is weakening.

We should remember that God never changes. He who was once so real and played such an important part in your life is still exactly the same God. You are to blame for the diminished quality of your spiritual life, not God. But the way is always open for you to return to a renewed and sparkling relationship with the Master.

If you have lost the freshness and sparkle in your religious life you should be determined to find the reason for this. Perhaps you are in a spiritual rut which is getting deeper as a result of stereotyped prayer and meaningless generalizations. Under the leadership of the Holy Spirit you should discover the true reason why your faith has lost its strength and lustre.

When the Holy Spirit has revealed this truth, you should obey His leadership and He will lead you back to the glory and richness of your initial faith.

Holy Lord Jesus, I thank You for the renewal of my spirit through the Holy Spirit and that I may again experience sparkling faith. Amen.

Read: Mark 1:32-39

February 20

Early morning is a golden opportunity

Very early in the morning, while it was still dark, Jesus got up, left the house and went off to a solitary place, where he prayed.
– MARK 1:35 –

A positive and meaningful faith can be maintained only by continued fellowship with the living Christ. The best time for doing this is before the rush and responsibilities of life start. Naturally excuses in this regard are many. The most common excuse is a lack of time. In some cases this really is valid.

When a mother has to see her husband off to work and get children to school, her meeting with the Master will be most beneficial when the house has become quiet. But to offer a lack of time as an excuse while you refuse to get up half an hour earlier is unacceptable.

It is a sad fact that when our comfort means more to us than our quiet time with the Master we are robbing ourselves of a dynamic source of energy. Our failure prevents us from experiencing an awareness of His living presence.

Although it is possible to pray wherever you are: in the street or in the factory; the office or while doing your chores, nothing can take the place of the prime time you spend with Him at the beginning of the day. Your indifference to this critically important meeting with Him at the start of the day is a source of great joy to Satan. He is skilled in undermining all spiritual discipline. Soon your time of prayer will become so neglected that it will be of no value to you.

Make time to be alone with the Lord and try conscientiously to keep this appointment. Then you will find increasing joy in your growing intimacy with Him. In this way you will discover a source of power at the beginning of every challenging and taxing day.

Loving Savior, I want to seek You early in the morning, so that I can taste the magnificence of Your presence all day long. Amen.

February 21

Read: Matthew 28:11-20

You are never alone

"And surely I am with you always, to the very end of the age"
– MATTHEW 28:20 –

An apparent awareness of the presence of the risen and living Savior is a basic prerequisite for meaningful discipleship. We should always guard against our faith becoming a tradition without any sparkling life and strength. It can so easily happen if we do not continuously experience the presence of the living Christ in our lives.

It does not matter how long you have been following the Christian way of life, you must know Christ as a living reality.

Christ reveals Himself in your life as a result of your simple faith and because you have invited Him to take control of your life. Many people find it extremely difficult to give themselves completely to someone they cannot see or hear. If you believe His Word completely, which says that you can know Him at all times in the strength of His resurrection, new horizons of spiritual experience will open up to you.

Realize that Christ is with you every moment, firmly believe this and live like someone who is in His loving company every moment. Faith is a firm belief in those things we cannot see (according to Hebrews 11:1).

Believing that He is with you every moment will give you strength for the demands of each day. In prosperity and adversity, in joy and in sorrow, His delivering presence will lead you to a life of abundant inner peace and strength. And this is not for today only, but also for tomorrow and the day after, and to the fullness of time.

I praise You for Your living presence, O Lord! It fills my life with certainty. Do not let the world around me ever rob me of this wonderful privilege. Amen.

Read: Matthew 6:25-34   February 22

Travel light through life

"Therefore I tell you, do not worry about your life, what you will eat or drink; or about your body, what you will wear. Is not life more important than food, and the body more important than clothes?"
                                        – MATTHEW 6:25 –

Are you one of those people who cannot throw anything out? Worthless items are saved because you think you may need them one day. It is also quite possible that if you should need them again, you would probably not remember that you have saved them. In time, this collecting becomes a real problem, if not for you, then for the people who must sort through all your things when you are no longer there.

The average person can accept with reasonable safety that if you have not needed an item during the past year or so, you will never need it. Discipline yourself and get rid of redundant items that have become useless. Someone else could possibly use them.

To do this, you will probably have to fight the "collection mania" that you have acquired over the years. You have collected everything that you could lay claim to until your space became restricted and your sense of values was lowered. You have perhaps become so hampered and impeded with non-essentials, that you are chained to the world. These things may be like treasures to you, but they bind you to the past in such a way that you can hardly see the beckoning future.

Rid yourself of these non-essential items and allow the Holy Spirit to determine your concept of values. Then you will gauge the value of the present and move freely and with self-confidence into the future. This also applies to obsolete, useless spiritual red tape.

O, *Holy Spirit, help me to free myself from the past and to reach out to the future so that I can win the prize in Christ Jesus. Amen.*

February 23

Read: John 14:1-4

Do you know the way?

Thomas said to him, "Lord, we don't know where you are going, so how can we know the way?"

– John 14:5 –

It is not always easy to know God's plan for our lives. Many roads lead in different directions ahead of you and you do not know which one God wants you to take. What should you do under these circumstances?

There are certain basic principles which you should consider and which will serve as guidelines in your search for Christ's will for your life. First, get to know God before seeking His path for your life. Live as close to Him as possible and do not allow anything to move Him from the central point of your life.

To live close to God implies that you have to spend much time in His holy presence. This should not be a boring act of duty but a wonderful privilege. Be sensitive to the thoughts passing through your mind while you are with Him. They are often filled with meaning. Write them down because one forgets so quickly. Allow your thoughts to be clear and relaxed in God's presence.

If you make a habit of this, you will be amazed at the ease with which new thoughts appear in your mind. You will taste the excitement of those who realize that they are partners in God's master plan for their futures.

These thoughts should, however, be checked against the revealed will of God in His Word. Obviously anything contrary to true love, purity, unselfishness and honesty will not be His will for your life. If the guidance, however, coincides with Scriptures, you should ensure that you are obedient and follow where He leads you through His Holy Spirit.

Heavenly Guide, I thank You for the assurance that You will lead me if I am sensitive and obedient. Amen.

Read: Galatians 2:15-21   February 24

Living faith

And I no longer live, but Christ lives in me.

– GALATIANS 2:20 –

Too many Christians do not experience the power and joy which the living Christ has promised them in their daily lives. They accept the viewpoints of the church, but lack the essential and dynamic personal experience with Christ.

God has many treasures available for those who trust Him. If you walk with Him through Christ every day and accept the gift of the Holy Spirit, you are spiritually strengthened in your faith and you can face daily demands with confidence. He gives you the discriminative ability to expose temptations and the strength to live victoriously. God is there to provide in every human need if only we live in dependence on His will.

God's greatest and most precious gift to humankind is Jesus Christ. If you have a hunger in your soul, and long for a spiritual experience which will enliven your tired spirit and give you courage to move forward confidently, you need God. You then have the assurance that you will never be alone. God has met your need by giving you Jesus Christ. Until, however, you have accepted Him as your personal Redeemer and Savior, He cannot work effectively in your life.

You must accept Christ in faith and love and serve Him with your entire being. Then you will experience the total satisfaction which only He can give you.

Living Christ, by accepting You and living in harmony with Your will, I experience complete peace and happiness. Amen.

February 25

Read: Psalm 62:1-12

Do you make time for God?

Trust in him at all times, O people; pour out your hearts to him, for God is our refuge.

– PSALM 62:8 –

Perhaps you are one of those Christians who long for prayer to play a deeper and more significant part in your life. You may realize that your spiritual and moral defeats, your frustrations and subsequent feelings of dejection are caused by your spiritual poverty as a result of neglected or inadequate prayer. Perhaps you have already pleaded with God to do something about it.

The fact of the matter is that God has already done everything that is needed. He loved you before you were aware of His love. Christ came to die to prove that love and He has promised to be with you always: never to leave or forsake you. This He does through His Spirit which He sent us as Comforter and intercessor. The question is: how much time are you prepared to give to Him?

The responsibility for developing a significant prayer life rests squarely with you. You determine how much time you spend in prayer. Only you can exercise the discipline of prayer in your life in such a way that it can lead to a fruitful prayer life; only you can determine a time and place for being alone with God.

Richard Newton said, "The most important cause of spiritual barrenness is an inexplicable unwillingness to pray. When I can get my heart into a state of courage and boldness to pray, all other things are relatively easy."

The experience of generations of God's children has proven the wisdom and value of time surrendered to God. This time forms the foundation of your spiritual existence and growth. Always remember: you can meet the Lord at any time and in any place by simply directing your thoughts to Him and opening up your spirit to the work of the Holy Spirit.

God of mercy, You who listens to the prayers of supplication from Your children, help me consciously and purposefully to make time for fellowship with You in prayer, so that I can experience the work of the Holy Spirit. Amen.

Read: Galatians 6:1-10   February 26

Appreciation creates two-way communication

Therefore, as we have opportunity, let us do good to all people, especially to those who belong to the family of believers.
— GALATIANS 6:10 —

Never hesitate to express sincere appreciation. It is so easy to take for granted the work someone did with great effort and sacrifice, or to appropriate as a right the sacrifices made with great effort on our behalf.

Appreciation does not only delight the hearts of those who receive it, but it also brings you joy.

Guard against being self-centered and taking more from life than you are prepared to put into it. If you make a conscious effort to be aware of things to be grateful for, you will realize that there are a number of blessings that you have taken for granted.

Love, loyalty and generosity of spirit are beautiful gifts people give to you every day. Recapture the God-given insight to see the glory of the daily acts of love that people perform for you continuously. Answer these with your own acts of grateful love.

Never forget God's acts of mercy to you. It is impossible to stand in gratefulness before our glorious God and still be depressed. Allow your gratitude to God to spread out into acts of unselfish love for your fellow man. This will become a rich source of blessing to others and to you.

If you have an urge to express your appreciation or do a kind deed, don't delay or postpone it. Act as soon as possible to show your appreciation.

Help me, heavenly Father, always to be full of appreciation for the love and help I receive from so many people, and especially from You. I thank You humbly for all Your blessings in Jesus Christ which I undeservingly receive. Amen.

February 27

Read: Luke 15:11-24

The moment of truth

When he came to his senses, he said, "How many of my father's hired men have food to spare, and here I am starving to death!"
— Luke 15:17 —

Many people refuse to come to a standstill and deal with personal issues they have with themselves. Deep down in their hearts various questions arise, but they refuse to listen to these or to handle them. Generally every possible effort is made to avoid the questions. These questions however, keep cropping up with monotonous regularity and demand answers.

Questions which most people have asked in one or other form, are: "What is truth?"; "Is my life governed by blind fate?" and "Can I really know God?"

These and other questions of vital importance need to be answered. There are no instant answers to these questions. Many students have devoted a lifetime to searching for the answers and trying to express them.

When you reach the moment of truth in your life and admit that the questions which touch the core of life are far beyond your understanding, the wise and constructive thing to do is to place yourself under the instruction of Jesus Christ. Accept His wisdom and guidance for your life. It requires the discipline of prayer, meditation, study of the Scriptures and self-discovery. He teaches you and guides you in your daily life.

Then you will find that, though you may not discover all the answers immediately, you will develop an awareness that God is guiding you to a more complete and richer understanding of life. Then your struggle with the vital questions is not in vain.

Perfect and all-wise Lord, because You control my life, I leave all the unanswered questions in Your hands. I am convinced that You will give all the answers to me in Your time and in Your way. Amen.

Read: Mark 10:13-16   February 28

In the school of love

I tell you the truth, anyone who will not receive the kingdom of God like a little child will never enter it.

– MARK 10:15 –

Most small children are pure, innocent and loving. They are also teachable and easily guided. Jesus Christ set these qualities as conditions for access to the kingdom of God.

Teachers will tell you that up to a certain age children believe that the teacher cannot possibly make a mistake or do anything wrong. Children have the same trust in most adults, especially in their parents. There are many aspects to consider if one desires a complete understanding of a child's faith.

Unfortunately evil and sinful things are taught to children. They believe the examples we set them. If these encompass prejudice, violence, hatred, selfishness and such qualities, then they believe that this is how they should live. The pattern of their lives then changes from loving to aggressive. If they are strengthened in their faith and have examples of love, nobleness, integrity and sympathy, they will then follow this example.

It is no wonder that adults have to learn afresh how to love. The world in which we live is not a loving place. But the true world, God's world, is a place of love. The love of Jesus Christ was not a weak, emotional love, but something powerful which could achieve great deeds.

Therefore we should purposefully focus on loving more every day; we should enroll in Jesus' school of love so that He can love through us.

We should learn to be tolerant and to allow others to differ from us. We should always be filled with compassion and be prepared to reach out to someone in need. Give other people a sense of self-worth by expressing appreciation and by encouraging them. Ultimately, through perseverance, you will be promoted to candidacy for the kingdom of God.

Teach me daily, O God of love, to love with a pure and sincere heart. Amen.

February 29

Read: Psalm 90:1-17

Your most precious possession

Teach us to number our days aright, that we may gain a heart of wisdom.

– Psalm 90:12 –

Today is an extra day we receive because the Gregorian calendar makes a correction every four years. The tropical year consists of 365.242 days and a day is added every four years so as not to lose the fraction of a day.

How will you use this day of grace? Will you allow it to pass unused while you are fully aware of it? Will it disappear into thin air without us being able to account for it? And how many of the precious days of every year are not wasted!

As the markers speed past on our path of life and the years increase, some people convince themselves that they have become obsolete. So they waste precious bonus time which God has added to their lives. It is the content of the years that determine the quality, and not the number of the years. We should never become too old for new experiences. We should live every day to the full. If you want to do something, do it now! If you want to go somewhere, go now! Do not wait until your God-given moment is wasted.

Be prepared for new experiences and new encounters. Do not become too old to delight and rejoice in the beauty of God's creation. Accept the restrictions that life places on you, but live productively from the gifts that God bestows on you. Do not waste a fraction of your time in self-pity and depression. Remember, life does not return wasted time to you.

Life is an exciting experience, especially when experienced with God. Then human weaknesses and age do not count. Remember the eternity of God; that He is with you every step of the way and that He expects you to use your time wisely.

Lord Jesus, give me such an appreciation of life that I will be able to evaluate my life according to acts and attitudes, rather than years. Amen.

MARCH

March 1

Read: Hebrews 11:30-39

Faith will carry you through

The prophets, through faith conquered kingdoms, administered justice, and gained what was promised.

– Hebrews 11:33 –

Many people worry themselves sick about the future. It seems as if there is unrest and disruption right throughout the world and everywhere people ask, "How much longer, how long can it continue like this?" Even if this attitude is understandable, it eventually only leads to depression and despair. And that worsens the situation. Then people ultimately lose all hope and they bow before what they regard as the inevitable. Throughout the centuries the world has been filled with conflict. Humankind has experienced every imaginable form of danger, hardship and catastrophic disaster. Through greed and lack of involvement, cravings for honor and man's digression has caused or contributed to every disaster on earth.

Nevertheless, history proves that there has always been a core group of believers who trusted in God. By His mercy they overcame stumbling blocks and the Lord God rewarded their steadfast faith.

However dark and disastrous your circumstances may appear, place your trust steadfastly in God. Hold on to the certainty of the risen Savior who triumphed over the world. Remember: "In the beginning God created the heavens and the earth. Now the earth was formless and empty, darkness was over the surface of the deep, and the Spirit of God was hovering over the waters. And God said, 'Let there be light,' and there was light" (Gen. 1:1-3).

Despite the anxiety and panic of the world, you should continue believing in the irrefutable fact of a loving and almighty God who can create order from chaos. He will protect everyone who trusts in Him. It is still God's earth, despite the fact that the world seems to believe the opposite.

Perfecter and Finisher of my faith, I place my complete trust in You under all circumstances and at all times. Amen.

Read: Matthew 19:16-30

March 2

God can do it

Jesus looked at them and said, "With man this is impossible, but with God all things are possible."

– MATTHEW 19:26 –

Despite the disbelief and cynicism of modern times, God is still capable of miracles. Unfortunately many of the modern miracles are ascribed to coincidence. Often when prayers are said for the sick and they recover miraculously, the prayers are forgotten and no thanks or acknowledgement is given to God. Many people pray when they face a crisis, but when the crisis is past and their worst fears have not materialized, they ignore the fact that they have prayed, or even feel embarrassed about it.

The evidence that God does answer prayer is overpowering. Many modern Christians can bear testimony of miracles that occurred in answer to prayer. Lives have been unrecognizably changed; illnesses have been miraculously cured; twisted human relationships have been restored. Many people personally discovered that God gives guidance when we ask for it.

Despite the miraculous power of prayer, God requires our cooperation for the answering of our prayers. God cannot solve your problem if you lay it before Him in prayer, but then take it back again with you. Hand the problem completely over to Him and do not try to solve it yourself. Let it rest there and allow God to unravel it like a pattern that has been incorrectly knitted.

Do not succumb in your extreme despair. At the right time and in the right way God will answer and you will be amazed by the result. Then you will rejoice in the fact that you did not interfere. In this way we gradually learn obedience in prayer and God increasingly works His miracles in our lives.

Not my will, Master, but Your will be done in my life. I once again place my life completely at Your disposal. Amen.

March 3

Read: 2 Timothy 4:1-8

Your best is good enough for God!

I have fought the good fight, I have finished the race, I have kept the faith.

– 2 TIMOTHY 4:7 –

The service of many people who are involved in God's work on earth, is influenced adversely by their own negative approach to their calling and task. Some do not feel capable of the task; others are discouraged because they consequently feel that they should have done better; then there are those whose best is never good enough for themselves. Such attitudes can influence you in a very negative way and subsequently influence the work of the Master you want to serve.

If you make a study of the life and work of the biblical giants of faith, you will find that they all, at one time or another also made mistakes. They all experienced moments of doubt in their own abilities. But despite this, they all gave God their best. They tackled their task in the strength of the Lord. They triumphed over all adversity and remained standing until the end.

Whatever task the Lord has given you, remember His promise that He will always be with you (Heb. 13:5) and that you are capable of everything through Him who gives you strength (Phil. 4:13). Accept the unchangeable fact that you cannot do anything without Him, but that all things are possible *with* Him. Let every effort you make be supported by prayer and commitment.

Execute your task then to the best of your ability and in prayer ask for the strength of the Holy Spirit. God does not ask for anything more – and nothing less – than your best. Then God can use you as an instrument for His great deeds.

I thank You, holy Father, that I can rejoice with the psalmist: "With Your help I can advance against a troop; with my God I can scale a wall" (Ps. 18:29). Amen.

Read: Ephesians 3:14-21

March 4

Privileges and responsibilities

So that Christ may dwell in your hearts through faith.
— EPHESIANS 3:17 –

There is no substitute whatsoever for a personal relationship with the living Christ. Doctrines and creeds are essential to clarify the Christian faith and rituals can help to bring you into the right frame of mind for an encounter with God. Unfortunately, many people place the main emphasis on the side issues, and forget that they are mere guidelines to bring us to a true meeting with the risen Savior.

The indwelling Christ is one of the great themes of the gospel of Jesus. The committed disciple of Christ should not use knowing Him intimately as an excuse to dissociate himself from the world. To isolate yourself from your fellow men because they do not share the same spiritual experience as you is merely spiritual arrogance. It leads to unproductive isolation. It cries out against the example Jesus Christ set when He lived and worked on earth.

Because Christ lives in you, you have specific responsibilities and privileges. You are responsible for reflecting the glory of Christ. To think that non-Christians allow their opinion of Christ to be determined and influenced by your life, should be an eye-opener. After all, they see the way you handle certain situations that they have to face themselves.

The great privilege in giving yourself to Christ, is the fact that He knows everything about you. He supplements your imperfection with His complete perfection; your weakness He strengthens with His power; your lack of love He transforms through His perfect love. Nothing can surpass the peace and love that He offers to those who are rooted and grounded in His love.

I praise You, Lord Jesus, for the privilege of belonging to You, and in Your Name I accept my responsibilities. Amen.

March 5

Read: Job 37:14-24

Not I, but God!

"Listen to this, Job; stop and consider God's wonders."

– Job 37:14 –

When you feel unworthy of and inadequate for the task that God has called you for, you can gain courage from the fact that many of God's greatest servants felt unworthy of the work God called them to do. The Scriptures tell of many people who tried to escape from the responsibility God placed on them.

If you are convinced that God gave you a special task and you are nevertheless unsure of your own abilities, you should do everything in your power to prepare yourself thoroughly for the task. Erase all negative thoughts and emotions from your mind and spend some quality time alone with God. Become quiet before Him and become aware of His living presence.

This spiritual discipline will make you aware of God's way of working. You will see God at work in changing circumstances and situations. This will give you confidence to face all the problems the future may have.

The inspiration and confidence you receive from God are more than just emotional feelings. When your spirit is depressed and the insight into what you should do for God is impeded, you should be alone with Him, the Energy Source. And while you draw on His power and wisdom, your spirit and thoughts can be renewed.

Lay your thoughts before Him and beg for His approval. Diligently follow His guidance through obedience to the Holy Spirit. In this way you will become a fellow worker in the miracles of God, while you will taste the deliverance that is part of those who live within the will of God. In doing this you will discover the purpose of your life and God, who accomplishes His miracles through you, will use you as a powerful instrument.

Merciful Father, make me receptive to Your inspiration through the Holy Spirit, so that I can accomplish Your task with confidence. Amen.

Read: Jeremiah 17:3-13　　　　　　　　　　　　March 6

Strength from hidden sources

Blessed is the man who trusts in the LORD, *whose confidence is in him. He will be like a tree planted by the water that sends out its roots by the stream. It does not fear when heat comes; its leaves are always green. It has no worries in a year of drought and never fails to bear fruit.*

— JEREMIAH 17:7-8 —

It is tragic that so many of Christ's followers lead superficial and barren lives. Unwilling to discard their pet sins, they mold their beliefs according to their own desires, and discover, in times of stress and tension that their faith is inadequate for meeting the demands. Great promises of a life committed in service to the Master, are tragically not kept.

You should constantly be aware of the unlimited resources of the living Christ. It is inalienably the inheritance of those who love Him and serve Him. These resources are: a purposeful faith that becomes stronger the longer it is practiced; a deep awareness of Christ's living presence, not only when you are alone with the Lord in private, but also in your busy day to day life; a certainty about where to go for inspiration and strength and a knowledge of His Word so that you can draw on a meaningful word in times of crisis.

The hidden sources of faith can only be effective when they are constantly utilized and employed. The more you draw on them, the more effective your life and service become.

If your faith is based on a fixed foundation, you will remain standing against superficial emotions in times of spiritual drought. When your spirit reaches a low-water mark, your faith will give you wings. Despite external circumstances, you will live in the land of victory because you are drawing on a hidden Source of power.

Savior and Redeemer, I thank You for the stable faith that the Holy Spirit strengthens in me that is greater than my unstable emotions! Amen.

March 7

Read: Psalm 57:1-12

Start the day right

My heart is steadfast, O God, my heart is steadfast; I will sing and make music. Awake, my soul! Awake, harp and lyre! I will awaken the dawn.

– PSALM 57:7-8 –

Many people do themselves injustice every day. They wake up in the morning and start grumbling and complaining. This sets the pattern for the morning and usually, for the entire day.

When you wake up in the morning, think of all the beautiful and good things that make life worthwhile for you.

Take pleasure in even the smallest privileges of life: birds that sing; dealings with valued friends; food to eat and clothes to wear. Counting your blessings is a wonderful way to start your day. Decide to have a positive attitude towards everything you have to do today and towards everyone you will meet.

Look forward with anticipation and excitement to what the day will bring. Be convinced that God intended only the best for you. Faithfully believe that the good Father will give you the self-confidence to face the day with calmness and joy.

Never underestimate the effect of your thoughts in relation to your daily life. Start every day with this unshakable belief: "This is the day the LORD has made; let us rejoice and be glad in it" (Ps. 118:24). Start counting your blessings the moment you wake up and your spiritual life will be elevated to a new, unknown level of joy. Then you will be able to meet every challenge of the day.

If you start the day complaining, you have only yourself to blame because your entire day could turn out sorrowful and sad. With a positive prayer and the right attitude, every day can be a psalm of praise, and you will be an inspiration to others.

God of mercy, I accept every day as a glorious gift from Your loving hand. Help me to fill it with grateful joy. Amen.

Read: Matthew 17:1-8   March 8

No one except Jesus

When they looked up, they saw no one except Jesus.
                                        – MATTHEW 17:8 –

Never before in history has there been such a fragmentation of the Christian religion and doctrine. Believers are faced with different interpretations that all purport to be true. This causes such a veritable Babel of confusion that people become unsure of what to believe.

If you experience such a dilemma, it is perhaps time to stop for a while. Examine your spiritual questions under the guidance and leadership of the Holy Spirit. Move all preconceived ideas to the background and open up your spirit for His guidance. Confess your willingness to be obedient to His will. If you allow the Holy Spirit to work freely in your life, you will discover that He will lead you to a deeper and more intimate relationship with the living Christ. You will also discover that Jesus will occupy the central position in your life.

It is the all-important sovereignty of Jesus Christ that has to be responsible for the germination and growth of a living faith. Everything that contributes to His glorification comes from the Spirit of the living God. Any doctrine that does not give Christ precedence is not inspired by God.

Whatever Christian belief you may have, whatever faith or doctrine you may support, remember that without Christ they are powerless and meaningless. Only when He truly rules as King in your life and heart, will your faith be alive and meaningful.

No one except Jesus – it is the emergency call of the human heart.

Central point of my longing, I thank You that my heart thirsts continuously for You. Protect me from anyone or anything that will threaten Your presence in my life. Amen.

March 9

Read: Job 37:1-18

God makes life good

"Listen to this, Job; stop and consider God's wonders."

– Job 37:14 –

We live in troubled and uncertain times. Consequently, most people bemoan their lot or find fault with the world. There are international, political and racial tensions. Moral standards are in decline and high principles in business are no longer valued. The sanctity of the family is no longer seen as the foundation of our civilization. The end result is, sadly, that a great number of people admit defeat and do not even try to swim against the tide, but just drift along aimlessly.

If you find yourself in this position, you should, like Job, stop to think for a while. Do not be prepared to accept defeat too soon. Worldly influences and opinions become insignificant when seen against the time span of centuries.

Reflect on the wonderful deeds of God. Out of chaos and darkness He called forth this beautiful earth. He granted us the privilege of living and working on it. From the dust of the earth He created Adam as the father of mankind.

His love for His creatures was so great that He wanted to save them from the bonds of sin and death. He came to live among us in the perfect Person of Jesus Christ. In this way He set us the example of a Christian way of life. Through His death and resurrection He triumphed over death and Satan. He achieved the promise of an eternal life for us. Through His Holy Spirit we are privileged to live with and in Christ – forever.

When you question life, become quiet and consider the wonderful deeds of God. Praise Him in gratitude for everything He does for you. Then life will flourish again.

Lord, how cheerful and full of abundant thanks You make my heart. Thank You for the glorious deeds you do in and around me. Guide me through Your Spirit to see only this and to appreciate it. Amen.

Read: 1 John 4:7-21

March 10

Love is indispensable

*Dear friends, let us love one another, for love comes from God.
Everyone who loves has been born of God and knows God.*

– 1 JOHN 4:7 –

There is no substitute for love. Love is essential to an abundant life. Have you noticed that there are people who at forty look as though they are more than sixty and many who at seventy look much younger? It is incorrect to say that the difference can be attributed to circumstances and events. This is true for people in all situations of life.

A youthful appearance is also not only the result of make-up. If one's spirit is bitter and unforgiving and if it gnaws at you continuously, the most skillful application of expensive make-up will never manage to bring a youthful sparkle to the eye or brighten a careworn appearance.

People who live life with a cheerful spirit have discovered that sparkling youthfulness is the product of a heart in harmony with God. To live in the awareness of His loving presence brings depth as well as joyfulness. The faith of such a person is a matter of great joy. It is based on the Rock of love and not on fleeting emotions.

If you share everything in your life with God, He shares the wealth of His spiritual treasure chamber with you. This means in particular His most precious and greatest gift – love. It lives in your spirit and is reflected through your entire life. No age can be linked to the spirit of love. Although, if your body is changed and even aged by the passing of time, your spirit will reveal a timelessness that is the unalienable share of all who love God and their fellow man.

It is beauty and youthfulness that wells up from a person's deepest and innermost being. For this, love is indispensable.

Perfect Father and Master, make me a distributor of Your love so that timelessness will radiate from me. Amen.

March 11

Read: Romans 8:28-39

Tossed between hope and despair

What a wretched man I am! Who will rescue me from this body of death?

— Romans 7:24 –

No, in all these things we are more than conquerors through him who loved us.

— Romans 8:37 –

Sometimes you will find yourself on the mountain top of spiritual exultation where the presence of Christ will be a living reality in your life. But Christ never promised His disciples that they would eternally remain on the mountain top. On the contrary, He Himself sent the disciples down to the valley where they became deeply aware of their powerlessness and incompetence.

It is encouraging to know that even Paul experienced the depths of spiritual depression. Yet, he also rose to great heights where he could praise God for victory and deliverance.

You will share in both experiences at different times, but you will have to decide in which of these worlds of experience you are going to live. God's will for your life is only good. He wants you to constantly taste the joy and strength that flow forth from the awareness of His loving presence in your life.

Too few of God's children see themselves as victorious children of the King. They are too aware of all their sins, failures and defeats and they are continuously occupied with hiding behind their spiritual unworthiness. It is time for you to look past your failures and discover the type of life that can be yours through the power of the indwelling Christ. As a worthy child of God you will have to live a worthy life. This will give a new quality to your existence.

You'll live to His glory and become a worthy vehicle for God's love and strength.

Lord, my God, I thank You in humility and amazement that I may be Your child through Jesus Christ! I make myself available so that Your Spirit can develop my life to its full potential. Amen.

Read: 1 Corinthians 15:42-58   March 12

Christ unlocks eternity

Now we see but a poor reflection as in a mirror; then we shall see face to face. Now I know in part; then I shall know fully, even as I am fully known.

– 1 Corinthians 13:12 –

When we suddenly have to face the great mystery of death and the hereafter, we more than ever become aware of our human limitations. In all honesty, we have to admit that there are lots of things we don't easily understand, even though we might know the answers to many questions.

Lancelot Andrews said, "If we could reach God only through knowledge and argument, the learned and gifted would be the only people to achieve this. But God changed the path leading to Him into a 'Via Regium' – a kingly highroad." Christ is the key bearer who unlocks new vistas for us on this highroad to God.

We do not know the future but we know Him who holds the future in His mighty hand. We do not know the way, but we know Jesus who is the way. Even though we cannot answer all the "whys?", through faith we know the God who has all the answers. We know that Jesus Christ is God's answer to all our questions.

That is why a personal relationship with the living Christ is so important. If we want to receive God's gifts of forgiveness and eternal life, we should, through our faith in Jesus Christ, stride out courageously on the unknown road. His glorious presence provides all the consolation we need.

Speak to God about your questions and your pain and accept the sovereignty of Christ – do it in the dark times in your life as well.

One day we will stand face to face with our glorified Savior. We will know Him as He knows us, and all the answers will be given to us. Until that day, we must have the courage in faith and the confidence to live without all the answers and yet hold on to Him inseparably.

Loving Savior, help me to calmly accept my limitations and to joyfully walk the path that Christ has set before me. Amen.

March 13

Read: Romans 14:1-11

Each for himself? No!

For none of us lives to himself alone.

– ROMANS 14:7 –

If we lead a normal life, we come into contact with other people all the time. At home, at work, on the sports field, in trade and in spiritual areas we are continuously confronted by the challenge of human relationships.

There are people whom we like and there are unfortunately people we do not like. It may be difficult for us to give a reason for this, but it is the plain and unpleasant truth. It is precisely those people whom you do not like who present a challenge to you as a Christian. Ensure that your attitude is not based on jealousy. This sin has destroyed more human relationships than will ever be known. Open yourself to the Holy Spirit and make sure that there is nothing in your life that can cause friction. If there is tension in your relationship, try and determine your part in this unhappy situation.

Perhaps you have been aware of the faults and weaknesses of the other person for such a long time that you no longer expect anything good from him. When you see each other, serious conflicts occur, and before either of you have said anything, there is a mutual feeling of antagonism.

As a Christian, it is your duty to defuse such a tense situation. Pray for the cleansing power of the Holy Spirit. Seriously pray to be saved from the spirit of antagonism and accept others in a spirit of goodwill.

If you persevere lovingly, you will conquer this destructive spirit and through your attitude you will bring forward the best in others. Only God, through the love of Jesus Christ, can enable you to do this.

God of love, with Your help and mercy I am going to build every relationship in my life with a positive attitude. Help me in this through the Holy Spirit. Amen.

Read: Romans 12:9-21   March 14

Unshakable trust

Be joyful in hope, patient in affliction.

– Romans 12:12 –

When everything seems to be going wrong for people, they are often tempted to act in either one of two ways. On the one hand they can be completely overwhelmed by their problems and collapse under them. On the other hand they can try impulsively to solve them in their own strength.

In both cases you have little chance of coming out of it unharmed. It is also possible that you will have to pay a very high price for your impulsiveness. The Lord has promised never to forsake or leave you. The Scriptures tell time and again of how God kept His promises. It is therefore imperative that you trust Him completely on your journey through life.

Nevertheless, you must have patience, because you cannot hurry God or prescribe to Him. He has His good time and method. His timing is always perfect. Even if you find it difficult to understand in your present confusion, you must accept that God sees the overall picture of your life. He is all-knowing and all-seeing. Your faith in Him must be of such quality that you will unshakably trust His promises and abide obediently by His judgment.

When dark days and difficulties cross your path, place your burdens in His care and keep on trusting. Seek the guidance of the Holy Spirit to teach you to wait patiently on the Lord. Ask Him for the discernment to see His answers to your prayers.

Having done that, you can, with childlike faith, leave everything in God's hands and believe that He will provide. He wants you to experience only the best and the most beneficial, and if this takes place in strange and roundabout ways, you should continue believing and trusting steadfastly. They who stand steadfast in affliction, receive God's most precious gifts from His treasury of mercy.

Lord and Father, I find peace of mind by trusting You completely. Keep me steadfast through my faith in You. Amen.

March 15

Read: Romans 8:18-27

Persevere in prayer

In the same way, the Spirit helps us in our weakness. We do not know what we ought to pray for, but the Spirit himself intercedes for us with groans that words cannot express.

– ROMANS 8:26 –

When one needs the healing power of prayer the most, you are often not able to pray. It is extremely difficult to pray trustingly when sorrow overwhelms you. Then the only prayer is often a lament: "I cannot pray!" But this sincere prayer is an admission of your own shortcomings, of your distress, of your willingness to change, of your willingness to be enriched by God's love. God does not answer prayers because they are perfect, but because He reaches out in love and sympathy to people in distress.

We should not think that a sorrowing heart cannot pray at all. It is not how much or how well we pray that counts, but simply that we do pray. With that we admit that God as the Good Shepherd, is with us, even in the dark depths.

Jesus says, "Ask and it will be given to you" (Lk. 11:9). Just whisper a prayer amidst your confusion, asking for comfort, strength, wisdom, calmness and peace, and you will feel the comforting touch of the Master. It will enable you to move through the dark valley and into the light.

You are not praying alone. The Holy Spirit intercedes for you with insight you do not have at such moments. In your confusion and uncertainty the Spirit prays for you according to the will of God. God asks only that you should keep your heart tuned in to Him, because this in itself is a form of prayer. "He will respond to the prayer of the destitute; He will not despise their plea" (Ps. 102:17).

The dark hour will pass. Do not rebel against your inability to pray. Hold on to this eternal truth: God's love for you never changes!

Lord, teach me to pray so that I can walk from the dark valley towards eternal sunshine. Amen.

Read: 2 Peter 3:1-18   March 16

Mature Christianity

Grow in the grace and knowledge of our Lord and Savior Jesus Christ.

— 2 PETER 3:18 —

Spiritual immaturity is a self-imposed characteristic. Many people call themselves Christians because they were born in a pious family or because they are part of a Christian civilization. Yet they have never personally surrendered their lives to Christ.

You become a Christian when you accept Jesus Christ as your personal Savior and Redeemer. From that moment on, you start a way of life which requires you to commit yourself daily to the Master. Without a daily commitment you can never significantly come to maturity. You cannot have a meaningful experience on a part-time basis.

When you confirm your faith in Him, the living Christ accepts you as His disciple. He keeps all His promises. The responsibility to develop a vigorous faith, however, rests with you. You may have a desire for a richer prayer life, but unless you devote time to deepen and improve your prayer life, even God cannot give you your heart's desire.

You may long for greater and stronger faith, but if you do not use the little faith you already have, you will not receive more faith. A sincerely developing Christian never stops striving for conformity to His Lord. This may seem like a high ideal, but no child of the Lord struggles on his own. The Master is always there to encourage, to inspire and to strengthen you, especially in times of weakness and frustration.

The Christian life is a continuing process of growth to maturity. If you stop working on it, your spiritual life will stagnate and eventually stop existing.

Enabling Master, I plead that Your Holy Spirit would stir me in moments of spiritual laxness. Amen.

March 17

Read: 1 Peter 2:11-17

Freedom has a spiritual quality

Live as free men, but do not use your freedom as a cover-up for evil; live as servants of God.

— 1 PETER 2:16 —

The word "freedom" is frequently misused. In the name of freedom disgusting crimes are committed. It calls embittered people to action. Those false leaders who promise freedom, find themselves unavoidably under a new form of bondage.

True freedom can only be enjoyed when a person's spirit is freed from all hate, pettiness and jealousy. True freedom has a spiritual quality known to and experienced by those who know, love and serve God.

The majority of people live in slavery. They may be unaware of the bonds that bind them, because they have already become accustomed to them. They are oppressed by the bonds of habit, preconceived notions and wrong thoughts. This is reflected in their gloomy attitude towards life and their fellow man. A negative attitude that is expressed through hate and bitterness reveals the bondage which binds so many people to powerlessness.

The good news of the gospel is that it brings freedom for everyone who was held captive by the destructive influences that apparently controlled their inner being.

Christ forgives sins and frees us from all the bonds of sin. This freedom is a gift of God's love. It is experienced when accepted in faith. While you enjoy the blessing of the freedom that Christ is giving you, you are being recreated to a new life of harmony, peace and an awareness of your connection to God.

God of mercy, through Your indwelling Spirit, I have been set free of all sin and undesirable habits. I rejoice in the freedom I have to worship You. Amen.

Read: Matthew 26:36-46　　　　　　　　# March 18

Spiritual depression

"My Father, if it is possible, may this cup be taken from me. Yet not as I will, but as you will."

– MATTHEW 26:39 –

A popular misconception among Christians is that sincere believers are supposed to always experience spiritual ecstasy. If they experience times when they are feeling down, there is a strong conviction that they are disappointing themselves and the God in whom they believe. When this happens, they try to cheer up their depressed spirit with all kinds of emotional tricks.

People seldom realize that spiritual depression can be a real spiritual experience. The mere fact that you are depressed, already serves as an indication that you know that something better is waiting for you. If you had not been aware of a better and nobler life, you would not have been depressed.

It is essential to let your faith rise above your emotions. Emotions fluctuate and if you allow them to control your life, your faith will become unstable.

When Jesus prayed in Gethsemane, He was confronted by a situation that He would rather have avoided. He even pleaded with God to free Him from the responsibility placed upon Him. At that stage His spirit was deeply upset. The power of the Savior's life lies precisely in the all-important fact that He placed God's will above His own will and desires.

The secret of a balanced and even spiritual experience lies in elevating God's will above your own desires, and to remember at all times that, whatever you may feel, the living Christ is always with you and He cares and understands.

Father who understands all, I thank You that my faith is a stabilizing reality in my life. Guide me through Your Holy Spirit to a balanced discipleship. Amen.

March 19

Read: Proverbs 17:1-10

Live in peace

Better a dry crust with peace and quiet than a house full of feasting, with strife.

— PROVERBS 17:1 —

For many people possessions and wealth have become the most important aspects of their lives. They follow the example set by others in our society where abundance and wealth are the most important priorities. The accumulation of material wealth and a luxurious lifestyle take precedence over having peace of mind and contentment.

These people become tense and pressurized, which in turn leads to worry, broken relationships, general restlessness and unhappiness. While thrift and thorough planning for future success are praiseworthy, they can become a problem if pushed to the extreme. They can lead to nastiness, jealousy, selfishness and dishonesty.

As soon as your material possessions become the most important thing in your life, your life loses its real purpose and meaning. Then it becomes a routine and a painful punishment, like being on a treadmill that just keeps going.

Do not fall victim to the temptation of giving wealth and a luxurious lifestyle top priority in your life. Rather seek a personal encounter with the risen Christ. Serve Him in obedience and surrender to Him. The peace of mind you will obtain from this, will enable you to experience that which no earthly possessions can equal.

The fullness of the new life in which Christ will guide you, will surpass anything this world can offer by far.

I praise Your Name, Lord Jesus, for coming to earth so that I may live, and that in abundance and with peace of mind. Amen.

Read: Romans 5:1-11   March 20

The Holy Spirit – cultivator of love

Because God has poured out his love into our hearts by the Holy Spirit, whom he has given us.

— ROMANS 5:5 —

The sure knowledge that Christ lives in you can bring about a powerful spiritual revolution in your life. It inspires your thinking, broadens your outlook, gives you new confidence, creates enthusiasm, and offers purpose and meaning to your daily existence. All of this is the work of the Holy Spirit in particular, who constantly assures you of your connection with the Source of true love.

However powerful and inspirational you may find this mutual love between you and your God, it should be firmly anchored in the foundation of reality and faith.

To say that you love Christ, and yet refuse to lighten the burden of an oppressed fellow human being, is a denial of that love.

If you truly love Him through the Holy Spirit, it will bring you to the painful awareness of the distress of others, and it will create in you the irrepressible urge to do something about it.

If you lay claim to the love of God in your heart, it will be revealed through your words, in your attitude towards others, and your willingness to serve others through His Spirit and in His strength. God is revealed through His Spirit's work of love in your life. Then you lovingly accept the full responsibility of your faith, by the help of the Holy Spirit, your Teacher.

This love enables us to look for the highest good in our fellow man, despite insults, hurt or humiliation. This includes the heart and the intellect, will and emotion. It is the purposeful attempt to seek nothing but the best for others with the help of the Holy Spirit. God Himself is the source of this love and this was demonstrated for us by Jesus Christ. The Holy Spirit cultivates this in our hearts.

Holy Spirit, love Divine,
Glow within this heart of mine,
Kindle every high desire,
Perish self in Thy pure fire.
Amen.

March 21

Read: Jeremiah 18:1-17

God can renew you

The pot he was shaping from the clay was marred in his hands; so the potter formed it into another pot, shaping it as seemed best to him.

— JEREMIAH 18:4 —

It is often difficult for the follower of Jesus Christ to bring his life in accordance with the will of God. So many of the characteristics of the old nature keep appearing. He often despairs that a life filled with Christ will never be revealed through his life.

Such a struggle originates in the human mind and is not from God. Although man desires a new life in Christ, he refuses to abandon his old habits and ways. It is a division of loyalties, with one half of his being longing to satisfy God, and the other half longing to live according to the directions of his own senses and will. It creates a divided Christian witness, which is ineffective. It eventually leads to the impoverishment and weakening of character and personality.

This conflict usually leaves a person intellectually and spiritually insolvent, to such a degree that he wants to renounce God, together with everything he knew and believed about Him.

In the midst of this destruction and depression, God can pick up the pieces, and with His loving artist's hands reshape them into an object of beauty. But certain conditions have to be met for this to happen. Because God can renew what has been destroyed by arrogance and self-righteousness, the only cooperation He asks for is that you unconditionally surrender yourself to Him; that you love and obey Him with your whole being.

As soon as you have dedicated yourself to Him unconditionally, He can start His plan for your recovery. He makes you into a new creature to become the person He wants you to be.

Savior and Transformer, I give myself to You completely and unconditionally. Reshape me according to Your will, to the person You want me to be. Amen.

Read: Ephesians 4:1-16　　　　　　　　　**March 22**

Growth through the truth

Instead, speaking the truth in love, we will in all things grow up into him who is the Head, that is, Christ.

　　　　　　　　　　　　　　　－EPHESIANS 4:15 –

It is a glorious and unsurpassed truth that faith in Jesus Christ saves you from sin. This is the starting point of the gospel. But we dare not forget that the growth process should start in your life after you have accepted Christ as your personal Savior and Redeemer.

If you don't think growth is necessary or important, it will not be long before your spiritual experience will be shipwrecked on the stormy seas of disappointment and despair. There must be growth and development, or else your spiritual life will diminish and die.

There are many resources that God has made available to us to improve our spiritual growth. But we should take care that the aids don't become goals in themselves. Fellowship with believers is necessary, but fellowship that is not centered around Christ serves no constructive purpose.

A study of the Bible will be a source of continuous inspiration and guidance, but the purpose should always be to point the disciple to Christ and to glorify Him. Good deeds and charitable work for the underprivileged undoubtedly find favor with God, but these are only the results of our acquaintance with Jesus Christ and can never take the place of our faith in Him.

There can only be spiritual growth if your main objective is to reflect the image of Christ more and more. It should be the heart's desire of every believing Christian disciple. In this way your spiritual life becomes more than emotion and it demands of you your very best for the Most High.

My Lord and Redeemer, let Your Holy Spirit take possession of me in such a way that I will live solely for Your glory. Amen.

March 23

Read: 1 Corinthians 9:19-27

Do you have an exercise program?

Everyone who competes in the games goes into strict training. They do it to get a crown that will not last; but we do it to get a crown that will last forever.

— 1 CORINTHIANS 9:25 —

One of the regular items in every news bulletin is a story dealing with someone's great achievements in the sporting world. Great emphasis is placed on an exercise program and the preparations of those wanting to win. They then also receive the tribute of a world crazy about sport. Later these people become only memories in record books when others surpass their performances.

Just as the athlete has to prepare himself with the greatest commitment, and has to practice if he wants to achieve anything, the Christian should commit himself totally to the task of answering to the high standards set for him by his Guide, Jesus Christ. He must do this in the face of temptations and enticing distractions. As with the athlete, it calls for courage and conscientious commitment as well as the iron will to continue to the very end. And this is where the comparison ends.

Sports people come and go as their records are equaled or broken. Titles are won with great fanfare and then lost again. The moment of glory is quickly forgotten on the vast plains of time. As a Christian you are, however, assured of the continued glory of living with God. His reward for your commitment and faithfulness is not a floating trophy, but the crown of life.

Steadfastly hold on to your faith and do not give up. Complete the race of life in the strength of the Master and enjoy the everlasting crown of eternal life that awaits you.

Perfecter and Finisher of my faith, in Your strength I will run and complete the race of life. Amen.

Read: 1 John 4:7-21　　　　　　　　　　　　March 24

Memories

This is love: not that we loved God, but that he loved us and sent his Son as an atoning sacrifice for our sins.

– 1 John 4:10 –

Our loved ones never die as long as their memories continue to live in our hearts. It is not hypocritical or sanctimonious to want to remember the good and to forget the bad. The degree to which we want to cherish the memory of our loved ones depends on the attitude that love evokes in our hearts. An artist has the right to position the subject of his work of art in such a way that a blemish is mercifully disguised.

Robert South said on occasion, "It is a noble and great thing to cover the blemishes and to excuse the failings of a friend; to draw a curtain before his stains and to display his perfections; to bury his weaknesses in silence, but to proclaim his virtues from the housetop." We are excessive in our forgiveness towards those who have passed away and merciless in our unforgiving attitude towards ourselves. We reproach ourselves so often about what we could have done or could have said. Feelings of guilt increase our sorrow and exceed the boundaries of all reason. If we can so easily forgive the faults of those who have passed away, think how easy they find it to forgive us in their perfect state of happiness.

Let us appropriate God's forgiveness. He sent His Son as a sacrifice to cancel our sins. If we accept this loving gift of mercy from God, our sorrow will be minimized and we will find peace of mind. God, in His boundless love, will forgive us our sins completely.

It is praiseworthy to cover the weaknesses of others under the cloak of love, and to pull down a curtain of forgiveness over imperfections; to remain silent about shortcomings and to forget them, and to recall virtues lovingly. Grant yourself the same space for living which you so generously grant others.

Holy God, who is my heavenly Father through Jesus Christ, teach me the values that I have to remember and teach me to forget the things You expect me to forget. Amen.

March 25

Read: Nahum 1:1-15

Problem solving

The LORD is good, a refuge in times of trouble. He cares for those who trust in him.

– NAHUM 1:7 –

There are many people who are overpowered by their problems and eventually succumb to them. They try to solve their problems in their own strength and soon find that they are not able to cope at all. Consumed with tension and worry, their spirit snaps because they have only their own strength to rely on.

Your faith in God is not a guarantee that you will never experience problems, but without a doubt it is the only way to handle your problems successfully. Complete faith in God's power is the key to victory over your problems.

One of the most general mistakes many people make is thinking that their problems will immediately disappear the moment they believe in God. When the problems then do not immediately disappear, they think their faith is not strong enough, or that God is refusing to answer their prayers.

To handle your problems in the best way, you should believe with unshakable trust that God loves you and cares for you; that He is always ready to listen to your call of distress, and is ready to protect you against the onslaught of your problems. If you place your trust in Him, He will lead you in handling the problems that may occur in your life.

This will give you the ability to act with self-confidence and determination, since the Holy Spirit will give you the peace that surpasses all understanding. Only then will you see the problem no longer as a stumbling block, but as a challenge.

Holy Master, You are my refuge and strength. Guide me from defeat to victory through Your Holy Spirit. Amen.

Read: Matthew 14:22-36

March 26

Joyous assurance

"Take courage! It is I. Don't be afraid."

– MATTHEW 14:27 –

Many of the Lord's children have forgotten how to be cheerful and care-free people. We live in a world that is overburdened with ominous things, and people find very little to be cheerful about. They identify with the spirit of the times and forget that, as Christians, they must have the ability to rise above the atrocities of our times.

Christian cheerfulness is more than sparkling emotions that ignore ominous events and shrug them off as insignificant. Christ commands His disciples to remain cheerful and courageous in their distress.

This implies that they should acknowledge the fact that things aren't going well, but still trust in the Lord. Know that in life's darkest hour the flame of hope still burns brightly and clearly. Even when you are afraid and despair stalks you, hold steadfastly to the truth that God is still in control of this earth.

Christians should be joyful and at peace because they carry a living hope in their hearts. Even so, this hope should be based on a positive and dynamic relationship with Christ, or else it is just wishful thinking. This hope is the mark of the true disciple of Christ.

If you share in the spirit and nature of Christ, you have the joyous assurance that the ultimate victory belongs to Christ, even though it may appear as if evil is triumphing in the world. Then you can face the future with courage because Jesus Christ has conquered the world.

Strong Redeemer, through Your indwelling Spirit I can face the future with joy and peace of mind due to my faith in You. Amen.

March 27

Read: Micah 6:1-18

Blueprint for Christlikeness

He has showed you, O man, what is good. And what does the LORD require of you? To act justly and to love mercy and to walk humbly with your God.

– MICAH 6:8 –

In the midst of all the theological and doctrinal arguments and discussions which are so common today, the question that is yet again asked is: "What is a Christian?"

All possible knowledge of the Scriptures does not necessarily make someone a Christian. There are many people who are experts in theology, but who are nevertheless not Christians. In the same way, good deeds alone will not make you a Christian.

The core of our Christian belief is the acceptance of Jesus Christ as our Redeemer and Savior and the placing of our faith in Him. Added to this is our readiness to open our lives to Him so that His Holy Spirit can work in and through us to His honor and glory.

When Jesus explained this truth to His disciples, He said, "Not everyone who says to Me 'Lord, Lord' will enter the kingdom of heaven, but only he who does the will of My Father who is in heaven" (Mt. 7:21).

To do God's will means steadfast obedience to the demands of God. We must obey the instructions that He has given us. We must follow Him and love Him and serve our neighbor in love as long as we may live – by letting justice take its course, by showing love and faith and living mindfully before God.

If the Holy Spirit guides and inspires us, it is possible to meet these strenuous demands. Then we begin to understand what Christian discipleship really means.

Heavenly Father, through Your strength and mercy I will follow the example of Christ, my Lord and Master, and in this way bring honor and glory to Your holy Name. Amen.

Read: Psalm 119:33-40

March 28

God's work according to God's instructions

Teach me, O LORD, to follow your decrees; then I will keep them to the end.

– PSALM 119:33 –

There are many servants of the Lord who report for duty, but withhold the love in their hearts from Him. Such people are working for the Lord in many different ways, but it is usually ascribed to their own haphazard choice.

They choose how and where they want to serve Him to suit their own needs. If they are challenged to service of a higher and greater spirit of sacrifice, they only work harder and more seriously at their own choice of service.

Although any work done for God is beneficial for the person who performs it, the only work that is really lasting, is work that is performed according to His holy will and decree. It is God's great mercy alone that blesses all work performed in His name. But quality work for the kingdom can be done only where God's instructions are precisely followed and His honor is sought.

To many people the problem is to know exactly what God's will is. Compassion with other people's distress, physically as well as spiritually, will lead you to a better understanding of God's ways. When the suffering of others compels you to action, you are certainly performing God's will. The Master was always deeply moved when He saw people suffering, especially when they were innocent.

If you become aware of a spiritual need in your fellow man and you offer your intellect, heart and support to alleviate their distress, you will be amazed by the reaction when God uses you in His service. For this, absolute obedience to His instructions is essential.

Teach me through Your Holy Spirit, O Redeemer, to serve You according to Your instruction. May my labor always contribute to Your glory and the well-being of my fellow man. Amen.

March 29

Read: Matthew 9:27-34

Faith that enables the blind to see

Then he touched their eyes and said, "According to your faith will it be done to you."

– MATTHEW 9:29 –

There is a fundamental difference between true faith and wishful thinking. Many people never learn to make this distinction. This leads to spiritual poverty and blindness.

There are people who desire certain things with all their hearts, but deep inside they believe that these things are really unattainable. This creates conflict in their hearts and they become colorless, ineffective people without spiritual strength and vision.

Sincere faith is the conviction that every holy desire is possible and is only waiting to be claimed in the Name of Jesus Christ. You do not strive in your own strength for the unattainable, but trust in the deployment of God's omnipotence in your daily existence. Faith that wants to see results must have its origin and inspiration in God. If we expect great things from God, we will receive great things from Him, and we will perform great deeds in His Name. This was the case with the two blind people about whom the Bible tells us today.

If your faith originates from God and is to His honor, you will become an instrument through which His powerful deeds are performed. A new world of active spiritual energy will open to you. A panorama of colorful possibilities will arise in your mind's eye.

Remember, you do not restrict His omnipotence through your lack of faith and unbelief.

By commitment to Him, your faith becomes a glorious reality.

Almighty God of mercy and love, I thank You for what I am to You and may do for You. Continue to strengthen me through the power of Jesus Christ, my Redeemer and Savior. Amen.

Read: 1 Corinthians 2:1-5 March 30

Christ only

For I resolved to know nothing while I was with you except Jesus Christ and him crucified.

– 1 Corinthians 2:2 –

It is a wonderful privilege to be assured in your heart of the living presence of Christ. To know Him as Lord and Master and to worship Him as the perfect revelation of God, are the most enriching experiences a person can have.

It is obvious that the method and nature of your meeting with Christ will be something exceptional to you. You must, however, guard against not confusing the path you took to find Christ with Christ Himself. The Christian path is in a certain sense also a very wide path. It is wide enough to contain the extremes of Christian thinking.

It is not important whether you follow the sacramental path, or the path of the fundamentalists, or the orthodox, or the charismatic. What truly matters is that these paths should all have *one* shared purpose, and that is to glorify God through the living and risen Christ.

Jesus Christ is the singular focus and purpose of the Christian path. If you allow yourself to be shunted onto a sidetrack through ways and theories and thus lose sight of Christ, you lose the essential part of your Christianity. Your living faith is founded on a personal relationship with Christ and not on theories relating to Him.

You need not defend Christ. You only need to worship and glorify Him and live and proclaim His love. Then you will lead a Christian life that is healthy to its core.

Lord Jesus, You are the Center Point of my faith and life. I love You sincerely and want to sing Your praises, always. Amen.

March 31

Read: Hebrews 11

What is of greater value

He regarded disgrace for the sake of Christ as of greater value than the treasure of Egypt, because he was looking ahead to his reward.
– Hebrews 11:26 –

It is very easy to develop wrong values. The world bombards us with certain values and standards that we unthinkingly accept as our own.

Before you became a disciple of Christ, you strived for those things society deemed valuable – possessions, status and wealth. They became the goals you strived to obtain, yet they gave you no satisfaction when you obtained them.

After your conversion and rebirth you underwent a transformation. Suddenly, you were able to see the essential value of your old objectives. You know now that they gave you a false sense of security. Worldly values can never satisfy your soul.

The most important things in life are the invisible things and they are often difficult to define. The heroes of faith in Hebrews 11 all realized what was most important. They faced persecution, rejection and death for the sake of their faith in Christ.

They knew that this world with its empty promises is transient and that an eternal reward beyond understanding awaits those who are focused on Jesus, the Author and Finisher of their faith.

Holy Redeemer and Lord, I thank You that my eyes are not focused on the world and its empty values, but on Jesus who promises eternal life. Amen.

APRIL

April 1

Read: Proverbs 3:1-18

God first

Trust in the LORD with all your heart and lean not on your own understanding; in all your ways acknowledge him, and he will make your paths straight.

– PROVERBS 3:5-6 –

Today is not only the first day of a new month. It is also the first day of the rest of your life. Therefore, your decisions and actions today may have far-reaching consequences for your entire life.

It is therefore wise to spend constructive time alone with your Creator. Review the past with the help of the Holy Spirit. Uncover and confess those hidden sins and weaknesses you wouldn't admit to, or which you felt you couldn't do anything about. Start the month with a period of honest and open confession.

If you do this earnestly and with sincerity, you will experience the deliverance of forgiveness. In this way you will make a new start with God who renews everything.

A new life is based on complete trust in the living Christ. Commit yourself to Him and surrender your life without reservation to Him because He will never disappoint you. Through His indwelling Spirit He will open new vistas on what life holds. Your sense of values will change as you come to see life as He sees it. The more intimately you walk with Him, the greater your understanding of His path and His love will become.

If you have a positive and sincere faith in Christ, you will discover that His Spirit works through you until such harmony comes into being that you only want to do His will. You will increasingly become a witness for Him in the world, while your own spiritual life will be immensely enriched. Then it is no longer you who are working, but His Spirit working through you. He will lead you on the right path.

Eternal God, draw me still closer to You through the power of Your Holy Spirit. Reflect something of Your glory through my imperfect life. Amen.

Read: 1 Corinthians 6:12-20

April 2

Reflected glory

Do you not know that your body is a temple of the Holy Spirit, who is in you, whom you have received from God? You are not your own; you were bought at a price. Therefore honor God with your body.
– 1 CORINTHIANS 6:19-20 –

The core of your life is not the doctrines that you support or on which you base your life but the glorious reality that God's Holy Spirit has come to live in you. The recognition and acceptance of this truth place a great responsibility on you.

You may never slight your body, but rather approach it with the respect that one of God's most wonderful creations deserve. You should show moderation in eating and drinking, ensure that you get enough sleep and relax enough and don't poison your body by using nicotine or other drugs. If you do these things you show a destructive attitude towards what God created.

Your body is a temple of God created to worship Him. Committing your body to God should never be an unbearable burden to you, it should create a healthy spiritual and intellectual view of life.

Since God's Spirit is living in you, your thoughts must be purified and approved by Him before any of them are released in your life. As you become increasingly aware of His indwelling presence, your outlook on life will not only be purified but also broadened. You will become more aware of the greatness and worthiness of His omnipotence. The path to spiritual greatness is to allow the Holy Spirit to work through you. This requires unimpeachable obedience at all times.

Almighty God, I open my life to the inflow of Your Holy Spirit and pray humbly that my life will reflect something of Your glory. Amen.

April 3

Read: Psalm 51:1-19

Deliverance of sin

For I know my transgressions, and my sin is always before me. Against you, you only, have I sinned and done what is evil in your sight.

— PSALM 51:3-4 —

Extreme feelings of guilt can become dangerous and destructive. They can cause you to do things you wouldn't normally do, and say things you will later regret. It can be like a festering sore that doesn't heal. But the greatest danger is that you can become so accustomed to the feeling of guilt that you accept it as a normal emotion. If this happens, your life loses many of its praiseworthy qualities. Your life becomes empty and dull, without spontaneity or enthusiasm for the things of God. If you suffer from a guilt complex you can no longer enjoy life in the way God intended.

If you are bowed down by a sense of guilt at this moment, you have reason to thank God. It shows that you are not insensitive to spiritual truth. To sin without feeling remorse, means that you have reached a terrible and dangerous point. It proves that you have become deaf to the voice of the Holy Spirit on purpose; that your spirit is no longer sensitive to God's will.

To confess your sins in repentance before God enables you to live a positive and constructive life. You thereby acknowledge God's power to forgive your sins through Jesus Christ and to renew your life so that you can live joyfully and in harmony with Him. This harmony removes feelings of guilt, even if it sometimes calls for restitution. It puts you in a new relationship with God and your fellow man and gives you a feeling of deliverance and joy.

I thank You that I may turn to You in repentance and with a confession of guilt every day, O Lord. I start my new life in Your strength and forgiving love. Amen.

Read: Psalm 56:1-13 April 4

Comfort through tears

Record my lament; list my tears on your scroll – are they not in your record?

– PSALM 56:8 –

Tears set one free and purify a grieving spirit. Shakespeare said, "To weep is to make less the depth of grief." Tears enable us to naturally rid ourselves of sorrow. Crying prevents sorrow from turning into despair. If we never cry, we'll lose out on inner healing. Christ Himself stresses the benefit of tears, "Blessed are those who mourn, for they will be comforted" (Mt. 5:4).

Tears are not only shed by the weak, but also by the strong, since they arise from love, tenderness and compassion. Washington Irving says, "There is a sacredness in tears. They are not the marks of weakness, but of power. They speak more eloquently than ten thousand tongues. They are the messengers of overwhelming grief, of deep contrition and of unspeakable love."

In His compassion God sees our grief and through our tears He provides us with something that is bigger than our grief. Through the tears of Jesus Christ, God sanctified our tears. He was godly enough to resurrect Lazarus, and human enough to weep with the mourning. He was powerful enough to remove the cause of their tears, yet human enough to shed tears Himself.

Thank God for the healing, delivering and purifying power of sincere tears. They soften grief, bring acceptance and eventually lead to joy. The soul would have known no rainbow if the eye knew no tears. In addition, we also have God's promise that there will be an end to our tears. John speaks of the new heaven and earth and says, "He will wipe every tear from their eyes" (Rev. 21:4). C. J. Langenhoven once remarked, "If you have to shed tears, may they shine like dew drops to introduce days of joy."

O, Holy Comforter, I thank You that I can find solace through my tears; they make my grief bearable and bring me closer to You. Amen.

April 5

Read: Romans 7:7-25

The divided self

For what I do is not the good I want to do; no, the evil I do not want to do – this I keep on doing.

– ROMANS 7:19 –

Every one of us has experienced inner conflict. Often it makes us ask in despair, "Who am I?" Then there are times when you have an overwhelming desire to lead an honorable and committed life. Spiritual matters appeal strongly to your inner soul. You are convinced not to think mean or unworthy thoughts. In such times, God is very real and very close to you.

It is possible that, even while you experience this certainty, spiritual pride and religious arrogance could start undermining your faith and God could be moved from the center of your life. Your quiet time could suffer as a result.

You no longer enjoy the spiritual strength you once had. It becomes increasingly difficult for you to maintain your spiritual enthusiasm. You know what you should do, but you are incapable of doing it. Your baser self is engaged in a struggle with your conscience. With every victory this baser self makes you a slave of sin. This continuing spiritual struggle between right and wrong, can only be resolved if Christ is in total control of every aspect of your life.

If you are completely committed to Him and surrender your life to Christ; if you have the unshakable certainty of His living presence in you, then His strength will be available to you. Then you will be a person who lives to glorify the Master; with His peace in your heart and in your mind.

Loving Lord, make me a fully integrated personality who lives to Your honor, through the inspiration and guidance of Your Holy Spirit. Amen.

Read: Matthew 6:5-15   April 6

Forgiveness: human and divine

Forgive us our debts, as we also have forgiven our debtors.
                                        – MATTHEW 6:12 –

We all need to pray this prayer and understand what we say
when we pray it. Literally it means: forgive us our transgressions to the extent that we forgive them who have harmed us. There
are specific requirements for having this Christian forgiveness in
our lives.

We should learn to understand. There is always a reason why people do certain things. It may be the result of a secret worry or pain or
it may be due to a misunderstanding. It may be the result of our surroundings or of our temperaments or it may be hereditary. To know
all is to understand all; and to understand all is to forgive all.

We should learn to forget. We often hear, "I will forgive, but I will
never forget." As long as we ruminate on insults and the injustices
done to us, there is no hope of forgetting. Only the cleansing Spirit
of God can redeem us of bitter memories, which gnaw at our souls
and make us spiritually ill.

We should learn to love. Love cannot be conquered, but love can
conquer all. We can only love if Christ, the Source of love, takes possession of our lives. He did not only teach us to love and forgive one
another, He also demonstrated this on the cross when He prayed,
"Father, forgive them, for they do not know what they are doing"
(Lk. 23:34). There is no substitute for love.

Love enables us to forgive to the extreme, but if we have no love
our efforts will be in vain. Therefore, we have to learn the divine art
of loving from the Source of love, Christ Himself.

*Redeemer, teach me today through Your divine example the
sublime virtue of forgiveness and love, so that we can also be
worthy of Your forgiveness in our lives. Amen.*

April 7

Read: Matthew 18:1-5

Believe like little children

He called a little child and had him stand among them. And he said: "I tell you the truth, unless you change and become like little children, you will never enter the kingdom of heaven."
– MATTHEW 18:2-3 –

It is quite possible to become so entangled in theological and dogmatic issues, that you can lose the simplicity of your faith. If that happens your faith will lose its effectiveness *and* the awareness of Christ in you will disappear.

If investigating everything is part of your personality, there will always be questions that need answers. While you study facts about God, nagging questions trouble you and you could end up in a spiritual wasteland. You seek, discover and demand answers that nobody can give. You become more and more frustrated. You may even feel inclined to abandon the Christian faith due to its demands.

The confusion caused by conflicting religions and convictions, is self-inflicted. But admitting that God exists is the simple foundation on which to build your faith. To say with conviction, "I believe in God", is to identify yourself with the greatest life-giving Power in the entire universe. If such a declaration is sincerely and honestly applied to your life, it will make God a reality for you. You'll discover that God reaches out past your doubts and uncertainties, and becomes a reality.

Although you may have doubts about God, He does not have any doubts about you at all. He sees and knows you for what you are and what you can become. He expects you to share your life completely with Him through a childlike faith. Then your life will be abundant.

Master, my faith in You is simple, but my trust in You is very real. Strengthen my faith through Your Holy Spirit. Amen.

Read: Ephesians 4:1-16   April 8

Your shortcomings do not restrict God

As a prisoner for the Lord, then, I urge you to live a life worthy of the calling you have received.
– EPHESIANS 4:1 –

It is startling to know that so many Christians have a poor image of themselves and their calling. They delude themselves into thinking that God praises those who think very little of themselves. Therefore, although they have many good and virtuous qualities, they never reach the heights God intended for them.

If, in your moments of being quiet before God, you have already convinced yourself that you will not be able to do anything of value for God, ask yourself why you have come to that conclusion. Be downright honest with yourself.

If you say that you know your limitations, it is possible that you may have looked at your own potential without considering what God can do through you. You may feel inadequate and have a poor opinion of yourself and your own abilities. However, if you use the resources God made available to you, the results will be exciting and unpredictable.

Do not waste your time and spiritual abilities on moaning about what you cannot do. Hold steadfastly and unshakably to the truth that if you commit yourself to the Master, He will use you in ways you have never thought possible. Place yourself in His hands and pray, "Use me, O Lord. Use even me!"

Such surrender to the will of God brings hidden talents to light. You'll discover gifts you never even knew you had. Those disciples who sincerely seek to work for Jesus Christ through His power, experience the highest fulfillment in life.

I can do everything through Him who gives me strength. Amen.

April 9

Read: Ephesians 4:25-5:5

The truth in love

Therefore each of you must put off falsehood and speak truthfully to his neighbor, for we are all members of one body.
— EPHESIANS 4:25 —

From time to time we face situations in our daily lives where we are compelled to say something. Our words may be an expression of encouragement or sympathy; of congratulation or reprimand or we may be called upon to criticize. Whatever we say, our words may have a far-reaching effect on human relationships and feelings.

Therefore, when we speak a heavy responsibility rests on our shoulders. We must choose the right time and the right place to speak. Most important is, however, the choice of our words. Whatever we say must be the truth. Our words should be spoken in sincere and honest Christian faith. Love without honesty is mere sentimentality; on the other hand, honesty without love can easily degenerate into mere brutality. Unless the occasion demands us to give public comment, we should do this in private, especially if it is negative criticism or a reprimand. Whatever we are called to say should be said at the most opportune time, or not at all.

The only way we can achieve this is to continuously keep in touch with Christ. In this way we will be sensitive to the guidance of the Holy Spirit, who will lead us and teach us in our communication with others. Then you will be sure that everything you say is inspired by Christ and will therefore be expressed in love.

Lord Jesus, guide my thoughts and control my tongue so that I will never hurt anyone's feelings on purpose. Let Your Holy Spirit guide me to speak the truth with love. Amen.

Read: John 21:15-19

April 10

Profit despite loss

When you were younger you dressed yourself and went where you wanted; but when you are old you will stretch out your hands, and someone else will dress you and lead you where you do not want to go.

– JOHN 21:18 –

It is painful to think that your youth is forever a thing of the past. Usually it also brings about endless loneliness: fellow travelers fall away along the road; your surroundings change from where you grew up and you only see strange and unknown faces everywhere.

Physical strength diminishes and leaves us in the lurch, our eyes can no longer dwell on the horizon, our hands shake when we lift the tea cup, our ears can no longer pick up all the sounds of life, the way seems long and there are many inclines, the heart does its work with effort and exertion.

Nevertheless, we may not sink into despair. God offers rich recompense for losses suffered. In Joel 2:25 God promises, "I will repay you for the years." How abundant and merciful is God's repayment!

Where the Lord takes away physical strength, He gives more spiritual strength. External strength is replaced by a new kind of exciting, internal strength. Then we really understand the word of the Lord in Zechariah 4:6, "'Not by might nor by power, but by my Spirit,' says the LORD Almighty."

We should guard against focusing on the losses which the transient years bring and start concentrating on the profits this time of life brings along. Thank the Lord for the positive things.

Lord, also the God of old age, thank You that I may trust in You throughout life. Be my power and strength every day through Jesus Christ, my Redeemer. Amen.

April 11

Read: Psalm 38:13-22

I am sorry

I confess my iniquity; I am troubled by my sin.

– Psalm 38:18 –

Three of the most difficult words to say in the English language are: "I am sorry!" Simple words that can bridge the gap between friendship and estrangement – and yet so difficult to express.

As you are about to say these words, many reasons for not saying them come up: you did nothing wrong; other people will think you're weak; it is humiliating and will affect your dignity; the person to whom you say these words will find pleasure in your discomfort. So the excuses will multiply, yet you will always feel the need to express the healing words, "I am sorry." Perhaps the estrangement between a friend and yourself is the result of one or other thoughtless word or careless action. You may not even be aware of the cause. But where love and friendship once flourished, there are now just misery and misunderstanding. And you will come off worse as a result of this unhappy situation.

It is possible to pretend that the collapse of a human relationship does not affect you. You can claim that it does not bother you. This attitude is often just another smoke screen to hide hurt feelings.

Every spoilt relationship is putting you at a disadvantage and that's something you cannot afford. However, if you apologize because you have allowed estrangement to happen, you will experience a wonderful feeling of being set free as well as the joys of regained friendship. This is worth the effort. Accept the challenge in the name of Christ's love.

Make me big enough, heavenly Master, to bridge the gaping abyss of a broken friendship by just saying, "I am sorry!" Amen.

Read: John 10:1-21

April 12

Abundant life

"I have come that they may have life, and have it to the full."
– John 10:10 –

Relatively few people really think of religion as a force with life-giving power. They have the idea that it will restrict the way they live. They look at the lives of Christians and are not at all impressed by what they see. Secretly they fear the surrender of their lives to a power that requires whole-hearted loyalty and commitment. Why, they ask, should they get involved in a way of life that is restrictive, unattractive and demanding?

If you consider Christianity with an open mind, you will discover that its apparent failure cannot be ascribed to faith, but to the presentation of it. It is unthinkable that the Creator of life will keep people from enjoying life. That He, who is the reflection of perfection and beauty, will make it unattractive to follow Him, that He will demand your love and commitment and not give you life in abundance.

Christianity is a way of life that includes the abundance of God through Jesus Christ. Because Christ promised to live in you and you accepted this promise, it is your privilege to allow the living Christ to live to the full through you.

If the revelation of Christ becomes the main objective of your life, you will experience the Holy Spirit working through you. The more your life reflects the glory of Christ, the more abundant will be your joy and peace.

My sincere prayer is, O Lord, that my life will reflect Your glory more and more through the work of the Holy Spirit in me. Amen.

April 13

Read: John 14:15-31

Peace unto you

"Peace I leave with you; my peace I give you. I do not give to you as the world gives. Do not let your hearts be troubled and do not be afraid."

– John 14:27 –

Tension, anxiety and worry have become part of our lives in such a way that we think we have to live with it.

The truth is that it was never God's intention to begin with. By allowing these things to rule in our lives, we restrict the working of God's mercy in our lives. Hence the instruction in Psalm 46:10, "Be still, and know that I am God."

Our spirit sometimes needs to be totally relaxed; to experience complete peace of mind. Therefore it is essential to put aside time for prayer and quiet meditation every day. It is the God-given way to find peace.

If we feel tense and heavy-hearted because we cannot stop thinking about our problems and what still has to be done, it is time we say to ourselves loud and clear, "Be calm, relax, let go and let God!" Allow the peace of God which surpasses everything to rule over your thoughts.

By allowing tension and anxiety to overcome you, or to collapse under the pressure, is to turn your back on God's loving offer of peace. And God's peace is the true product that differs completely from anything and everything the world has to offer.

The never-ending human search for peace is not passive or negative: the search for peace is a powerful activity through which we glorify God and increase the quality of our lives unrecognizably.

I thank You, faithful heavenly Father, that You make the anxiety and tension disappear from my life, with the comfort of Your Word. Help me to give these things to You regularly in prayer, through Christ, who is my peace. Amen.

Read: 1 Kings 18:1-21 April 14

Definite decision-making

Elijah went before the people and said, "How long will you waver between two opinions? If the LORD is God, follow him; but if Baal is God, follow him."

– 1 KINGS 18:21 –

Many people find it difficult to make firmly calculated decisions. When handling responsibility, they hesitate and waver between two thoughts in the hope that someone else will make the decision for them.

Life offers its treasures to those who can make positive decisions. These people are determined and are not swayed by every new way of thinking or set of circumstances. Once they have made a decision they do not change their minds.

The predominating fear of making the wrong decision causes hesitancy, tension and a feeling of uncertainty. It is better though to make wrong decisions and learn from your failures than to hesitate. Unless you have the courage to make definite decisions, you will constantly be frustrated by indecisiveness.

If you accept God as your Guide and Leader, you have a Source of wisdom that becomes more efficient the more you use it. Consider every decision in prayer before God, spend time with Him, consider alternatives and be open to the guidance of the Holy Spirit. When you intuitively feel in your heart that you should go in a certain direction, go forward decisively, aware of His presence. Through the working of the Holy Spirit, indecisiveness in your life will be laid to rest so that you can lead a free and abundant life.

Stand by me, O Lord, and help me to make wise decisions through the guidance of Your Holy Spirit. Amen.

April 15

Read: Ephesians 3:14-21

Do you doubt your abilities?

Now to him who is able to do immeasurably more than all we ask or imagine, according to his power that is at work within us, to him be glory.

– EPHESIANS 3:20-21 –

We determine our abilities by the opinion we have of ourselves. If we truly believe that we can do something, we usually manage to do it. If we are told that the task is beyond our reach, we do not even make an attempt. Since most people are not sure of their true abilities, they underestimate themselves. Gradually they convince themselves that they will never be able to establish anything of any worth.

People often have double standards: there are things they feel they can manage on their own, and then there are things they can accomplish with God's help. It is only when they rise above their own abilities and realize what they can achieve through the wisdom and power of the almighty Father that they enter a new and exciting life of faith.

With their still hesitant faith they try the seemingly impossible and then to their astonishment find that it is indeed possible. Bright horizons and new possibilities open up for them. At the same time, they become conscious of growth and a deepening of their spiritual lives. With a growing faith the need for a complete dependence on Jesus Christ arises.

As you discover that you now manage things which you previously thought impossible, you discover that it is not you who are doing it, but Christ who works in and through you.

You become an instrument in His hands and a new relationship starts developing between you and the Lord. You learn to understand His ways better and you develop the courage to do things in faith and in His name. Things you previously regarded as impossible. Only then do you really excel in your God-given abilities.

Heavenly Lord, in faith I reach past my own limited abilities and lead a fuller, richer life through the power of Your Spirit. Amen.

Read: Philippians 1:1-11 April 16

Priority number one

And this is my prayer: that your love may abound more and more in knowledge and depth of insight, so that you may be able to discern what is best and may be pure and blameless until the day of Christ.
— PHILIPPIANS 1:9-10 —

There are so many important things that demand our attention and energy every day. Our work, full-time studies, the routine of running a home and bringing up a family, caring for the sick and aged – these are but a few of the demands made on our time and energy. You can probably add your own important issues to this list.

Nevertheless, we are called to assess our priorities: the essential issues in life. We should be able to place first things first on the agenda.

God is the First and the Last; from Him and through Him and in Him are all things. Therefore, God's position in our lives is the essential issue. He claims the highest priority in our lives, not only because He has the right to it, but because this will increase the quality of our lives. If God is the center of your life, He can affect all the other aspects in your life to His glory and to your immeasurable advantage.

Honor God with your time, your talents, your possessions and your plans. Allow His Spirit to rule in all areas of your life. Then you will make the exciting discovery that when God is first in your life, all the other issues fall into place. This is to be at peace with yourself. Then your life develops an exceptional quality of joy and peace.

Heavenly Father, teach me through the Holy Spirit to make You the center of my life at all times. Do this for me through the grace of Jesus Christ, who lived and died to glorify You. Amen.

April 17

Read: Genesis 4:1-16

Do you have the courage to care?

Then the LORD said to Cain, "Where is your brother Abel?" "I don't know," he replied. "Am I my brother's keeper?"

– GENESIS 4:9 –

No one lives in isolation and only for himself. You are dependent on others for the food you eat and the clothes you wear. It is unrealistic to say, "I am self-sufficient." People are created to depend on one another, that's just how it is.

Due to this basic fact, human beings are essentially divided into two groups. Those who want to receive without giving: the takers; and those who find joy and fulfillment in making themselves available to others in service: the givers. It requires great courage to give of yourself through the act of love. It means that you must identify very closely with the person you want to help. This identification can be very expensive in terms of time, energy and emotion.

If you question the wisdom of becoming involved in the distress of someone who needs your help, what is the alternative? Will it make you happy to turn your back on someone who needs your help and love urgently? The knowledge that someone needs you should give you the courage to react without considering the cost.

It is an inspiring truth that when you react to the deepest distress of your fellow man, the almighty God will give you the wisdom and strength to do what must be done. You can never care for someone in distress without experiencing the blessing of the Lord on your efforts.

This is the inheritance of those whose philosophy in life is: "I am not only my brother's keeper; I am my brother's brother!"

I bow in humble gratitude before You, my God and my Provider, in the knowledge that I am blessed in a unique way by helping others. Amen.

Read: Numbers 11:10-20 April 18

Delegated responsibility

"I will take of the Spirit that is on you and put the Spirit on them. They will help you carry the burden of the people so that you will not have to carry it alone."

– NUMBERS 11:17 –

There are many dedicated children of the Lord who serve their Master and their fellow man with dedication and enthusiasm, even putting their own health on the line by doing this.

They never refuse when they are asked to serve on a committee; they volunteer to do any task that arises, even when they are not fully equipped to carry it out. Eventually they have so many divergent responsibilities that they cannot do anything properly.

The intellectual and spiritual tension on their lives then becomes so big that it visibly affects the condition of their health, resulting in them collapsing under the strain.

Many pastors and church members are so conscientious and concerned about their God-given task that they are not willing to share it with anyone else fearing that it will not be done according to their standards. Therefore they stubbornly refuse to delegate the Lord's work to other talented Christian disciples.

In the end these poor people have so much to do and so little time in which to do it that nothing is done thoroughly. They then become frustrated and discouraged.

If God has called you for a specific task, it is your privilege and duty to do it to the best of your ability. This does not mean you cannot ask for help from others. Accept your God-given responsibility, but never regard a request for help as neglecting your duty. With the help of others you can most likely serve God more effectively.

Master, when You give me a task, teach me to cooperate with others to complete it. Amen.

April 19

Read: Philippians 4:2-9

Develop a sense of humor

Rejoice in the Lord always! I will say it again: Rejoice!
– Philippians 4:4 –

Life would have been very dull and monotonous without humor and smiles. But we were not all born with a well-developed sense of humor. As with any other gift, it too has to be nurtured and developed.

The ability to be amused by life is an art that can keep a person's mind balanced and even save one's life. Anyone who has experienced suffering will confirm this truth.

A smile or a burst of laughter can ease tension. Laughing is excellent exercise for the respiratory system. The old saying that laughter is the best medicine, holds much truth. To have a good sense of humor implies much more than the ability to laugh in the right place when someone tells a joke. It much rather means to have sympathy towards other people's misfortune and to never take your own success or failure too seriously. People who play practical jokes on others are not necessarily the ones with the purest sense of humor. It is rather those people who find pure joy in the thrill of life itself and in the humor of everyday events. True humor never laughs at a fellow human being, but with him. That is why humor has been defined as laughing with a tear.

A person who is only concerned about himself most probably has no sense of humor. We have to be sincerely interested in people and be sensitive to their mindsets and distress before we can see the humor in their situation. Then we are bringing a little sunshine into the world around us.

Do not allow your sense of humor to grow rusty because you don't use it. Ask God to put some sparkle into your life through the Holy Spirit.

Heavenly Father, thank You for the joy You bring even in the darkest circumstances and situations. Thank You especially for the joy I find in being Your child. Amen.

Read: Psalm 42:1-11   April 20

Make time for God

As the deer pants for streams of water, so my soul pants for you, O God.

– PSALM 42:1 –

How sincere is your desire to really get to know God? Are you only expressing an empty sentiment when you say that you long for God, or do you really thirst for Him and call to Him in your distress? If you earnestly and sincerely desire a deeper spiritual relationship with God, you will find no sacrifice too large in order to reach your goal.

One of the first sacrifices God will ask from you is to give of your time. It is an incalculable asset, yet many people recklessly waste their time. If you use your time wisely, it will coincide with God's purpose for your life. You will realize how significant time is.

The most time-consuming, but also the most profitable exercise to undertake is to increase your knowledge of God through prayer, Bible study and reflection. When you read about the experiences of other children of God it can influence your growth. However, it can never take the place of a personal relationship with God.

The main reason why you don't have a better understanding of God's love, may lie in the fact that you do not give enough time to God. The longing you have in your soul for God is one of His gifts of grace to you. If you react to this yearning and seek Him, you will find to your surprise and delight that He is already waiting for you with all His richest spiritual blessings.

Lord God, You are the only One who can satisfy my deepest longing. I come to You to relieve my deepest distress. Amen.

April 21

Read: Psalm 24:1-10

What are we doing to God's world?

The earth is the LORD's and everything in it, the world, and all who live in it.

– PSALM 24:1 –

We live in chaotic and turbulent times and many people wonder what the future holds for them. Evil is all around us, and destructive forces have an apparently invincible effect. In contrast to this, order and justice seem insignificant and ineffective. However, do not allow appearances to deceive you. The world still belongs to God. He created the universe and has not yet given up on it, although erring humankind is doing its level best to damage God's handiwork. When people reject God's will and follow their own heads, sin floods the world through disobedience and rebellion.

God's great mercy and love is revealed in the fact that He has not yet rejected humankind totally. He came to earth in the flesh through Jesus Christ to reconcile the world with Him (see Col. 1:20). Such an amazing revelation is too big for the human mind to fathom. Our superficial observation of this truth unfortunately reduces its impact on us.

To vaguely philosophize about the redemption of the world will leave our inmost being untouched. However, when we realize that spiritual renewal should start in our own lives and not in the outside world, we begin to understand something of God's challenge to humankind to live a more committed life.

Scriptures teach us that the world and everything in it belongs to God. If we accept this glorious truth and allow Christ to rule in our lives, the responsibility is ours to maintain the noble and eternal values of God. Then the question is not, "What is happening to God's world?" but, "What am I personally doing for God and His world?"

Creator God, help me through Your grace to be Your ambassador through Jesus Christ on this earth. Amen.

Read: Job 5:1-7

April 22

Spiritual decline

For hardship does not spring from the soul nor does trouble sprout from the ground.

– Job 5:6 –

God has only good intentions for all of us. You may be surrounded by difficulties and think there is no way out. Your faith may have reached rock-bottom and you may even doubt the love and mercy of God.

To lose the assurance of Christ's living presence that was so real to you once, is a painful experience caused by uncertainty and despair.

Knowing what God intended you to be and realizing what you are, lead to a heart-searching challenge. Where did your spiritual life go off the track? Why do you experience defeat and frustration instead of a life of growth and victory?

This unhappy situation does not arise without cause. God's love for us is eternal and undying. Therefore the fault lies with us and not with God.

We should never take our spiritual condition for granted. We should never think that we've reached our destination and that we have a guarantee that we'll not revert to our old way of life. The spiritual path is a never-ending pilgrimage that leads to an increasingly pure love for and understanding of God.

The only way to stop your spiritual decline is through serious prayer and meditation, until you experience the presence of the living Christ in your heart again. You will find the strength to live in the land of victory and know the joy of true peace of mind.

O Holy Spirit of God, I praise You because You established energy, growth and enthusiasm in my life. Lead me to Christ through purposeful growth. Amen.

April 23

Read: Psalm 73:15-28

Over-sensitivity brings its own pain

When my heart was grieved and my spirit embittered, I was sense-less and ignorant; I was a brute beast before you.
— PSALM 73:21-22 —

A sensitive spirit often hides behind a rough exterior, because many people think that to show sympathy is a sign of weakness. Yet it is sensitive people who serve their fellow man best, and who bring back the sparkle in lives that have lost all joy and gladness. Being sensitive to the distress and needs of others is the foundation of effective Christian service. It should be regarded as a source of inspiration and a way of helping and motivating others.

Unfortunately, to be sensitive to the demands of God and the distress of your fellow man may cause you pain. When this happens, you should thank God that you can be still before Him. His sensitive Spirit knows the pain of rejection and the pain that loved ones cause when they choose to follow the road of self-destruction.

As the awareness of the presence of the living Christ grows in you, you will increasingly become aware of the distress of others and have great compassion for them.

Although it is true that Christ gives joy, peace and strength, there is an element in His teachings that can be understood only if we are sensitive to the consequences of sin. If you become increasingly sensitive to sin and discover how this separates you from God, you will long for an increasingly deeper relationship with Him. To deviate from His ways will now be a painful experience.

Merciful Lord and Redeemer, make me sensitive through Your Holy Spirit so that I can avoid the pitfalls of sin and live in harmony with You and my fellow man. Amen.

Read: 1 Corinthians 13:1-13   April 24

Love triumphs

And now these three remain: faith, hope and love. But the greatest of these is love.

– 1 Corinthians 13:13 –

This chapter is rightly called "Hymn to love!". As poignant and as beautiful as it is, many Christians would rather want to side-step or avoid the demands outlined therein. It contains overwhelming challenges and prescribes a way of life that is idealistic rather than practical.

We are told to be patient and friendly; never to be envious, boastful or arrogant; never to act improperly or in one's own interests; and never spitefully or stubbornly remember the wrongs done to us by others; to forget injustices and to rejoice in the truth. This, as well as many other difficult demands, seem to show how impractical the Christian faith is.

People see the spiritual shortcomings of others and even though they do not judge their actions, they only confirm to you how impractical it is to meet the demands of this chapter of Scripture.

The challenges of the gospel are mainly directed at the individual. It deals with the individual's personal relationship with God. It is not concerned with the personal success or failure of people on their pilgrimages. The big question is not whether others are leading Christian lives of love, but whether you are doing it.

To lead a life of triumphant love, you must experience the living Christ in your spirit. Only if His Spirit rules your spirit and Christ is reflected in you, can love become the watermark of your Christianity.

I love You truly, O Lord. Let love overflow into every facet of my life – and then flow over to my fellow man. Amen.

April 25

Read: Mark 16:1-8

Overcoming stumbling blocks

Very early on the first day of the week, just after sunrise, they were on their way to the tomb and they asked each other, "Who will roll the stone away from the entrance of the tomb?"

– MARK 16:2-3 –

It is terrible to be caught up in fears about the future. Difficulties and problems seem unconquerable. The realization of your own inability and the fear of failure, have a crippling effect on your thoughts and your spirit.

Perhaps this fear has been with you for as long as you can remember. When you look back and determine which things you feared most, you will find that in all probability, they never happened. Or the consequences were not nearly as destructive as you feared they would be.

If you fear something that is supposed to happen in the future, and it's weighing you down, reduce the effect by determining what it is that scares you so much. Are you afraid of what people may think? Do you fear that your prestige or social standing will suffer?

When the women reached Jesus' tomb, their biggest problem was finding someone to roll away the stone from the entrance to the tomb. Only then would they be able to carry out their task. But God moved out in front of them and removed the stumbling block for them.

Even if it is your ideal to live within the will of God, you are not indemnified against difficulties. But you can face them with confidence in the knowledge that He is with you and that He will enable you to overcome your stumbling blocks. Difficulties met in the power and wisdom of God are never too great to overcome.

I praise Your Name, Lord and Master, because I can face and overcome every difficulty in Your wisdom and strength. Amen.

Read: John 11:17-32

April 26

A friend we fear

As for man, his days are like grass, he flourishes like a flower of the field; the wind blows over it and it is gone, and its place remembers it no more.

– PSALM 103:15 –

At one time or another, every one of us has to face the great mystery of death. Death is with us as a "Friend we fear" every day of our lives. Bacon says in one of his essays, "Men fear death as children fear to walk in the dark!"

We see signs of death in our own bodies: the eye that darkens and the physical strength that decreases.

This world holds an addictive enchantment for us. We shrink in fear at the thought of death and we see the grave as a cruel bottomless pit, while in reality, it is the door to God's brightly lit glory – heaven. It is the passing from this fragile life to immortality.

When we die in Jesus Christ, death introduces a new and better beginning. He has prepared a place for those who love Him. Even if death seems final, He assures us, "I am the resurrection and the life. He who believes in Me will live, even though he dies and whoever lives and believes in Me will never die" (Jn. 11:25-26).

This should be our comfort when we have to bid farewell to a loved one: Jesus went to prepare a place for us and we will meet again. Even when we enter the valley of death we will be able to say confidently, "I will fear no evil, for You are with me" (Ps. 23:4).

Then we know the final victory and are set free from that last great fear called death.

I thank You, risen Savior, that You have defeated death and that You have unlocked eternity for me. In faith, I accept the comfort of immortality. Amen.

April 27

Read: Romans 5:1-11

Spirit of Love

Hope does not disappoint us, because God has poured out his love into our hearts by the Holy Spirit, whom he has given us.
— Romans 5:5 —

People across the entire earth can testify of their love for Jesus Christ. These people differ in nationalities, traditions and cultures. Nevertheless, they bear witness of their love and faith in Jesus Christ who died on a cross two thousand years ago. They are convinced that He is alive today. How is this possible? They've never even seen Him. His earthly ministry lasted about three years and the reports on that are rather fragmentary.

The secret of His unique attraction does not lie in one or other theological formula or religious organization – regardless of how important these things may be in their right context. But Jesus promised to grant His Spirit to everyone who accepts Him and confesses that He reigns over all the earth.

Through the ages He has kept His promises. He said that His Spirit would live in every person who loves Him and who serves Him. Countless followers of this century believe that this experience with the living Christ is valid and true today.

If you want to stand on the sideline, remember that Christ can convert your life. A new, unparalleled strength will take possession of your spirit. It will enable you to do the things that are pleasing to God and will reassure you of Christ's life-changing presence in your life.

If you have the Spirit of Christ in you, you will know the reality of His holy presence. Love for Him will radiate from your heart and life.

I praise You, Lord, that I can experience the power of Your living presence through the work of the Holy Spirit and that I may love You with a pure heart. Amen.

Read: 2 Peter 3:14-18   April 28

Growth is essential

But grow in the grace and knowledge of our Lord and Savior Jesus Christ.

— 2 PETER 3:18 —

The Christian's spiritual life may never stagnate, since this can so easily cause dreariness. If you are not continuously growing towards a more intimate relationship with Christ, you are allowing your love for Him to cool down and your communion with Him to fade away.

Do you know Christ better now than a year ago? An honest answer to this question will indicate the direction that you are moving in spiritually.

Peter encouraged the disciples of the early church to grow in grace and knowledge of Jesus Christ. Grace is a gift bestowed on us by the Holy Spirit. As your experience of the risen Lord deepens and grows richer, His nature is reflected in your life and is directly linked to your commitment to God.

A disciple who lives according to Christ's example is never too conscious of this development taking place in his life. On the contrary, he will deny this since he is very much aware of his own shortcomings. Nevertheless, denying this can be proof of his spiritual growth.

Growing in the knowledge of Christ can be understood only in view of the knowledge God gives His disciple through the Holy Spirit and through His Holy Word. The Christian reacts to this knowledge and grows in his resemblance to his Perfect Example, Jesus Christ.

Help me, my Redeemer and Example, to grow through grace in such a way that the world will see something of You in me, to Your honor and glory! Amen.

April 29

Read: Romans 12:9-21

The Christian businessman

Never be lacking in zeal, but keep your spiritual fervor, serving the Lord.

— ROMANS 12:11 —

Many people make the mistake of thinking that Christianity and business are irreconcilable. They suppose that it is impossible to be part of the business world and be a Christian. However, the fact that there are prominent business people who confess their trust in God openly and who follow in Christ's footsteps despite a strongly competitive business world, show that this school of thought is totally incorrect.

The failure of Christians to apply their religion to the business world is not due to the fact that they find Christ's doctrine impractical. The cause is the lack of commitment to Christ.

It can be very difficult to satisfy both God and an indifferent and aloof employer, especially if the latter is hostile to everything a Christian regards as precious. However, if the employee lives and works to honor God and carries out his task to the best of his ability, he can confidently leave the result in God's hands.

In the business environment, God is not impressed by profits but by the service rendered. The Christian businessman, in imitation of the holy Managing Director, should not seek to be served but to serve others. Although this point of view may sound idealistic, it is in fact good business acumen. More and more firms focus all their energy on service to their clients.

It is not a question of being either a businessman or a Christian. If one understands the principles of faith, one can be a Christian businessman to the honor of God.

Spirit of God, help me to demonstrate my faith in all my business activities. May I work faithfully to serve You and my fellow man. Amen.

Read: 2 Corinthians 4:7-18 April 30

Outward decline – internal strength

Therefore we do not lose heart. Though outwardly we are wasting away, yet inwardly we are being renewed day by day.
– 2 CORINTHIANS 4:16 –

To be fascinated by a new-born baby; the surging expectations of the spring of life; the fullness of adulthood; the composure, wisdom and peace of age – these things are all part of that great choir of God that we call "Life"!

One can easily collapse from the burden of memories and suffer from the awareness that you are getting weaker. Particularly when it is memories of your weaknesses and sin – the sin of worldliness; that time when the world and its delights meant everything to you. Or the sin of lust, when your passion and desires burned red-hot. Or perhaps the sin of unfaithfulness when you said, like Peter, "I don't know Him!" (Lk. 22:57).

As you grow older, the world means less and less to you and God means more and more. Your obedience and faithfulness to God are now so much greater and with Peter you can say, "Lord, You know all things; You know that I love You!" (Jn. 21:17).

Your outlook on eternity is now so much purer, since, with Peter, you can say, "Now we know that if the earthly tent we live in is destroyed, we have a building from God, an eternal house in heaven, not built by human hands" (2 Cor. 5:1).

I thank You sincerely, beloved Lord, that You have not deserted me in my old age. I accept old age as a gift of love from Your hand and I praise You for every new day. Amen.

MAY

Read: Zechariah 14:12-20 May 1

Piety and peace

On that day HOLY TO THE LORD *will be inscribed on the bells of the horses, and the cooking pots in the* LORD's *house will be like the sacred bowls in front of the altar.*

– ZECHARIAH 14:20 –

"Piety" is a word that has become outdated. Referring to someone as "pious" makes it seem as if you are describing someone who is hypocritically virtuous. Yet, piety is a quality which God loves. True piety is not an act you put on in order to create a certain impression. It is a way of life. It is the result of a life anchored in God that reflects His will and Spirit in every situation.

It implies furthermore that all the aspects of our lives should become committed to God. Zechariah captured this vision of piety when he remarked that across the everyday things of life would be written: "Holy to the Lord."

To many, this way of life holds no attraction, but there is a rich reward for those who honestly and sincerely seek to live for God. To consciously live in the presence of God, will sanctify your entire life. God leads you on paths He has prepared for you; the strength He gives to your spirit enables you to obey Him. The greater your love for Him, the more you will understand His will and the life to which He has called you.

When you include God in every aspect of your life, you become a co-partner of His peace. Then you possess a treasure which only God can give.

O Prince of Peace, mercifully grant me the peace which is the result of a pious way of life. Do this through the working of Your loving Holy Spirit. Amen.

May 2   Read: 1 Samuel 30:1-8

Equipment for life

David was greatly distressed ... But David found strength in the
LORD his God.

– 1 SAMUEL 30:6 –

A pparently every generation seems to think that life is more complex in their time than it was for previous generations. This has been the case in past years and will undoubtedly be the case in the future.

Life is never easy. Through the ages man has had to deal with droughts, famine, plagues, war and a multitude of situations which create feelings of fear, helplessness and despair.

History tells the story of humankind and its continuous struggle for survival in the face of obstacles, pitfalls and misfortune. Nevertheless, man has survived and continues to deal with life to the best of his abilities.

In many cases it seems to be a hit-or-miss game. To many people life is mainly a question of "fate". To ensure that you overcome the unpredictability and uncertainty of modern life, it is essential that you enter into an intimate relationship with the living Christ. Cultivate this through an in-depth study of His eternal Word, through prayer and by spending time in the quietness of His holy presence.

By doing this, the strength of Christ which flows into your life will nurture your spirit. Through His peace and His gift of grace, He gives you the self-confidence you need to lead a life of victory every day.

Lord my God, in my time of need You have been ever-faithful.
You deserve the praise and glory for all eternity! Amen.

Read: Zechariah 13:1-9

May 3

Purified like gold

This third I will bring into the fire; I will refine them like silver and test them like gold.

— ZECHARIAH 13:9 —

The fire that consumes coal also purifies gold. Both are minerals from the earth, but gold has certain qualities that are absent in coal. These qualities make gold so much more precious than coal. Gold can withstand high temperatures; gold is malleable and pliable; gold glitters and reflects light.

There is also a marked difference in people who have been placed in the melting-pot of life. Those who trust the Lord faithfully are purified and strengthened through suffering. As with gold, the image of the Goldsmith is increasingly reflected in them.

Those who refuse to trust God are consumed by their own bitterness and rebellion. The strengthening and development of character are the end-results for those who faithfully trust God with their problems, disappointments, trials and sorrow. Those who doubt and question the omnipotence of God, face confusion, depression and eventually self-destruction.

Trials and tribulations will never leave you at a disadvantage permanently, unless you harden your heart against God, or become embittered and rebel against His will.

What ultimately makes the difference, is how you react to certain situations in life. Do you blame God and turn away from Him or do you move closer to Him so that you can avail yourself even more fully of His mercy and comfort?

If we turn to Him in prayer and surrender, pain is relieved, and suddenly we arrive at green pastures and quiet waters. Then we know: the stars have always been there, it only had to become dark for us to see them clearly. Trusting in God during dark hours, is the highroad to God's strength and solace. For them who trust in Him, He unlocks the heavenly treasury of comfort.

May the melting-pot in my life bring me closer to You, the heavenly Goldsmith, so that my life may bring forth purified gold which will reflect Your glorious image. Amen.

May 4

Read: Romans 8:18-31

All things to the good

And we know that in all things God works for the good of those who love him, who have been called according to his purpose.
– ROMANS 8:28 –

When our lives are on the verge of being destroyed by problems, sorrow or affliction, we find it extremely difficult to believe that God can and will make all things work out for the good of those who love Him. Even if only a little hope remains in our lives, it is sufficient for God to fulfill His plan for our lives. We can never lose so much that God cannot create something good out of what remains. There is no loss that God cannot compensate for.

God is so much greater than our understanding. His omnipotence is not limited and His love is infinite. How will we, with our limited ideas, ever completely understand His perfect plan for our lives if we do not have a burning faith in our hearts? God does not only want us to accept His intervention in our lives, but also to understand it.

After overwhelming sorrow or disappointment it may sound inappropriate to say that God can make it work out for our good. Yet believing this is an integral part of our healing and solace. If it had not been for this Christian hope, we would all have had broken hearts. Hope for tomorrow is today's inspiration. For those who love God this is the most glorious knowledge: that God wants only the best for us and that He wants everything to work for our good. Silent and solid trust in God sets His power free on our behalf.

Phillips Brooks stated, "We believe as we love and where we love. If we love Christ very much, we will surely also trust Him very much".

Out of our love for Christ, good is born. Therefore we should impress love on ourselves since this will increase our faith in God all the more.

I thank You, Comforter, for this glorious promise that You will make everything work out for the best. In this I will love and trust You, today, tomorrow and every day You grant me. Amen.

Read: John 14:15-31   May 5

Royal love

*"Peace I leave with you; my peace I give to you. I do not give to you
as the world gives. Do not let your hearts be troubled and do not be
afraid."*

– John 14:27 –

People are always longing for peace. The nations of the world
discuss this in conferences; citizens want to escape the tumult
and confusion of their daily routine; everyone is looking for a place
where he can find this much sought-after peace. All are searching
for peace, but it often eludes us because we are looking for it in the
wrong places.

True peace can only be experienced when inner tranquility and
balance take hold of one's spirit. You might be fortunate to flee from
the confusion, but if your spirit is restless and unbalanced, peace
will escape you.

Peace arises from a heart that is in harmony with God and with
itself. This peace is not achieved as a result of external circumstances. Mother Theresa had it, even in the slums of Calcutta; mis-
sionaries have it in danger zones of uncivilized worlds; persecuted
Christians have it in parts of the world where the reality of God's
peace is still unknown.

Godly peace is a gift granted to those who love Him and who
walk with Him. It is also a reward for living according to His standards.

The amazing thing about godly peace is that it is not affected by
external circumstances. As the pressure and tension of life increase,
the peace that God gives also becomes more powerful. If you live
close to the Father, the peace of God which transcends all understanding will become a fixed part of your life.

*I worship You, King of peace, and I thank You that I may expe-
rience Your peace in such a practical way through my Redeemer,
Jesus Christ. Amen.*

May 6   Read: Joel 2:28-32

You have a part to play

And afterward, I will pour out my Spirit on all people. Your sons and daughters will prophesy, your old men will dream dreams, your young men will see visions.

– JOEL 2:28 –

Despite the fact that we live in an age of astounding scientific and technological development, there are many of us who will admit that something is lacking. In this sophisticated era, we are rapidly being degraded to figures without names. Electronic devices do our work for us, instant solutions are found for every problem imaginable, even our relaxation and entertainment are provided for us!

It is absolutely certain that progress and development have a place in the history of humankind and in many cases this has been of incalculable importance. The essential danger to man, however, lies in the fact that he can slowly fall victim to the temptation of not thinking for himself. His thinking is done for him by highly developed machines.

Since creation this earth has been established on the foundation laid by God and by people who put their faith in Him. After seeking His will, they went out in the power of the living Christ and obediently carried out His great instruction.

Despite the temptation of begin carried away by the masses, you should never neglect waiting on the Lord. His inspiration will enable you to carry out the task He entrusted to you. Always remain open to the guidance of the Holy Spirit and be sensitive to the prompting of God. Like the great men in history, you will then also have a part to play in making this world a better place – to the glory of God!

O Holy Spirit of God, inspire me every day so that I will play a productive role in building and developing Your kingdom today and wherever You may lead me. Amen.

Read: Psalm 55:1-24 May 7

Fleeing or trusting?

I said, "Oh, that I had the wings of a dove! I would fly away and be at rest."

— PSALM 55:6 —

Cast your cares on the LORD and he will sustain you; he will never let the righteous fall.

—PSALM 55:22 —

The way in which people deal with problems reveals much about their Christian character. The psalmist points out two methods in which people try to deal with their problems.

There is the "flight method", in which you try to escape or evade your problems. Then there is the "stand fast and trust the Lord method" in which you deal with your problems and overcome them in the name of the Lord.

Jonah started by running away. God sent him to Nineveh but he fled in the opposite direction. He did not like the people of Nineveh. He bought a ticket at Joppa for a voyage to Tarshish, far away from his responsibilities. But Jonah never reached Tarshish. Tarshish remained a mirage. Jonah didn't want to accept that there is no place on earth we can go to escape our problems completely.

Instead of solving his problems, Jonah only multiplied them. You can never escape from yourself, your responsibilities or problems. When Jonah eventually chose the path of obedience and went to Nineveh to carry out his task, the Lord gave him strength and he performed miracles in the Name of the Lord.

At one time or another we all face the temptation of trying to flee from our problems or to sidestep our responsibilities. Even Jesus was confronted by temptation in the desert. However, He accepted God's will for His life and did what He had to do. If we are obedient and trust God completely, He *will* support and help us.

Holy Trinity, I trust You with my life and my problems. Make me obedient and faithful through Your Holy Spirit and through the power of my Redeemer, Jesus Christ. Amen.

May 8

Read: Romans 7:15-24

Strength for victory

For what I do is not the good I want to do; no, the evil I do not want to do – this I keep on doing.

– ROMANS 7:19 –

The old saying: "Know yourself" is often quoted, yet seldom completely understood. Man's personality is very complex and a distinct characteristic is his unwillingness to admit unpleasant truths. Bad habits or sinful behavior is disguised behind intellectual terms and is in that way excused.

The teachings of Christ, seen in the illuminating light of the Holy Spirit, reveals your true self. To be completely understood by the Holy Spirit is a heart-searching experience. His sinlessness reveals your sinfulness; His strength accentuates your weakness; His holiness makes you deeply aware of your own unworthiness.

We should, however, guard against continuously placing our lives under a magnifying glass in search of real or imaginary sins. If you faithfully accept the forgiveness of the Father, you should rejoice in it. Through the power of His redeeming love and the gift of the Spirit, you are delivered from the binding power of sin and you can live in victory.

If you live in this freedom, you can see yourself as you are in Christ. This will open new prospects of inner potential and you will look forward to life with joy. You will develop exciting and satisfying expectations.

Do not keep on fretting about sins which God has already forgiven. It will only weaken your thinking and depress your spirit. Do not allow them to have a hold over your life. Rather rejoice in God's forgiveness and in the strength He gives to you to live victoriously.

God of mercy, I thank You for the gift of repentance and the confession of sins through Jesus Christ. Help me to live victoriously every day through the strength of Your Holy Spirit. Amen.

Read: John 15:1-8

May 9

Growth through pain

He cuts off every branch in me that bears no fruit, while every branch that does bear fruit he prunes so that it will be even more fruitful.

– John 15:2 –

God often uses pain and sorrow to teach His children important lessons. By doing so He also strengthens our character and gives us the opportunity to grow spiritually. Sorrow is a fruit and God does not allow this fruit to grow on branches that are too weak to carry it.

Christ tells us that God is the great Gardener who lovingly prunes His children. The right pruning methods result in vines, shrubs and trees growing better and bearing more fruit.

In our lives, there are many infertile shoots: bad habits; wrong thoughts and sinful inclinations. Therefore, the pruning-shears of God are sometimes required. Christina Rossetti stated, "Although today He prunes my twigs with pain, yet doth His blood nourish and warm my root; tomorrow I shall put forth buds again and clothe myself with fruit."

Our heavenly Father is a Master Pruner. He knows all about our shortcomings. His pruning promises growth and abundant fruit. Under the tender care of the Gardener, the wounds heal and new life breaks out everywhere.

He who has learnt to carry his cross will find peace. You will be a conqueror and you will stand strong in this world. Christ did not come to make all pain disappear, but to teach us to bear it with dignity and to glorify Him through it. Then you become a participant in Christ's suffering on behalf of the whole world. It is through the positive contributions of those who have experienced suffering and pain that this world becomes a better place to the glory of God.

Father of abundant grace, help me to accept the pain in my life as part of Your loving pruning and enrich me through Your healing mercy, so that I can bear abundant fruit. Amen.

May 10

Read: Luke 12:13-21

Man's evaluation system

Watch out! Be on your guard against all kinds of greed; a man's life does not consist in the abundance of his possessions.

– LUKE 12:15 –

Appearances can be deceptive. You may see someone who radiates cheerfulness, yet his heart may be broken; someone may seem prosperous, yet his business may be on the point of bankruptcy; someone may appear in the best of health, but be the victim of some incurable disease. Judging someone on his appearance is to forget that there are hidden and secret depths in every personality.

Do not be overwhelmed by appearances, since possessions may just be a front to hide moral weakness or spiritual failure. The essential value of a person is the loving compassion he has for his fellow man. When a person has risen above the desire to impress other people and seeks to serve them in a way that would enrich their lives, he has discovered his real value and then people will recognize his place in society and value it.

It is a person's character that ultimately determines his value. An unimpeachable character is not the result of a fleeting emotion, but the end product of a life built on the highest principles, a firm spiritual foundation and a positive and practical belief in God.

If your life is ruled by God and inspired by His Holy Spirit, your inner life develops and brings about deep satisfaction and enrichment. This life has its origin in God. To live consciously in His presence will develop a way of life that is not only beneficial to you, but also to those around you.

Heavenly Teacher, may my life reflect true spiritual values through the blessed work of Your Spirit in me. Amen.

Read: Matthew 6:5-15

May 11

Principles for prayer

When you pray, go into your room, close the door and pray to your Father, who is unseen. Then your Father, who sees what is done in secret, will reward you.

– MATTHEW 6:6 –

Prayer is not meant as a means to obtain things from God, but rather as a means to hear God's point of view about the most important things in life.

Prayer is to seek God's will, rather than to command Him to do what you want. Prayer is to give yourself to God completely and not to use God for your own selfish goals.

It is just as much "listening" to God as it is "talking" to God. Prayer is a dialogue, not a monologue.

It is patiently waiting on God and not expecting everything to be done immediately. It is not an emergency button that you press in times of crisis, but it is a way of life.

Prayer is creating joy by spending time with God; and is not a hasty ceremonial duty to be performed before you quickly return to the world.

It is not a list of requests presented to God with the monotonous introduction, "Give me"; it is a total commitment that honestly asks, "Lord, what do you want me to do?"

Prayer is never "Do it now!" but to confess, "Thy will be done." It is through mercy that God keeps us waiting, and does not always give us what we ask for.

We are like small children who ask for machine guns or time bombs. We are not equipped to use the things we often ask for. The main purpose of prayer is to honor God, to glorify His name, to carry out His will and to edify His Kingdom. True prayer is simply to know God!

Our Father in heaven, hallowed be Your Name, Your Kingdom come, Your will be done. Amen.

May 12   Read: Mark 11:20-25

Let go of your grievances

When you stand praying, if you hold anything against anyone, for-
give him, so that your Father in heaven may forgive you your sins.
                                              – MARK 11:25 –

There are many people who stubbornly refuse to bury their grievances. They are found in all walks of life. They nurse their so-called pain and wounded hearts and with self-pity tell everyone about their unjust treatment.

Some people are so over-sensitive their feelings are hurt if you just look at them funny. Even if no harm was intended, they feel insulted and retreat into their shells. Then they nurse their pain and refuse to forgive the "sinner".

Christians who act like this forget two important facts. Firstly, they have lost sight of the Christ of the cross. He was robbed of all human dignity, He was renounced and betrayed, He was ridiculed and despised by many. Nevertheless, in the midst of people's bitterness and hatred towards Him He asked His Father to forgive them.

Take your petty grievances and pain you find so precious; compare them to the Cross and see how insignificant and unimportant they become. Let them disappear in the love and strength that radiate from the Cross.

Another aspect of the foolish nursing of grievances, is the damage it does to our thoughts, our spiritual lives and our health. By nursing your grievances, you create a pattern of thought which prevents you from positive and constructive thinking. Still greater damage is done to your spiritual life by harboring grievances. It destroys the harmonious relationship between you and your heavenly Father.

Compare your hurt to the pain Christ suffered. Shame will drive you to your knees.

Merciful Master, enable me through Your Holy Spirit to surren-
der my grievances to You and to exult in Your cross. Amen.

Read: 1 Corinthians 3:9-23   May 13

A firm foundation

For no one can lay any foundation other than the one already laid, which is Jesus Christ.

— 1 Corinthians 3:11 —

Over the years people have held widely divergent opinions regarding the education of children. Academic experts have written volume upon volume, teachers have based their ideas on years of practical experience in the classroom and parents have experienced family life with all its trauma and crises. Every generation is convinced that they carry out the task better than the previous one, and every child is sure that he will handle the situation better than his parents.

There is, and always will be, just one method of ensuring that your child is educated in such a way that he is able to face the uncertain future with confidence and has a balanced outlook on life. Making sure your child's life is based on the well-tried foundation of the Christian faith. This necessarily means that you should lead a Christian life.

When your child's life centers around Christ, he will be filled with love, joy, peace, patience, kindness, goodness, gentleness, faithfulness and self-control while growing up, as well as later in his life (see Gal. 5:22-23).

All these things Jesus will communicate to His children through His Spirit. In which better way can a child be equipped to walk out into an ever-changing world? Your child will have a firm foundation to build his life on.

Father, by building my life and my house on the Rock, I will ensure that my children also find fulfillment in life. Thank You for entrusting them to me with this glorious purpose. Amen.

May 14   Read: Matthew 5:3-12

Comfort from mourning

"Blessed are those who mourn, for they will be comforted."
– MATTHEW 5:4 –

It is reassuring to know that we are not at the mercy of blind fate, but that even our mourning serves a holy purpose. It is not coincidental that the world is called a "valley of tears". Sorrow does not allow itself to be brought out or prayed away. It brings emptiness to our hearts, homes and world. That is why it is like a wave of heavenly music to hear Christ tell us, "Blessed are those who mourn!"

The greatest loss in a person's life is to come out of your hour of darkness without any permanent gain. God wants to give you the treasures that come from darkness:

I walked a mile with Pleasure,
She chattered all the way.
But left me none the wiser
For all she had to say.

I walked a mile with Sorrow
An ne'er a word said she;
But, O, the things I learned from her
When Sorrow walked with me! (Anonymous)

There's a saying, "If you always experience sunshine, you are in the desert." There are certain spiritual benefits that can only be born from suffering.

Sorrow does two things for us: it teaches us the embracing mercy of God's love and it shows us the goodness and love of our fellow man. Through our sorrow, we rediscover our God and our fellow man. Sorrow teaches you that you do not stand alone; that you are escorted in your hour of distress when you need loving encouragement.

God of comfort, the darker the night, the more we long for the stars. Let the light of Your countenance shine in the dark places of our lives. Amen.

Read: Philippians 1:12-26　　　　　　　　　　May 15

The crown of life

For to me, to live is Christ and to die is gain.
— PHILIPPIANS 1:21 —

There are many people who have grown old without ever really enjoying life. Since they were children, they have never come to any positive conclusion that was of any importance. They have always accepted the mood of the moment. They have existed, yes, but they have never energetically lived life to the full. Their lives are without the inspiration that hope and positive thinking bring about.

Life is a gift of God, but you must learn how to use it, otherwise you will lose its essential value. The foundation of true life is knowing Christ. The recognition and acceptance of the reality of God is the first lesson which you have to learn if you want to move from mere existence to a full and satisfying life.

If you have given Christ His rightful place in your life, you will discover that He expects complete obedience from you. This requirement may sound overpowering, but you will discover that it is not something you have to fear. Everyone who obeys the living Christ will experience His blessings and his life will take on new meaning.

Acceptance and obedience are two core values of a true Christian life. They are also God's gifts that crown a sparkling and adventurous life to His glory.

Through the love and grace of God, it is possible for us to experience the presence of the living Christ in our lives. When we have Him, we "live" in the true and pure sense of the word.

I give myself in complete surrender and obedience to You, O Master. I thank You that I may live completely and victoriously, because I know You and love You. Amen.

May 16

Read: Genesis 1:26-31

To love ... in spite of

God created man in his own image, in the image of God he created him.

– GENESIS 1:27 –

Some people radiate sparkling sunshine. Other people only bring problems and cause frustration, especially when you, as a follower of Christ, are called to love them. In His wisdom, God did not create any two people alike: He made no duplicates. This causes human relationships to become challenges.

In your life you will get to know people who are difficult to understand. Regardless of how you approach them, you never experience harmony in your relationships with them. As time passes and no mutual understanding develops, you start losing patience. A complete break in the relationship may seem unavoidable.

We have all been created in the image of God. God is Spirit and man was created as a spiritual being. Deep in the spirit of even the most depraved person there is a trace of the Divine which can never be extinguished.

"Come unto me, ye weary,
And I will give you rest!"
O blessed voice of Jesus,
Which comes to hearts oppressed.
It tells of benediction,
Of pardon, grace and peace,
Of joy that hath no ending,
Of love that cannot cease.

The realization of this truth enables us to love the innermost being of a fallen person; that part of him which reacts to the divine love of Jesus Christ.

Teach me every day, loving Master, to love even the most difficult people I meet. Amen.

Read: 2 Corinthians 5:11-21   May 17

Who am I?

Therefore, if anyone is in Christ, he is a new creation; the old has gone, the new has come!

– 2 CORINTHIANS 5:17 –

One's immediate reaction to the above question is: "I'm me of course!" In a certain sense it is entirely true. Nevertheless, there is not a day that passes during which you are not affected by the influences that surround you. In so many subtle ways ideas, expectations, disappointments and many other influences shape your thoughts and character. You may eventually reach a point where you are no longer in control and can't make decisions for yourself anymore.

It is wise to realize that this takes you back to the basic principles of understanding yourself. To find an answer, you need someone other than yourself with a set of standards that enforce respect, who will not excuse your self-centeredness, who will expose your unfulfilled aspirations, who will set a challenge for you to accomplish. God is that agent. He reveals you to yourself in a powerful and clear way. He expects you to react to His challenge by committing yourself to Him completely.

Through the guidance and direction of the Holy Spirit, you will come to realize that you are a child of God. Perhaps you have always believed it, but have you had the courage to act on this belief?

The moment you realize your holy inheritance and kinship, life takes on a new meaning for you. You will have confidence in identifying with the Father. You know who you are and where you are going.

Heavenly Father, I praise Your great Name that I have come to know myself as a new person through the realization of my unity with You, by the grace of Jesus Christ. Amen.

May 18   Read: Matthew 6:5-14

When we pray

"When you pray, do not keep on babbling like pagans, for they think they will be heard because of their many words."
                                        – MATTHEW 6:7 –

There are many people who associate prayer with pompous eloquence. They seem to be under the impression that prayers should necessarily be long, that they should be complex and that the language of prayer should be formal and very correct.

The prayer most acceptable to Christ is in fact a childlike prayer. It should be simple, humble and sincere. The Afrikaans poet N. P. Van Wyk Louw speaks of the "honesty of deathbed words". The parable of the Pharisee and the tax collector is a classic example of this. Very often long drawn-out prayers are said more for the effect than out of sincerity. The cry of distress, "Father!" which comes from a repentant heart full of love, will be heard by God.

Pay attention to the instructions of Jesus in your prayers. He placed a high premium on simplicity and childlike faith. He also taught us to pray in private which is just as important – if not more important – than praying with others.

When you pray, speak to God in simple everyday language as you would speak to a trusted friend. Jesus is your Friend, after all. Pour out your worries before Him; share your anxiety and joy with Him. Wait on Him in silence. He will hear you and answer your prayer, often in the simplest and most surprising way. Truly believe this for He gave you His Word.

O Holy Spirit, guide my thoughts and words when I pray. Help me when I do not quite know what to pray. Amen.

Read: Daniel 3:13-26   May 19

Christ in the center

We do not need to defend ourselves before you in this matter. If we are thrown into the blazing furnace, the God we serve is able to save us from it and he will rescue us from your hand, O king.
— DANIEL 3:16-17 —

To experience true success and to realize your highest ideals, Christ should be at the center of your life. Whether this is true of your life, will have to be settled with God in prayer.

When Scott Mills was sent to the stake by Queen Mary, he was told to renounce his faith in God to save his own life. His answer was, "Renounce my faith? I am wheat and not chaff that is blown away in the wind. I belong to Christ." This is the test we will be subjected to, just like Daniel and his friends. Then we will know that Christ holds the position of honor.

"The Sistine Madonna", an immortal painting by Raphael, the world-famous painter, was once shown in the palace of the king of Dresden. In great excitement it was brought to the throne room so that the king could see it. The problem was to find the most suitable place for it: the light, the background, the curtains, everything had to be just right to display the painting in its full glory.

It then appeared that the best place would undoubtedly be the spot where the throne stood. But one does not move a throne! Then the king came forward and pushed the throne aside, saying, "Make room for the immortal Raphael!" It was a fine gesture. But of course the king was wrong. Only one is immortal – Christ!

Who will take the position on the throne of our hearts? The self? The world? Pleasure? Enjoyment? Wealth? Lust? Sin? Or will we say, "Make room for the immortal Christ!" Then He will become the focal point of your life and all other things will fall into place. To have Christ at the center is the highest success in life.

Take my love, my Lord, I pour at Thy feet its treasure-store. Take myself, and I will be ever, only, all for Thee! Amen.

May 20   Read: Matthew 27:21-26

The choice is yours

What shall I do, then, with Jesus who is called Christ?
                                    – MATTHEW 27:22 –

If I should ask you what the vital questions of the day are, I assume I would get divergent answers.

Some people would say ecology is the greatest question of the day. What are we going to do about the pollution of our planet? Others would say that inflation is the burning problem of our time. How are we going to deal with rising costs and devaluation of money? Some people feel that elderly people present the most pressing problem of this century. How are we to care for the increasing number of aged people? Then there are those who see the youth as the greatest single problem of our time. With almost half of our population under the age of 25, we wonder how their energy can be channeled in the right direction.

These issues and problems are definitely important, but there is one question which is much more important: "What am I to do with Jesus Christ?"

It is not a new problem. Pilate had already asked the same question 2000 years ago. So much depends on your answer. The wrong answer can consequently mean that you lose everything of any worth. To keep quiet and not answer is to reject Christ.

Some people ignore Christ. Like Pilate, they theatrically wash their hands in innocence and announce that they do not want to have anything to do with the matter. Some people oppose Christ. With their voices or lives they shout, "Away with Him! Crucify Him!"

Others praise the Lord, choose Him as their Redeemer and King. By accepting Christ, they find redemption from sin and death. They gain peace, joy and eternal life.

Yes, Lord Jesus, my heart chooses You as King for eternity! Amen.

Read: 2 Timothy 3:10-17 May 21

Tradition and renewal

But as for you, continue in what you have learned and have become convinced of, because you know those from whom you learned it.
— 2 Timothy 3:14 —

Every era of human history has one or two buzzwords. At present the buzz word is "change". In many areas of life there are currently calls for change: in politics; in the cultural and social fields and with regard to our moral codes. It is of the utmost importance that we will maintain a healthy balance between tradition and renewal.

Change is not necessarily to be rejected straight away. On the contrary! The changes that have taken place in the world under the influence of science and technology are astonishing in many respects. One should, however, always ask what the basis for the change is and where it will lead. Change purely for the sake of change often leads to chaos and ends in revolution. Tradition is an essential element of human culture. It specifically includes the customs, practices and morals that order our lives. As such, tradition is not something that you can shake off like dust. It was not established in one day, but is often the result of values developed over generations.

Tradition is both an "anchor" and a "compass". As an anchor it binds us to the best and most noble things of the past, so that we are not blown about like tumbleweed by winds of change. As a compass it gives direction to our lives and helps us to keep on course through the crises we face. Tradition is the most effective obstacle in the way of radicalism that wants to uproot and destroy man's ties with the past.

Therefore, we should guard against presenting positive tradition in a bad light due to spitefulness or a lack of knowledge. For this we need the guidance of the Holy Spirit.

God of history, I thank You because Your Spirit teaches me which traditions inspire me to renewal and growth. Make me faithful to You, so that I will serve and follow You obediently. Amen.

May 22

Read: Ephesians 4:17-24

Anchor and compass

You were taught, with regard to your former way of life, to put off your old self, which is being corrupted by its deceitful desires: to be made new in the attitude of your minds; and to put on the new self, created to be like God in true righteousness and holiness.
— Ephesians 4:22-24 —

Because tradition serves as anchor and compass, it is not something that can remain static. It should be open to the demands of the present and developed further by every generation. After all, we cannot act like our ancestors did in similar situations. Upholding tradition for the sake of tradition (traditionalism) can only lead to stagnation and alienation from real life. You keep on facing the past with your back turned on the future.

Renewal is therefore not foreign to tradition. In fact, tradition offers the only basis for true renewal. Without the basis of tradition, every renewal constructed is just a form of opportunism.

The renewal of tradition is not only necessary because of the demands every new period brings, but it is also a calling on man's life. As a calling, renewal of tradition can take place only on the basis of pure and fixed principles. Principles are those things which help us to distinguish between what is important and what is not; what should be conserved and what can fall away.

Naturally, the principles that we use to distinguish between issues are contained only in a Christian ideology and view of life. That enables me, for example, to determine that I need not necessarily wear raw-hide shoes because my ancestors did, but that I should dress properly as they did.

New times bring new demands. New demands can only be evaluated in the light of the eternal principles of God's Word in which His will for our lives is revealed.

Almighty Father, give me the wisdom through Your Holy Spirit to distinguish truly, so that I can live for those things which really matter. Amen.

Read: Hebrews 11:1-10   May 23

Faith that sees the invisible

Now faith is being sure of what we hope for and certain of what we do not see.

— HEBREWS 11:1 —

To many people faith is a mystical, almost hazy quality that is entirely removed from everyday life. People desire more faith, yet they are deeply aware that they lack the ability to believe in everyday spiritual things. They continuously ask God to give them more faith and yet their spiritual lives remain ineffective.

We should realize that faith is an integral part of human nature. Everyone possesses some degree of faith, but the tragedy is that many people use it incorrectly. They believe in their inability to achieve a worthy goal; they believe in their fear which obstructs their view of life; and, strangely, they believe more in defeat than in success.

It is therefore not so much a question of more faith, but of the ability to use what I already have in a right and positive way. Everyone can believe in "someone" or "something", but without faith in Christ, no one can be a Christian.

Without faith we cannot have fellowship with God. Faith is trust in God and it thrives on the fruit it brings forth. Through Jesus' instruction that His disciples should have more faith in God, He wanted them to progress to a life of positive and constructive faith in their daily lives.

The most delicious fruit of Christian faith is the certainty of God's living presence and the assurance that He loves you. Then you can live positively because you see the unseen.

I thank You, Father, for the faith Your Holy Spirit awakens in my heart. It assures me that I am Your child by the grace of Jesus Christ. Amen.

May 24

Read: Matthew 14:22-32

When you are afraid

But Jesus immediately said to them: "Take courage! It is I. Don't be afraid."

– Matthew 14:27 –

Never be scared or embarrassed to show that you are afraid. Those who say that they are never afraid, either have insensitive spirits or they are not truthful. It is the fear of giving in to fear which makes us so anxious. If fear takes over, our lives start disintegrating, our thinking becomes chaotic and our behavior becomes irresponsible. That is why it is essential to control our fear.

Fear is a reality and takes on many forms. To name but a few: the fear of disappointing those who rely on you; the unknown future; it also includes the fear of death.

It is important to prepare yourself well to cope with fear in times when you do not experience any fear. To be afraid is a natural reaction and if you have no spiritual reserves, your reaction can have serious consequences. Reserves are necessary for your spirit to control fear that arises as a result of external circumstances.

If you want to prepare your spirit to handle circumstances that create fear, you have to accept the living Christ in every area of your life. If Christ controls your thinking and fills your spirit with His Holy Spirit, you will, despite the fear caused by circumstances, have inner peace, which is stronger than any fear, even the fear of death.

Christ has proved that life conquers death; that for those who love Him, death is only the gateway to life.

Merciful Master, I thank You that through Your Spirit, I can conquer all fear that threatens to overwhelm me. Amen.

Read: Romans 7:15-25

May 25

What you are meant to be

What a wretched man I am! Who will rescue me from this body of death? Thanks be to God – through Jesus Christ our Lord!
– ROMANS 7:24-25 –

There are many disciples who have become satisfied with substandard Christianity. Perhaps they gave and committed themselves to God years ago. For some time they experienced a powerful Christian life. Then the experience started to fade until only a memory remained. The glory of their faith deteriorated into something insignificant.

Nevertheless, even when their faith was ineffective, they knew instinctively that this was not God's will for them. God's will for His people is only the best. God wants to strengthen us so that we can live triumphantly. In addition, He offers inner peace which will drive away uneasiness and make it possible for us to have a balanced and positive life.

God is willing to give us this and many other spiritual gifts from His treasury, if our commitment to Him is absolute.

God did not remove Himself from you. Your deep desire for spiritual growth is just an inspired restlessness that God gives. He is calling you back to Him, so that you can become what He meant you to be.

You know what you can be through the power of Christ. God does not call you to an unfulfilled life. That is why He is calling you to renew your commitment today, so that you can regain the fullness of your faith. By doing that you will experience the glory of the power of the living Christ in your spirit and life.

O Master, through my total commitment to You, I rediscover the glory of my faith. Continue to guide me through Your Holy Spirit to a deeper life of complete commitment and obedience. Amen.

May 26

Read: Romans 2:1-11

Can you afford disobedience?

But for those who are self-seeking and who reject the truth and follow evil, there will be wrath and anger.

— ROMANS 2:8 —

Obedience to God is an aspect of the gospel that is toned down in order to make it more popular and acceptable. It is, however, a very important component of Christ's challenge to those who want to be His followers. He stresses the demands of obedience that the eternal God has always made on those who serve Him.

Unfortunately, obedience to God is often presented as something one has to endure, instead of a glorious privilege to be enjoyed. The cause of this misrepresentation is conflicting interests: your own self-interest and God's will for you.

Most followers of Christ know that He wants only the best for them. Due to God's grace and love people think, however, that their disobedience will be left unpunished. This belief originates in the hearts of people who play off God's love against His righteousness. They say that He will never punish people because He loves people so dearly. They think of God as a lenient Father with spoilt children.

God is the Creator of a universe ruled by fixed laws. Keep these laws and they will be a source of rich blessing to you. Break them and they break you. No one can be disobedient to God and His holy instructions and hope to evade the consequences. Going to God with a repentant heart is to be saved from the destruction caused by disobedience. Then you are living in harmony with His holy will.

Almighty God, I live to obey Your instructions and to do Your will. I thank You for the help of Your Holy Spirit. Amen.

Read: Psalm 27:1-14   May 27

Firm convictions

Though an army besiege me, my heart will not fear; though war break out against me, even then will I be confident.

— PSALM 27:3 —

It is impossible to satisfy everybody. Trying to do this creates a lack of trust and chaos. There are times when you have to take a stand regarding important issues. Neglecting to do so resembles a poor character and doesn't accomplish anything.

It is especially true of our spiritual lives. Unless you can say with unshakable conviction, "I believe!" you are missing out on an immeasurable source of spiritual strength. It is only firm convictions that can have a molding influence on your life.

Since you are a Christian disciple, Christ should be the focus of your life. He is the Lord. This statement is a conviction that doesn't allow compromise. Such a strong point of view may, however, never result in narrow-mindedness. The moment fanaticism takes the place of conviction, reason and love, your faith becomes unattractive and powerless. That is why you should allow the Spirit of God to come into your life.

It is essential to have a strong inner conviction if you want to lead a true Christian life. But just as important as conviction is the spirit of love. It creates a spirit of mutual trust and understanding despite mutual differences in thought.

Strong beliefs without love, make us aggressive and this alienates people from us. Hold on to your convictions, but make sure that your love is just as strong.

Redeemer and Savior, I will be strong and loving in my convictions through the strength of Your indwelling Spirit. Amen.

May 28   Read: Philippians 4:10-20

The impossible becomes possible

I can do everything through him who gives me strength.
— PHILIPPIANS 4:13 —

Through faith and the grace of God in our lives, the unattainable becomes attainable and the impossible becomes possible!

You have probably experienced moments of intense disappointment. To become more like Christ seems unattainable and in humility you realize your own inadequacy. Then you start wondering whether the struggle for good is still worth the trouble.

What God expects of you and what you currently see revealed in your life are worlds apart. It creates a feeling of frustration and spiritual inferiority. With Paul you want to cry, "Who is equal to such a task?" (2 Cor. 2:16).

If God should leave you to yourself in this condition, you would stay deeply unhappy and unfulfilled. But God never puts a hunger in one's spirit that He cannot satisfy. The exact hunger that so often upsets you and leaves you discontented, is one of God's precious gifts to you. It creates in you a desire for a better and deeper spiritual life. You cannot reach this in your own strength; God can fulfill every need of your spirit. This promise we find in Romans 8:26, "The Spirit helps us in our weakness."

God called us to a life which is unattainable in our own strength. But He promises His assistance and strength to help us reach those heights through the gift of the Holy Spirit. If you accept this gift gratefully, you can also achieve those things He called you to do.

Loving Lord, I thank You that it is not through my own limited strength that my life becomes what You intended it to become, but through Your divine strength. I thank You for Your Spirit who guides me in all truth. Amen.

Read: Job 32:6-22

May 29

The source of inspiration

But it is the spirit in man, the breath of the Almighty, that gives him understanding. It is not only the old who are wise, not only the aged who understand what is right.

— Job 32:8-9 —

It is a fact that you are spiritually, morally and intellectually strengthened or weakened by the foundation you are building on. If you are a committed Christian, positive behavior should strengthen your spiritual life. Your Christianity should be stronger and richer than at the time of your surrender and commitment to Christ.

If you are conscious of spiritual poverty or inner weakness, you should purposefully do something to enrich and enhance your moral life. If you are intellectually at the point of the Christian religion but are offering superficial arguments why you cannot accept it completely, you should ask yourself if you are not suppressing your faith.

True inspiration requires complete honesty. Without it, there is no challenge to spiritual growth; moral standards are lowered and the intellectual search becomes a mockery.

But to be brutally honest with yourself is not as easy as it sounds. Personal desires, changing circumstances, greed and many other negative factors combine to cause you to deviate from total honesty and to be satisfied with a second-rate compromise. The consequences are always frustration, dissatisfaction and disappointment.

The true Source of inspiration and honesty is revealed in you if you allow the Holy Spirit to show you who you really are. This is a challenging experience. You will discover that many things block the free flow of the Holy Spirit in your life and prevent Him from working through you. Live in the light of God's Holy Spirit and you will find yourself at the Source of the most noble inspiration.

Faithful Guide, let me live close to the Source of pure inspiration, through the grace of the Holy Spirit. Amen.

May 30   Read: Psalm 46:1-12

The discipline of silence

Be still and know that I am God; I will be exalted among the nations,
I will be exalted in the earth.

— PSALM 46:10 —

One of the most difficult disciplines for the Christian is to be still in the presence of God. It is reasonably easy to sit and believe that you are in His presence, but soon you start thinking of urgent matters or your thoughts exclude God from your meditation.

Many Christians find a solution by speaking to God continuously. While they converse with God, their thoughts are more or less on Him, but as soon as they stop they experience an uneasy silence. The silences with God create problems for them. However, if we cannot understand the silences with God we will never understand His words.

One of the most precious assets to possess in your search for the presence of God in silence is a thorough knowledge of His immortal Word. However, this does not mean long periods of academic or theological study. It implies that you are familiar with the great texts of the Bible, which over generations have helped God's children to experience the reality of His presence.

Different texts speak to different people in special circumstances. Look for those texts that have a special meaning for your spiritual progress and that you can easily recall.

No normal person can have a totally empty mind. Choose texts which can challenge, inspire and strengthen you. It should also give you inner assurance that God is with you in a special way and that you are close to Him. Memorizing specially selected texts that are remembered with love, will help you greatly to experience the presence of God as a reality when you meet Him in the silence.

Holy Master, I thank You that I may become aware of Your living presence through Your living Word. I thank You for the silences spent with You. Amen.

Read: Psalm 16:1-11

May 31

My heritage is beautiful!

LORD, you have assigned me my portion and my cup; you have made my lot secure. The boundary lines have fallen for me in pleasant places; surely I have a delightful inheritance.
— PSALM 16:5-6 —

In Psalm 16 David states unequivocally that he believes there is no good in life outside the will of God. This is also applicable to the times and fates of all people and nations. David takes this theme to a rejoicing climax when he praises God for the beautiful inheritance given to him by God's loving hand.

The same is true for us today for our history and for our country. Our heritage is outstandingly beautiful, "Soli Deo Gloria!" – To God be the glory! We have abundant reasons to be grateful. Just think of the beauty of our land, which defies description: blue heavens, towering mountains, the moving ocean, fertile valleys, an abundance of minerals, plant and animal life, sunshine and rain. When we think of all these things our hearts break out in a song of gratitude to our God.

That is why we kneel in thanksgiving before God. Like David, we confess to the Lord, "You have made known to me the path of life" (Ps. 16:11). We commit our family life to God because if He does not build the house, they who build it work in vain. We recommit our work, relaxation, culture, politics, economy, the entire lives of our people, and place it under His blessing.

We give our love anew: to our country, to our fellow man and to our God. We serve this love with a pure heart: a love that seeks unity amidst diversity; that seeks morality without hypocrisy; that seeks dignity that is not self-righteous; that seeks truth and not propaganda; that seeks justice which has not been bought with injustice; that seeks faith which is not vague sentimentality. With such a love, we can live with dignity in the place that God assigned to us.

Creator God, I thank You for the beautiful part of Your Kingdom that You have assigned to me. Make me worthy to occupy it to Your honor and glory. Amen.

JUNE

Read: Isaiah 40:27-31   June 1

A conditional promise

But those who hope in the LORD will renew their strength. They will soar on wings like eagles; they will run and not grow weary, they will walk and not be faint.

— ISAIAH 40:31 —

Now that we have reached the halfway mark of the year, we need assurance once again that we will be able to complete the race and fulfill our duty right up to the end. The hurry-scurry of life today poses a threat to our spiritual pilgrimage. There is so much to do and so little time. Life demands skill and speed in order to stay in the race, and there is no time to rest along the way and think about the reality and truth of God.

When you lose your spiritual balance, the detrimental outcomes are seen in all areas of your life. If you refuse to make time for God, your view of life becomes twisted. You start striving only for what you can do instead of realizing what God can do through you. When you stop waiting on the Lord, you start to limit your potential. You lose the joy granted to those who strive to inherit eternal life.

If you spend time in the presence of your heavenly Father and purposefully put this discipline before the passing demands of life, you will feel a new strength flowing into your life. Your spirit will sparkle and you will experience a surging expectation for the future. You will face life with greater confidence. While God daily becomes a greater reality in your life, you will develop a new sense of values. You will realize that He not only strengthens you, but that He also guides you lovingly in all your ways.

The conditions for this new, surging and inspiring strength include that you should steadfastly trust in the Lord. If you do this now, already halfway through the year, you will experience the wonderful sensation of soaring like an eagle.

I wait trustingly on You, my Lord and Guide. Thank You for Your power that permeates my spirit. Thank You for Your loving guidance in my life. Amen.

June 2

Read: Deuteronomy 10:10-20

When strangers meet

You are to love those who are aliens, for you yourselves were aliens in Egypt.

— DEUTERONOMY 10:19 —

There is a popular song with the title: "A stranger is just a friend you do not know." This reveals one of life's great truths.

You are constantly meeting strangers on the way. In shops and in busy streets you meet people you may never see again. Like ships in the night you move past each other. Yet, circumstances sometimes force people to spend time in the presence of strangers, even if it is only for a short while.

You might stand in an elevator with strangers today. Each person is caught up in his own train of thought and nobody says anything. But when one person suddenly says something pleasant, the reticence suddenly vanishes. A friendly word more often than not draws out a friendly reaction.

Many people protect themselves in a cocoon of isolation. They believe that the less contact they have with other people, the less the chances of getting hurt. Such private people are very sensitive to the moods of others and react to them easily. When you move amongst strangers, it is of utmost importance that you, as a Christian, radiate a positive and loving attitude. You don't have to say anything, but if you love people for the sake of Christ, they will instinctively feel the love and react to it.

The signals you send out by your unspoken thoughts and attitudes will come back to you. Estrangement and petty complaints among people would almost not exist if we would just spread Christ's love to strangers. With the attitude of Jesus Christ visible in your life and behavior, there would be more sunshine and joy in this harsh and unfriendly world.

Lord Jesus, You are my example, You showed infinite patience and love towards strangers, even when I was still a stranger. Help me to respect others and to accept them in love. Amen.

Read: 1 Corinthians 12:1-11　　　　　　　　June 3

Discover God's will for you

Now to each one the manifestation of the Spirit is given for the common good.

– 1 Corinthians 12:7 –

Have you ever experienced the feeling that you are drifting through life without any purpose and that it does not seem to matter whether you are here or not? Day after day passes by without you achieving anything of worth. Your spirit lost its sparkle long ago.

God is not to blame for the unhappy condition of your spiritual life. Firstly, you should rediscover the exciting reality of a spiritual experience with God. Then purposefully seek God's plan for your life, so that you can have a positive goal. If the living Christ is in control of your life, you will stop drifting aimlessly and start fulfilling the purpose of your life. You will become an inspired and positive Christian disciple.

The renewal of your spiritual life starts when you allow the Spirit of Christ into your life and invite Him to take control of your thoughts and actions. You will then discover that you live in harmony with Jesus Christ and that new areas of service are opening up for you. You will realize in astonishment that through the Spirit you are entering a new level of spiritual enrichment which you regarded as impossible before.

When you make the joyful discovery that you are under God's guidance, confirm this with God in prayer. Have the courage to act with confidence and to trust God steadfastly. Discovering God's will for your life does not only require steadfast faith, but also positive action. A life of unprecedented purpose will open up for you and allow you to meet the future with confidence.

Spirit of Grace, I thank You for the dynamic strength and inspiration You bring to my life. I accept the challenges of tomorrow with my eyes fixed on Jesus Christ, the Author and Perfecter of my faith. Amen.

June 4

Read: Psalm 32:1-11

Be sensitive to God's guidance

I will instruct you and teach you in the way you should go; I will counsel you and watch over you.

– PSALM 32:8 –

It is not always easy to distinguish the will of God. There are those few who know, without a doubt, exactly what God expects of them. However, most people hesitate and often ask, "What is God's will for me in this situation?" Of course we all know that God expects us to obey the Ten Commandments and to uphold the commandment of love. But when it comes to the personal complexities of life it's much more complicated to distinguish the will of God.

To know God's guidance so that you can do His will requires a particular and intimate relationship with Jesus Christ. This intimacy develops a sensitivity surrounding obedience. Every time you act contrary to God's will, a certain uneasiness will creep into your heart. You'll know irrefutably that you are acting contrary to His will.

Living close to God means a continued study of His Word, because there we find the revealed will of God and His answer to humanity's problems. To have a practical knowledge of the Scriptures makes it much easier to know and understand God's principles as they apply to you.

Living in fellowship with Christ and obeying His Word assure guidance through the prompting of the Holy Spirit. Then your words and deeds are brought into accordance with God's will for you.

Lord Jesus, You are King of my life, and through my fellowship with You and the knowledge of Your Word, I am constantly conscious of Your guiding love. Amen.

Read: Psalm 37:23-40   June 5

Justice will triumph

I was young and now I am old, yet I have never seen the righteous forsaken or their children begging bread.

– PSALM 37:25 –

Renouncing and compromising your principles and standards inevitably results in unhappiness and failure. A lack of integrity and dishonesty in business will ultimately result in disaster.

Nevertheless, it is difficult to understand that people so easily fall victim to these temptations to enrich their own lives. The reason is usually because they want to gain more possessions and status. Often enough it ends in sorrowful failure and humiliation.

History has proved time and again that justice always triumphs. While striving to lead a just and honorable life by keeping to your principles, you will be ridiculed and you will possibly suffer hardship. Remember that this is only temporary and what you believe in will ultimately be proven right. You will be respected for taking a stand.

If it seems to you that these demands are too high to meet, just think of the life of Jesus Christ. He never deviated from the path of justice. His love remained burning bright and could not be extinguished. Despite rejection, humiliation, suffering and crucifixion, His eyes were fixed on what was right and noble.

Consequently, He is still being worshiped two thousand years later and He has millions of followers. He is accepted as Lord because of His blameless life. On Him justice is based.

Lord Jesus, I will look up to You for strength and guidance in everything I say and do. Amen.

June 6

Read: Isaiah 58:1-7

Daily commitment

For day after day they seek me out; they seem eager to know my ways, as if they were a nation that does what is right and has not forsaken the commands of its God.

— Isaiah 58:2 —

If you have seen a vision of what you can be through the love and power of the living Savior or if you've experienced the inspiration of the Holy Spirit, then you must try to express that vision in your practical life.

For a while your spiritual life may prosper, but suddenly you will realize that you have not achieved your spiritual ideals. In one way or another your spiritual ideal has faded and you know with certainty that you are not the Christian that Christ meant for you to be. Something has disappeared from your life. The reality of your spiritual experiences are slipping away from you.

This is highly upsetting to the sincere and sensitive follower of the Master. There are two ways in which you can deal with this situation. Think of all the times in the past when the same thing happened, and decide to throw your spiritual life overboard and break with all spiritual ideals. Or see it as a serious call of the Holy Spirit to give yourself completely to Christ and His principles.

A fading faith should be seen as a challenge to a more complete surrender and commitment to Jesus Christ. Do not accept it as insurmountable. Every mature Christian has at one time or another on his pilgrim's journey, experienced moments of uncertainty and failure. Mature victory can be achieved only by continuous surrender to the Redeemer.

Redeemer and Lord, only through daily commitment to You can I have a living and victorious spiritual experience. Enable me to achieve this through the work of Your good Spirit in my life. Amen.

Read: Isaiah 62:1-12   June 7

God cares for you

For the LORD *will take delight in you.*

— ISAIAH 62:4 —

Extreme self-consciousness, feelings of guilt and feelings of inferiority can affect your life very negatively. Your spiritual growth and progress can be severely restricted. Many children of the Lord have degenerated into pathetic, colorless individuals filled with self-pity, because they have allowed feelings of total unworthiness to overcome them.

As a Christian you dare not forget that you are a child of God, a child of the King, a prince or princess in the family of the Most High. Whatever happens to you, remember that God loves you and that His love does not depend on whether you deserve it or have earned it, His love is infinite and unlimited.

Never forget the glorious truth that it's your privilege and joy to call God your Father; to know that He cares for you always and to know that He is continuously pouring out His love over you in every unique situation. He is concerned about your well-being. He wants to guide you on the path of true life and wants to ensure that you avoid the pitfalls on the path. When you feel depressed, praise God, because He is your Father and because His love for you is so great in life, death and eternity.

He sent Jesus as your Redeemer; He gave the Holy Spirit as your Comforter. May this be a continuous source of encouragement, comfort and strength. Take heart: God cares for you. God loves you.

I will rejoice in Your love and faithful care all the time, Lord my God! I thank You that Jesus Christ guarantees me this and that Your Holy Spirit keeps reminding me of this. Amen.

June 8

Read: Joshua 24:13-18

You determine the quality of your life

Then choose for yourselves this day whom you will serve.
– Joshua 24:15 –

You may perhaps blame other people or your circumstances for what you have become, but you cannot evade the responsibility of determining the quality of your own character. You are honorable or dishonorable; you are honest or dishonest; you live according to the truth or you are a liar; you are sincere or insincere – this is how you have chosen to live.

You may say that circumstances forced you to be dishonest, but the final choice between honesty and dishonesty, is yours. Your character is built on the choices you make. Every day of your life you have to make decisions and choose between right and wrong. What you decide can be affected by the need of the moment if truth becomes subject to comfort. Or you can keep to your principles without thinking about the sacrifice your choice might require. If you make decisions on the spur of the moment, to save yourself from embarrassment, you are motivated by self-interest. Your understanding of truth fluctuates according to the demands of the present situation.

Truth is eternal. It is the creator and foundation of a strong and decisive character. To serve the truth requires that high standards be met. If your understanding of truth varies with every changing mood and situation, you will always hesitate and the quality of your character will grow weaker.

If you have accepted Christ as your Redeemer and Savior, if His path and His will are your highest ideals, you will in due course develop a character that will reflect Him. This is the highest ideal of any life.

Loving Master, I steadfastly choose You every time, through the power of Your Holy Spirit that works in me. Amen.

Read: Job 6:14-30   June 9

Become aware of your emotions

Do you mean to correct what I say, and treat the words of a despairing man as wind?

– Job 6:26 –

Many people's lives are ruled by their emotions. Because they had a bad night's sleep, they start their day in an unpleasant mood. Someone upsets them slightly and for the rest of the day they are depressed and difficult to deal with. Perhaps jealousy has brought bitterness into relationships with others and they accept this unpleasant condition as inevitable.

The moment you accept moodiness, you become the victim of every changing emotion. It causes deep unhappiness. It is unfortunately true that many upsetting incidents occur in life. Many people are not stoics and they feel these things deeply.

If you experience times when you are highly stressed, relief and deliverance can be obtained by talking openly to a trusted friend or pastor. Sharing your burden changes it to half a burden and talking about your emotional confusion can often result in peace of mind.

However upset you may be, learn to see the bigger picture. It is very easy to become worked up about issues of lesser importance and to make a mountain out of a mole hill.

In your dismay you should become quiet for a moment and ask yourself, "How does God see this matter that is upsetting me so much?" Then eternal values will suddenly become part of the game. The things that upset you so much will become less of a problem and will soon vanish from your life.

Lord my God, through Your presence in my life, I can gain victory over all destructive emotions. Amen.

June 10

Read: 1 Corinthians 13:1-13

"If you love me, you will ... "

And now these three remain: faith, hope and love. But the greatest of these is love.

– 1 CORINTHIANS 13:13 –

Love has many shades and interpretations. Often it is degraded to suit our passions and comfort. Many people who are in love often abuse the phrase, "If you love me, you will ... " This is not love; it is nothing but extortion demanding total surrender. True love is not demanding, but accepts the loved one unconditionally.

True love bestows unlimited forgiveness on others. It has no limits and should never be confused with so-called love that dramatically declares, "I will forgive, but I will never forget." True forgiveness erases the past so that no sign of resentment remains. False pride, fanaticism and other destructive influences must be eliminated. It is a betrayal of true love to always dig up old grievances and use them heartlessly.

True love seeks no reward. It is satisfied with giving, as the myrtle-grove freely and richly gives off a lovely scent to the surroundings without receiving anything in return. Love carries on giving until it no longer needs to give. Saying, "I gave so much and never received a word of thanks," is not an expression of love, but a revelation of a hunger for appreciation and self-glorification. True love can only find expression in the Spirit of the Lord.

There is no such thing as "conditional love." Love gives everything. Its only concern is the well-being of your loved one.

Holy Lord Jesus, Your omnipotence and love enable me to love purely. Cultivate it in me through Your Holy Spirit. Amen.

Read: Proverbs 15:1-15   June 11

Cutting remarks

A gentle answer turns away wrath, but a harsh word stirs up anger.
– Proverbs 15:1 –

Were you hurt recently by an inconsiderate person who made a harsh remark? What was said hurt you deeply, perhaps. You now find it difficult to forgive, and almost impossible to forget. You record the injury in your memory and refuse to let it go. You place the insult on a pedestal and walk around with it in your heart. You look at it from all sides, until it has been pulled out of proportion.

This is a very human thing to do, but it is not wise at all. If you allow unforgiveness to settle in your thoughts and embitter your spirit, you lose every time. An embittered spirit is reflected in a dissatisfied approach to life. It is impossible to live in peace with yourself and in harmony with your fellow man if you carefully collect all the grievances you encounter, and then nurture them as well.

When someone is out to insult or hurt you, that person can only do it if you allow him to. He may make harsh, unfriendly and untrue remarks about you, but if you can find the grace to say as our Lord, "Father, forgive them, for they know not what they are doing," it will not cause you pain.

Obviously, someone who enjoys making cutting remarks has a twisted sense of values. Such a person needs your prayers more than your condemnation. Only those who do not have the Spirit of Christ in them will hurt a fellow human being on purpose.

Divine Teacher, teach me in the power of Your Holy Spirit to deal with unfriendly and painful words in prayer and forgiveness. Amen.

June 12

Read: Proverbs 13:15-25

Tell me who your friends are

He who walks with the wise grows wise, but a companion of fools suffers harm.

— PROVERBS 13:20 —

The well-known idiom, which alleges that one becomes like the friends you favor, is very true. It applies to every area of life, but especially to the spiritual area. After your conversion and acceptance of Jesus Christ as your personal Redeemer and Savior, you entered a new life with new principles and new interests. Since the interests of your previous friends have remained the same, there is estrangement between you. It is inevitable, but you may find it so upsetting that you try to compromise with them.

Your motivation for maintaining old friendships is most probably the desire for them to have the same spiritual experience that you have had. This motive is worthy of a Christian disciple, but if your faith is young, it is also a minefield of dangers.

The language, emotions and behavior of your old self still come reasonably easy to you. Out of your own will you still visit the old meeting places. Suddenly you realize that you are losing your grip on your faith. Eventually you are back where you started before your conversion. Old habits die hard. If you have accepted a new life, you should make a clean break from your old life and habits as soon as possible.

If God has burdened your heart with the spiritual welfare of your previous friends, accept the responsibility, but first ensure that your spiritual reserves are strong enough to face the opposition and ridicule on the way. Start by laying your concerns about them in prayer before God and ask Him for wisdom in your actions.

Master, give me a holy concern for others and the strength to help them in their distress. Amen.

Read: Isaiah 41:8-20　　　　　　　　　　　　　June 13

Discover yourself

You are my servant, I have chosen you and have not rejected you. So do not fear, for I am with you.

— ISAIAH 41:9-10 —

When you feel spiritually inadequate or despondent it is always good to remember that God does not feel that way about you at all. Your inadequacy and depression were not created by Him; you caused it yourself. It will be good to remember that, even if you feel like a complete failure and of no good to anyone or anything, the Lord knows that this is not the real you. He will never accept your view of yourself as inadequate and unworthy.

The living Christ called you to live in harmony with Him. This in itself is proof that He values His friendship with you highly. He called you because He needs you. If this seems like an amazing revelation to you, this next fact will be even more amazing: He sees something in you which you didn't know existed!

For far too long you have been saying to yourself, "I know myself and my limitations!" You accepted this untruth about yourself easily and started believing that you were incapable of creative and productive things.

If you determine your value according to your own standards and the criteria of those around you, you may have reason to feel depressed and deeply dispirited. However, if you allow the Spirit of Christ to develop your hidden potential, incredible changes may take place in your life.

Do not sink into self-deprecation and depression. God's hand is stretched out to help you up, to reach self-fulfillment and joy.

Christ Jesus, I open my entire life to Your Holy Spirit and ask that my hidden potential may be developed fully. I thank You once again for making my heart sing. Amen.

June 14

Read: Psalm 90:1-17

Act your age

Teach us to number our days aright, that we may gain a heart of wisdom.

— PSALM 90:12 —

Dr. Kathleen Heasman says in her book *An introduction to Pastoral Counselling* that there are three stages in a man's life.

The first reaches its climax during youth, when achievements are reached in the fields of physical strength and speed. The second is middle-age, when a condition of maturity and self-confidence is achieved and the pinnacle of a chosen career is reached. The third is old age, when qualities of reasoning and experience are of the utmost importance and wisdom comes into its own.

One of the biggest mistakes one can make in life is trying to stay in a phase when you should have moved on a long time ago. It is a terrible mistake to stubbornly try to remain a teenager. It is good to know when competitive games have come to an end. And it is still better to know when young people should be left to themselves. "A man amongst children, is a child amongst men!" Youth is a wonderfully beautiful time, but it passes. We must accept this fact.

Middle age is the age when we have reached the top of the ladder in our careers. Here we are also tempted to linger for too long. No one is indispensable. Leaving while at the pinnacle of success, is a clear form of success in itself.

Old age also has its own problems. One can so easily become self-centered and difficult. To be yourself and to constantly clash with others are recipes for loneliness and unhappiness. Remember that your children are maturing and that you should treat them as equals and not as little children. Only the grace of God and the Spirit of the living God can give you this wisdom.

I thank You, Creator Lord, for the phases of life. Give me the wisdom to move from one to the other with dignity. Amen.

Read: Mark 6:1-6   June 15

Well-known, but not well-respected

"Isn't this the carpenter? Isn't this Mary's son and the brother of James, Joseph, Judas and Simon? Aren't his sisters here with us?" And they took offense at him.

– MARK 6:3 –

Familiarity makes a relationship relaxed. You know someone inside out and he knows you. Between you there is such an intimate relationship that you can almost feel and think for each other.

Even in such an intimate relationship it is essential to respect individual personalities. There are moments when all of us wish to be alone. If you refuse someone this right and smother him or her, even in love, you threaten to destroy the friendship between you.

When Jesus visited His home town, the citizens thought they knew everything about Him. Had He not grown up among them? Even though they had listened to His divine wisdom and saw how He healed the sick, they rejected Him because He was too familiar to them. Not for one second did they think what this rejection on the basis of familiarity would cost them or the privilege they were refusing.

Familiarity is a danger to many modern disciples. Perhaps you were born and bred in a Christian home. You feel that you know everything there is to know about Jesus. You know the Bible inside out. You are no longer inspired or challenged by the living Christ. Holy things have lost their glitter for you.

Shake off this spiritual lethargy. Be determined to discover the freshness and the wonder of a living faith through the work of the Holy Spirit who lives in you.

Precious Lord, keep me from becoming so familiar with holy things that Your living presence is dimmed. Amen.

June 16

Read: 1 Thessalonians 5:12-28

Make prayer a way of life

Pray continually.

– 1 Thessalonians 5:17 –

The great benefit attached to putting aside time for prayer and quiet meditation is undeniable. Rich spiritual blessings flow forth from such times of prayer: inner peace; spiritual strength; determination and purposefulness. They form anchors in life and are founded in those quiet moments spent alone with the Master. This gives meaning to life.

It should be clear to every Christian disciple that true prayer is infinitely more than saying your prayers, which usually consists of a few skimpy moments where a series of requests are mumbled. The motivation is a desire to satisfy God, or to prevent something unpleasant from happening to you during the day. When prayer is used like this, it is only a safety catch or a superstition.

True prayer is a relationship with life; an attitude that overshadows the nuances of everyday life. The ordinary humble tasks that have already become the routine can become hallowed by regarding them as practical prayers to the glory of God.

During those moments, when your thoughts are not occupied with a specific task, it can be tuned in on the Master. He is your ever-present Traveling Companion through life. Wherever you are, you can know that you are in His presence and that you can talk to Him as to a friend.

The power and beauty of prayer lie in its simplicity. Even though traditional prayer has its place in our worship, it is the heart-strengthening childlike prayer to God, that makes Him a living reality in your life.

I thank You, Example and Redeemer, that I can develop a living and practical prayer life that can become a way of life through the help of the Holy Spirit. Amen.

Read: Luke 6:6-11   June 17

Builders of bridges

They were furious and began to discuss with one another what they might do to Jesus.

—LUKE 6:11 –

It is a tragedy when the Christian religion becomes a restricting influence instead of a liberating force. When Jesus healed the man with the shriveled hand, He encountered bitter opposition from the theologians and church leaders of His time.

It is quite possible that these people listened to His doctrines and even agreed with most of what He said. But when He did someone a kind deed on the Sabbath, which went against their religious convictions, they became His enemies.

Although creeds and doctrines play an important part in the expression and definition of the Christian religion, these do not mean much if they do not convey the spirit of divine love to those who try to understand the doctrine.

The spirit and nature of Jesus is an essential component of the Christian faith. Where His Spirit enjoys full and unrestricted freedom in the lives of His disciples, His message is also understood more clearly. However, if the Holy Spirit is prevented from making the Scriptures clear as a result of hardened hearts, the gospel is deprived of its joy. Then it becomes a restricting message that is difficult to understand.

Christianity is a liberating faith. Through the power of Christ's divine love awakened in you, you are able to conquer dogmatic differences. You enter spiritual harmony with children of the Lord who have the same mindset as you. The Spirit of Christ is the only force that can enable you to build bridges of understanding between fellow believers.

Immanuel, strengthen my love for You so that I can also love those with whom I do not always agree. Amen.

June 18

Read: Galatians 6:1-10

See yourself in perspective

If anyone thinks he is something when he is nothing, he deceives himself. Each one should test his own actions. Then he can take pride in himself, without comparing himself to somebody else.
— GALATIANS 6:3-4 —

It is important to have a true appreciation of your own worth. It gives purpose and meaning to your life to know what you are good at and to experience the joy received from a task well done. Nevertheless, you should guard against your satisfaction turning into negative pride.

Sometimes people in key positions see themselves as indispensable. Yet, they will be forgotten within a few years, except for a few faded photographs against boardroom walls, or a signature on an old document.

It is a fact that no one is indispensable. However, this does not mean that you are not important. You are a child of the eternal Father and He loves you. If you are willing and obedient, He can use you as a powerful instrument. This glorious fact elevates you above the temporary and emphasizes your spiritual importance. If you are self-centered and always engaged in feeding your own ego by telling yourself and others how wonderful you are, your feelings of importance will have no foundation for a lasting greatness. Eventually it will crumble.

If you humbly assess your own worth, you will achieve your goal in life. To God you are important. This truth should inspire you to be grateful for the fact that the Almighty is willing to use you to do His work.

Father of love and grace, everything I have and everything I am, are merciful gifts of love from You. Teach me to use them humbly to Your glory! Amen.

Read: Psalm 27:1-14   June 19

Remedy for loneliness

Though my father and mother forsake me, the LORD will receive me.
– PSALM 27:10 –

Loneliness has been a problem since the days of Adam and Eve. There are people who feel lonely in a crowd. There are even thousands of people who are hopelessly lonely in their marriages. People try to flee from the pain of loneliness through various escape mechanisms.

This is undoubtedly one of the universally unsolved problems that confronts man. However hard we try to ease the pain by working harder and harder, the pain will always re-emerge. It is often worse in the early morning hours of sleeplessness, at times when we have problems or when we feel sick.

Make an active attempt to drive loneliness from your life by being positive about who you are, your abilities and your acceptability. Learn to like yourself. Enjoy your own company. Praise yourself when you feel good about something you did. Do things for yourself which you would like others to do for you. Every now and then buy yourself flowers or a special little gift. Groom yourself and dress tastefully. Each day, plan something special that you can look forward to. Make your living environment attractive and comfortable. Discover new things to do on your own that will enrich your spirit.

Try to be purposeful in cultivating meaningful relationships with other people. You have to be friendly to make new friends. Be interested in other people, give of yourself to them, surprise people with simple deeds of love. Do favors for others without being asked.

Develop a deep awareness of the living presence of Jesus Christ. If He is your constant Friend and Guide, you can never be lonely.

Friend of lonely people who knew loneliness in its worst form, I thank You for being my best friend. I gratefully worship You. Amen.

June 20

Read: John 14:15-27

The final test of your love

"If anyone loves me, he will obey my teaching. My Father will love him, and we will come to him and make our home with him."
– JOHN 14:23 –

Often sentimentality is mistaken for spiritual experience. Some followers shout out the name of Jesus repeatedly and monotonously. This causes a form of self-hypnosis and creates the impression that they honor and glorify Christ in a special way.

There certainly are moments of spiritual elevation when Christians have a mountain-top experience that leaves them lost in wonder and love for the Savior. However, emotions alone cannot reflect Christ's true spirit and cannot confirm the practical application of His doctrines either.

If you love Christ unconditionally, your behavior will confirm that love. If you gain strength from God's love for you, your whole life will be ruled by love. This love is not revealed in fanatical behavior that pushes away rather than attracts. Christ possesses a certain attraction that awakens a natural love in people and makes it pure joy to be in His presence.

Practical obedience to Christ and His commands, is the final test of your love for Him. This is a challenging truth. You may be capable of crying "Hallelujah", but do you love your fellow Christians of other races and colors with His love in your heart? Is the priority that you give to Christ in your life greater than your emotions of pettiness, bitterness and hatred?

The real test of your love for your Savior is evident through your obedience to Him.

My mind is set, Lord my God, to express my love for You in a practical way according to the example of Jesus Christ, my Redeemer, through the power of Your Spirit. Amen.

Read: John 21:15-25

June 21

I love you truly, O Lord!

"Yes, Lord," he said, "You know that I love you."

– John 21:15 –

It is foolish to accept certain things as a matter of course, like the love and regard your family has for you. Too many people think they have a right to the love and respect of all the family members just because they are part of a family. Being born into that family does not give you the right to demand their love. It is something that has to be earned. Parents should give love to their children in order to receive love and vice versa.

A huge weakness in many marriages is that love is never expressed. The parties accept one another as a matter of course, as if they are part of the landscape or the furniture in the house. Something very precious is lost in that marriage. Saying to your partner, "I love you" and showing this through your deeds, strengthens the marriage bond in a special way.

In the spiritual sphere of life, the expression of love and appreciation has enormous power and value. When last did you tell the Lord that you love Him? You may argue like Peter, "Lord, You know all things; You know that I love You."

Not only does it gladden your Father's heart to hear you confirm your love for Him, but it also strengthens your spirit and your inner joy and peace. Tell God in your quiet time that you love Him and you will feel how strength and inspiration fill your spirit when He responds to the declaration of your love. It brings spiritual growth and enrichment.

Lord Jesus, I love You with all my heart, my mind and all my strength. I rejoice in our growing relationship of love. Amen.

June 22

Read: Ephesians 4:17-24

Call to perfection

You were taught, with regard to your former way of life, to put off your old self, which is being corrupted by its deceitful desires; to be made new in the attitude of your minds; and to put on the new self created to be like God in true righteousness and holiness.
— Ephesians 4:22-24 —

The living Christ poses an enormous challenge for His followers. It is the challenge of a new life with changed attitudes, resulting in a righteous and holy life. Unfortunately, to the layman this appears to be a way of life that is totally removed from the realities of our practical existence. Leading a holy life is unacceptable to many people.

However, the core truth is that we were created to be like God and to strive for perfection. It can bring rich fulfillment to your life. It is the greatest challenge that you will ever face in your life. When this is demanded, you may initially hesitate or even shrink back. Deeply aware of your inner weakness and sinfulness, you are convinced that Scripture makes a demand that you cannot meet.

Otherwise this calling can be inspiring and challenging. Despite the awareness of your own shortcomings, you know instinctively that you desire to rise up in your strive for perfection. Although you are conscious of your sin, you realize that you are meant to walk with God and to live in fellowship with Him. It is your highest goal in life and the source of your purest joy.

When you experience this deep desire and longing to walk with God, do not allow sin or shortcomings to rob you of it. Accept the help of the risen Lord. He offers you forgiveness of sins and the support of His Holy Spirit. With Christ in your life, you will not be perfect like God, but you will be on the right path to a holy life.

Lord Jesus, I praise Your holy Name for the serious desire You have placed in my heart for a higher, more noble and more perfect life. Let Your Holy Spirit work in me. Amen.

Read: Ephesians 4:25-32

June 23

Anger is destructive

In your anger do not sin. Do not let the sun go down while you are still angry.

— EPHESIANS 4:26 —

Anger can be more damaging than a serious illness, because it is an illness of the spirit. It can obstruct your good judgment, twist your thoughts, embitter your spirit and affect your emotions to such a degree that you will start suffering spiritually, physically and intellectually. If feelings of anger are not rejected, they will fester like a sore. The longer you harbor them, the more difficult it becomes to free yourself from their grip and to regain control over your life.

The best way of combating anger is to exercise forgiveness and love. Right through the gospel you can read about the many times that Jesus was provoked, threatened, ridiculed, humiliated, rejected, and eventually tortured and killed, but He never showed a sign of anger. Instead He radiated loving forgiveness, even when His persecutors did not want to accept it.

In this way, Christ could remain faithful to the reason He came to earth: to show God's forgiving love to the world and to give humankind hope of salvation and eternal life.

However angry you may become, plead with Jesus to free you from these feelings. Ask for forgiveness in the power of His Holy Spirit and forgive others in your relationships. To delay doing this will only worsen the situation. If Christ has delivered you from your anger, you will experience peace that surpasses all understanding. It is the gift Christ gives to the peacemakers among His children.

Almighty God, help me through Your Spirit to be big enough to forgive those who trespass against me, as You forgave me. Amen.

June 24

Read: Psalm 9:1-20

The majesty of God

I will be glad and rejoice in you; I will sing praise to your name, O Most High.

– Psalm 9:2 –

We are so used to hearing about everything that is wrong with the world that we are at risk of not believing that there is any good left in the world. The media and various people place emphasis on the fact that man has many weaknesses and shortcomings. However, little time and effort go into finding the good in life. Subsequently, we are in danger of becoming cynical and skeptical with a pessimistic and negative outlook on life.

There are hopeful signs that there is still good in this world, if you would just take the time to look for it. You will find warm-hearted, generous people who really care. People who offer their service to their fellow man out of love and not out of personal motives of gain. The creation of God is still the wonder it was at the beginning of time. Science and progress have made an unprecedented lifestyle possible.

When life seems depressing and it appears that everything is going wrong, if a spirit of despair descends on you, if you feel powerless against the evil of the world, when you feel that all is lost, then take note of the breathtaking achievements of science and art.

Think how the seasons come and go, and how each season offers its own enchantment and beauty, listen to the carefree laughter of a child or the pure song of a bird. Behind all these things you will see the majesty of God. Then praise Him and glorify His holy Name.

How great You are, O Lord, and how glorious is Your Name in all the earth. Amen.

Read: 1 Corinthians 15:12-28 June 25

Christ lives!

Christ has indeed been raised from the dead, the first fruits of those who have fallen asleep.

— 1 CORINTHIANS 15:20 —

Through the ages Christianity has been fragmented by divergent doctrines. So often the spirit of love and understanding has been replaced by fanaticism and bitter conflict. There remains, however, a bright light that can never be extinguished. It is the glorious truth that Jesus Christ conquered death and that He is alive today, just as He was alive when He appeared to His disciples after His death on the cross.

Whether we understand the "how" of this powerful spiritual phenomenon is not important. Because we know undeniably that it revealed a new dimension of the power and inventiveness of God. To acknowledge that Christ lives, that He lives today, and to shape your life according to this overwhelming fact, is to touch on the deepest Christian experience.

Although Christ is alive and always present, He can only work in the lives of His disciples if He is recognized as their Master, Lord and Guide. The core value is that, although He is always with you, you are not always with Him. Often your thoughts and deeds deny His invisible presence. If you could be in God's presence, you would not even consider doing half the things you are doing in His invisible presence.

How you react to the truth that Christ lives is proof of the sincerity and the quality of your faith. The living Christ Himself said, "Blessed are those who have not seen and yet have believed" (Jn. 20:29).

Risen and living Savior, help me to never live as though You are dead. Amen.

June 26

Read: John 16:5-15

The Paraclete

"Unless I go away, the Counselor will not come to you."
– John 16:7 –

The Greek word "Paraklëtos" is difficult to translate. The King James Version gives it as "Comforter" while the New International Version gives it as "Counselor". These translations are rich in encouragement but yet do not give us a true interpretation of the word. When we study the word "Paraclete", we begin to understand something of the wonderful gift of the Holy Spirit.

Paraclete means "someone who is called in to testify in our favor." How comforting to know that when Satan, our conscience or our fellow man accuses us before God, the Holy Spirit acts as advocate for us and pleads on our behalf.

He is also called to inspire those who are despondent, so that they can continue the struggle with enthusiasm and inspiration. We who dwell in earthly tents really need someone to give us courage and act as mediator and intercessor. The Paraclete is also called in to help in times of distress and suffering, doubt and confusion. Each time when the mystery of suffering, the pain of longing, the confusion of depression or any negative experience enters your life, remember that you have an Intercessor at the throne of grace.

This gives us new strength and courage and leads to a life of victory. The Paraclete also steps into the breach for us in times of danger. He walks, in a manner of speaking, on the side of the abyss and protects us against dangers. He holds our hands to keep us from stumbling. He gives us courage to walk on even in the darkness. He intercedes for our imperfections and mercifully enables us to deal with life's unknown secrets. That is why the Holy Spirit is essential and indispensable in the lives of God's children.

"Be with me when no other friend the mystery of my heart can share; and be Thou known, when fears transcend, by Thy best name of Comforter." Amen.

Read: Psalm 31:1-16

June 27

Victory over sorrow

Be merciful to me, O LORD, for I am in distress; my eyes grow weak with sorrow, my soul and my body with grief.

– PSALM 31:9 –

All of us have experienced grief and it is always very intense and personal. It causes emotional torture. The death of a loved one, the slow wasting away in sickness of someone who is near to you, a family member's deviation to the dark paths of sin and addiction – all these things cause almost inconsolable grief.

We must make concessions because some people grieve in their own particular way. There is no set pattern. Some people become highly emotional and show their sorrow visibly, while others are stoic and suffer in silence. If you are trying to help and comfort people in grief, always be understanding and sympathetic.

When grief threatens to overwhelm you, make sure that self-pity does not worsen your distress. Do not become overly concerned with introspection. Always remember that life goes on. Accept your responsibilities towards yourself, your family and your community.

Seriously guard against blaming God and developing a resistance to Him in your heart. The Father's heart is full of love and sympathy for you, His child. He wants to embrace you in His love. He wants to heal your broken heart and your distressed spirit.

To resist emotional pain will bring you nowhere. Take the cup of suffering and empty it courageously; resignation will replace your bitterness. Time will help to heal the wounds. The most important thing is, however, that you should encourage yourself in the process of healing.

God can deal with the worst that can happen to you. This assurance can deliver you from the bonds of grief. God comforts through His power and through the Holy Spirit.

God of Comfort, I thank You that You never leave Your children without comfort. Thank You, Lord Jesus for the Comforter, Your gift to us in times of grief. Amen.

June 28

Read: Psalm 122:1-9

God is present here

I rejoiced with those who said to me, "Let us go to the house of the LORD."

— PSALM 122:1 —

There are many people who go to church out of mere habit. For many years, possibly from early childhood, church attendance has become a custom and routine. Nobody is saying they should not go to church, but it is possible that little benefit is gained from a custom. Going to church has just become an accepted pattern that is practiced only because it is expected of them and because they have always done so.

Your presence at, and participation in, a service should be a noticeable joy. It is, after all, the time when you, with fellow believers, meet the Lord God in His house. You should experience the splendor and glory of His presence and be filled with excited anticipation. You are in God's presence and you are on holy ground.

If it brings you no joy to worship in a service, it is time you examine the motives for your church attendance and your reasons for participation. Do you attend the service merely to be seen, or do you selfishly want to receive something? Do you make a purposeful contribution to the worship by doing your bit for the fellowship of believers?

When you start giving of yourself, your most noble and your best, it is the start of an exciting journey of discovery into the joys that worshiping in spirit and truth in the house of the Lord brings.

Then you will leave church with rejoicing in your heart and courage to face the demands of life.

I rejoice, O Lord, in the privilege of worshiping You in beauty and holiness. Amen.

Read: Psalm 55:16-24 June 29

A loving invitation

Cast your cares on the LORD and he will sustain you.
– PSALM 55:22 –

It is not easy to define cares. It can be the awareness of sins, sorrow over a loved one, poverty, illness, a deformity of the body, an unbearable responsibility or many other negative things. Whatever you may see as a care only becomes a care once it becomes too heavy for you to bear alone.

While you can still plan and handle a problem, it is a challenge and not a care or burden. It is when the care becomes unbearable, when you lose control over it and when you feel that it depresses you and ruins your spirit, that you start getting desperate.

The old saying that man's embarrassment is God's opportunity, contains an underlying truth. When you have reached the end of your abilities and when you cannot go any further, you must pray. Obviously you should have been praying to God long before, even before the situation became desperate.

But the mystery and wonder of God's love is that He is always ready to help, even if you did search for other solutions before you turned to Him. Hand over your cares and burdens to the great Bearer of burdens. Do this in serious and sincere prayer. Do not seek your burdens again, forget about them. Leave them with God and trust Him. He will give you a solution if it is necessary. He will lead you in your confusion.

Freed from your cares, you will be able to face life with confidence. God will care for you by giving you confidence, calmness and renewed faith. What a glorious Father we worship. Praise Him, O my soul!

I place my burdens before You, O Holy Provider, and I am determined not to pick them up again. Amen.

June 30

Read: Ephesians 6:18

Prayer and service

Pray in the Spirit on all occasions with all kinds of prayers and requests.

– Ephesians 6:18 –

Many disciples of the Lord are so busy working for God that they have no time or desire to pray. They support Martha's argument and leave prayer to those who share Mary's attitude. They wrongly believe that their actions can replace prayer. This attitude ignores the fact that prayer is the source of inspiration for Christian service. Without the motivating power of prayer, there can be no inspired or creative discipleship.

In social and political fields, there are many people and organizations who have adopted the Name of Christ, but who know nothing about His enabling grace. Such people and organizations may be engaged in noble work, but as long as they are using the name of Jesus Christ as a front, they will never be as efficient as He expects them to be.

The Christian church is full of busy disciples who are eager to serve God and who jump at any opportunity to do good deeds. Nevertheless, they are often not serious about prayer. They do not ensure that what they do really constitutes God's plan for them. What they do might be important and praiseworthy to their fellow man, but God has a greater and more meaningful task for them.

An ever-growing prayer life must be linked to all Christian service. These two should supplement each other. There can be no Christian service without the support of prayer; and prayer without the practical outlet of good deeds is incomplete.

Lord, who hears my prayer, make my service to You the tangible part of my prayer life. Amen.

JULY

July 1

Read: Philippians 3:7-21

Do something with your life

But one thing I do: Forgetting what is behind and straining toward what is ahead, I press on towards the goal.
— PHILIPPIANS 3:13-14 —

Within a person there are many forces at work which all strive for recognition and fulfillment. The complexity of human nature is emphasized by the fact that within every person there is a parent, a financier, a politician, a religious person, a student and many other characters.

During your life, you move from one phase to another without being aware of it. You are constantly moving between different forces which strengthen or weaken your character.

Successful people know the importance of focusing on goals and striving to achieve them. Make sure that your goal is worthy of your very best. You will never be completely satisfied with your life if you lower your objectives.

Some people strive for success in the academic world, while others strive to obtain it in commerce or the arts. If you are a disciple of the Master, you would want to make the world a better place simply by living in it.

The highest goal in your life is to conform to Christ more and more. Perhaps it sounds too idealistic, but it is possible. Christ calls you to the most noble way of life that you can ever achieve. He does not only call you, but He equips you to achieve heights that you would not have been able to reach in your own strength. Let your life be meaningful and achieve its utmost potential through the power of the indwelling Christ.

Guide and Lord, help me to achieve the goal that You have for my life, through the work of Your Holy Spirit. Amen.

Read: Matthew 9:27-31

July 2

Faith and wishful thinking

Then he touched their eyes and said, "According to your faith will it be done to you."

– Matthew 9:29 –

There is a fundamental difference between true faith and wishful thinking. Many people never learn this distinction which results in spiritual impoverishment. Such people desire something passionately, but in their heart of hearts they believe that it is unattainable, unless they are lucky. This creates conflict in their innermost being and they become colorless, ineffectual people without spiritual strength.

Sincere faith is convinced that every hallowed wish is possible and waiting to be claimed in the name of the Almighty. You do not yearn for the unattainable in your own strength; it only happens when God's omnipotence is revealed in Your life every day.

Faith which wants to show results should always have God as its inspiration and source. If we expect great things from God, we will receive great things from Him and do great deeds in His name. As was the case with the two blind people of whom we read.

If your spiritual life has God as its source, you will become a channel through which His mighty deeds are done. Then a new life of powerful energy will open up to you. You will no longer limit His omnipotence by lack of faith, disbelief or wishful thinking. Through your surrender and commitment to Him, what you long for in faith becomes a glorious reality.

Almighty and merciful God, thank You for what I am able to do through faith in You. Strengthen me constantly through the power of Jesus Christ, my Redeemer and Savior. Amen.

July 3

Read: 1 John 4:7-21

In the school of love

Dear friends, let us love one another, for love comes from God. Everyone who loves has been born of God and knows God.

– 1 JOHN 4:7 –

For many people it is not easy to love. Perhaps they work with people who have become a continuous source of irritation to them; some people have habits which they find disgusting; others again have character traits which repel them. Living and working with such people makes Christ's instruction to love one another an apparent impossibility.

John says that we should love one another. Perfect love is not something which is attained immediately or all at once. It is a process of growing in Christ. It should, however, start somewhere.

When you meet someone whom you find difficult to love, remind yourself deliberately of the truth that this person was created by God in His image. Remember that despite the revolting appearance, there are eternal values waiting to be released. Compassion can touch these closed doors and tenderly open them up. The results will often put us to shame and fill us with humility.

Never judge people by appearances. See them as individuals whom God deems worthy of being His friends and whom He loves with undying love. When your attitude towards them changes from irritation to understanding, you will see growth in your own spiritual life. Gradually, you will start appreciating even those whom you at first found difficult to love.

God of love, I want to love unconditionally, also those people whom I find difficult to love. Help me to grow in mercy and understanding through the example of Jesus, my Lord. Amen.

Read: Luke 12:13-21   July 4

Passing values

I'll say to myself, "You have plenty of good things laid up for many years. Take life easy; eat, drink and be merry."
– Luke 12:19 –

It is interesting to note what people find important. Determining values is just as diverse as human personalities. Reaching a social or commercial peak is considered so important by many people, that no sacrifice is too great to achieve it. The accumulation of possessions and wealth and the influence it gives are seen by many as the highest ideal.

The things that people consider important reveal their spiritual state. What happens once you have reached the top, gathered more possessions than you can handle, and are moving in the elitist social circles?

Since man is basically a spiritual being, material possessions can never satisfy him. Only when he admits his spirituality, and strives for the development and fulfillment of his spiritual needs, is he tasting the satisfaction of an inspired life.

It is man's innermost spirit that makes him realize his eternal goal for which God has created him. No one, no matter who he is or what he owns, can attain complete fulfillment if he denies the reality of his spiritual needs.

Guard against basing your confidence and satisfaction exclusively on the possessions you have inherited or accumulated. Do not allow this to blind you to the spiritual wealth which gives balance to your life. The wonder of Christ's love, the experience of the indwelling Christ and the gift of the Holy Spirit, are but a few of the riches from the treasury of God.

He gives it freely to all of those who have given Him control over their lives.

Thank You, heavenly Treasurer, for the wonderful gifts You give to those who love You. Amen.

July 5

Read: Luke 12:13-21

Intelligent fool

"Watch out! Be on your guard against all kinds of greed; a man's life does not consist in the abundance of his possessions."

– Luke 12:15 –

Examined closely, speaking of an "intelligent fool" is not a paradox. Foolishness has very little to do with intelligence. The opposite of foolishness is wisdom. A person can be intelligent yet lack wisdom or be intellectually less endowed, yet have much wisdom. Foolishness and wisdom deal with the spirit of man; especially with his relationship with God.

We can deduce that this man was intelligent because he was capable and rich. This he achieved through planning and common sense. Wealth in itself is no sin; neither is poverty a virtue. He was hard-working, otherwise he would not have had any harvests. In addition, he was ambitious. When ambition is subject to God's approval, it can be a motivating force. He was undoubtedly also honest. He earned his possessions through hard work.

Why do we then label him a fool? Because he neglected his soul. He was so busy accumulating wealth that he neglected God. Every man who does not keep God in mind at all times is a fool.

He was especially foolish since he did not prepare for eternity. He did not have the insight to look past this world. He could only see as far as his old age. And because he did not take God into account, he missed out on both his old age and eternity.

Do your duty prayerfully every day. Make room for God when planning your life's agenda and your future, otherwise your labor could perhaps be in vain.

Take eternity into account, because it does man no good to gain the whole world, yet forfeit his soul. Guard against the danger of being materially rich, but poor in God.

I praise You, Creator God, for the pure treasures from Your bountiful storehouse that You give Your children. Help me never to exchange these for the superficial treasures of this world. Amen.

Read: Genesis 2:4-10; John 18:1-11   July 6

Two famous gardens

Now the LORD *God had planted a garden in the east, in Eden; and there he put the man he had formed.*

– GENESIS 2:8 –

When he had finished praying, Jesus left with his disciples and crossed the Kidron Valley. On the other side there was an olive grove, and he and his disciples went into it.

– JOHN 18:1 –

Two of the most well-known gardens are Eden and Gethsemane. They are more than just geographical localities, they are symbols of human experience. They are in truth the poles between which man leads his moral life. They are not only historic, but also prophetic. They do not only tell of what happened, but of what is still happening.

In the garden of Eden we see how man takes something of which the beauty cannot be described and changes it through his selfishness and moral decline into something ugly and unattractive.

In the garden of Gethsemane we see how a Man goes through a tragic experience and, through the nobility of His spirit, changes it into something indescribably beautiful. Adam and Eve do the obvious and easy thing; Jesus does the exceptional and difficult.

On the one hand we see how man fails and on the other hand we see how Jesus triumphs. Eden is the place where we try to evade our responsibility. Gethsemane is the place where we learn to accept our responsibilities. Eden damns man and Gethsemane redeems him. Note that God was in both gardens. In Eden, Adam and Eve hide from God; in Gethsemane Christ seeks God. Adam flees before God because he has done the wrong thing; Jesus seeks God so that He can be strengthened to do the right thing.

From one of these gardens we take our approach to life. We reveal the spirit of Eden or the spirit of Gethsemane.

Source of beauty to all gardens, Creator God, I thank You that I may wait on You in Gethsemane to find strength to accept my spiritual responsibilities. Amen.

July 7

Read: Ephesians 5:6-20

With a song in the heart

Instead, be filled with the Spirit. Speak to one another with psalms, hymns and spiritual songs. Sing and make music in your heart to the Lord.

— EPHESIANS 5:18-19 —

We are told to sing a new song to the glory of the Lord. A song involves joy and love. A person who does not sing, is like springtime without blossoms; like a world without bird song; like a day without sunshine. Augustine of Hippo said that, "A new person, a new song and the New Testament all belong to the same kingdom." The song and gratefulness go hand in hand. A grateful person sings and a person who sings is happy, regardless of his circumstances.

Music is present everywhere in God's creation: the wind singing through the trees; the rhythmic movement of the waves; the sound of raindrops against the window; the waving wheat fields. To them who want to listen, there is singing all around us.

Singing proves that the sovereign God is present in our hearts. When the king is not at home, no flags are hoisted at the palace. The world can tell by our singing that God is present in our hearts and lives.

Angels rejoiced at the birth of Christ. Jesus sang a song of praise with His disciples on the Thursday evening before He was captured and crucified. One day in heaven there will be continuous singing by the redeemed. Meanwhile we must practice our songs.

Singing gives us courage in times of suffering. Like Paul and Silas we should sing in times of trial. We are witnesses of the Cross, as well as witnesses of His glory.

Encourage and strengthen other believers with your song.

I greet you with an old Irish blessing, "May the road rise with you; may the wind always be at your back; may the rain fall softly on your fields. And may God keep you in the hollow of His hand."

Holy God, and heavenly Father, enable me to encourage others. Never let my song be silenced. Amen.

Read: Mark 14:32-42

July 8

A difficult prayer

"Yet not what I will, but what you will."

– MARK 14:36 –

It is extremely important to be single-minded when praying. The majority of people tell God about their needs. They continue asking for what they want without considering what God wants. True prayer is asking God to provide in all your needs.

Prayer means bringing your spirit in complete harmony with the perfect will of the Father and to continue working obediently to let His will take place in your life.

Complete subjection to the will of God is the key to meaningful prayer. It should not be confused with fatalism. Fatalism implies that it does not make any difference whether you pray or not. Prayer means the search for God's will for your life through contemplation, discussion and Bible study. It is opening yourself completely, and allowing God to achieve His purpose in your life.

Initially, it may lead to inner conflict and you may wonder why God does not answer your prayers. He is perhaps teaching you the greatest of all spiritual truths – that His will, and not your own, is the very best for your spiritual and physical well being.

Being able to pray, "Let Your will be done in my life" in complete surrender not only means praying a difficult prayer but also an essential one. One that will bring you unparalleled blessing.

Master, let Your perfect will be done in my life. Amen.

July 9

Read: John 10:1-21

Giver or taker?

"I am the good shepherd. The good shepherd lays down his life for the sheep."

– JOHN 10:11 –

A Christian cannot live for himself alone. Every day we come into contact with others. As a result of this contact we have an influence on their lives, even if it is unconsciously. If you should decide to live relentlessly for yourself alone and not to help anyone unless you can gain something from it, you will soon find that you live among similar people. Then your life becomes a mere existence without the mystic quality that makes it worthwhile.

The secret of true life does not lie in what you can grab and collect, but in what you can give. This involves giving not the inexpensive things, but those things that are most precious and valuable. You must give your love freely and unconditionally first before you can be loved by others. In order to receive a blessing, you should be a blessing to others first.

By giving His life for others, Christ became the Redeemer of the world. If this Christian requirement sounds too idealistic and too far-fetched, the only way to test it would be to experience it.

First try living in such a way that your life becomes an unselfish source of blessing to everyone you come into contact with. Be willing to listen and not only to talk. Be interested in others, cultivate a spirit of goodwill, sympathy and thoughtfulness.

Let the joy of the indwelling Spirit of Christ flow through you to others, enriching and encouraging them.

I plead for Your vital blessing, heavenly Lord, so that I can be a blessing to others You send across my path. Keep me from selfishness and insensitivity towards others. Give me, above all the attitude of my Master, Jesus Christ. Amen.

Read: John 15:1-17　　　　　　　　　　　　July 10

Joy in labor

"If a man remains in me and I in him, he will bear much fruit; apart from me you can do nothing."

– John 15:5 –

Sometimes your life's work becomes exacting, uninteresting and boring. When this happens, inspiration and joy disappear from your daily task. Your outlook on life becomes negative and bitter. There are many reasons for this: perhaps you do not allow yourself enough rest and relaxation; you possibly carry a burden of responsibility which is far greater than can be expected of you or of which you are capable of. Consequently, you become tense. Your fraying nerves start exacting their toll and you end up grudging your life's work in your heart.

If this is your experience, it may be that you are trying to live and work without the power of Jesus Christ. Your work has possibly become more important than your relationship with the Lord. Your life has become like a piece of machinery – cold, insensitive and monotonous.

The solution to this problem lies in the meaningful pronouncement of Jesus, "Apart from Me you can do nothing."

A sure method to achieve the peak of your productivity is by making Christ a partner in your life. Place every aspect of your life under His all-wise control. He understands life much better than you. Start every day by spending time alone with Him and then you will experience the assurance of His continued presence.

Go out into the heat of the day and carry out your task with a steadfast hand, while you look up in prayer to your Guide and Friend. Then you will discover the astonishing wonder of joy and pride in your labor.

Thank You that I may trust You regarding my daily task, O Lord. Help me to do it every day as if I am doing it for You, in the name of Jesus Christ. Amen.

July 11

Read: 1 John 1:1-10

The point of departure for spiritual healing

If we claim to be without sin, we deceive ourselves and the truth is not in us.

– 1 John 1:8 –

You cannot possibly build a healthy and effective spiritual life on the ruins of a decayed belief which declined as a result of stubborn and deliberate disobedience to God.

The cause of our lack of spiritual strength is in many cases our unwillingness to discard those things which damaged our relationship with God. You can never lead a dynamic life as long as you cling to the influences and forces which undermine you spiritually. Nurturing destructive forces, as many people are inclined to do, has catastrophic consequences for your spiritual development.

The basis of spiritual fitness is opening up your life to the influence of God's Holy Spirit. It can be a humbling experience, sometimes even painful. When the Spirit reminds you of old and pampered sins which are festering in your spirit and are blocking your spiritual growth, the time has come for you to confess them to your heavenly Father.

An active deed of confession is necessary. Not only because God requires it from you, but also because it will deliver you from the paralyzing influences that have been torturing you for so long. Confessing your sins, is the first step on the path to spiritual healing.

When you have placed the past in God's care and begged for His mercy, you enter a new phase of life. You can then meet the future with joy and confidence.

I thank You, Lord and Master, for Your forgiveness, which brought deliverance and freedom into my life. Keep me in Your love so that I will never stray from You again. Amen.

Read: Matthew 22:34-40   July 12

Be a blessing to others

"Love your neighbor as yourself."
– MATTHEW 22:39 –

We all run the risk of becoming self-centered. You perhaps speak and so often think of what you want and what you have, that you later think that God has created the world especially for you. When this happens, something priceless dies in your innermost being. You will find that people are no longer eager to spend time in your company. Egotism can destroy the beauty and strength of your character.

If you want to lead a fulfilled, free and satisfying life, you need other people around you. People whom you can love and serve. It is only through loving service that you can grow to spiritual and intellectual maturity. Jesus emphasized this fact when He said, "For whoever wants to save his life will lose it, but whoever loses his life for Me will find it" (Mt. 16:25). Live to be a blessing to other people and you will be amazed by the quality of your life.

If you desire your life to have meaning and purpose, it is essential that you lose yourself in an issue which is greater than you. It is on this level of existence that Jesus Christ has revealed Himself as the perfect inspiration to people like you and me. He said, "Remain in Me and I will remain in you."

Strengthened by this interaction of power, we are able to love our enemies, to bless those who curse us, to do good to those who hate us and to pray for those who bear false witness against us and persecute us. To be a blessing to others in this way, in the strength of the Lord, is to experience life at its highest level.

Mighty Lord Jesus, in Your omnipotence, I strive continuously to be a blessing to my fellow man. I thank You for enabling me to lead a full and satisfying life through the strength of the Holy Spirit and to Your glory. Amen.

July 13   Read: Job 21:1-16

Do you question the power of prayer?

Who is the Almighty, that we should serve him? What would we gain by praying to him?

– Job 21:15 –

It generally happens that when people's prayers aren't answered they wonder whether prayer is worthwhile and if it serves any purpose. They know the painful feeling of disillusionment after they have prayed urgently for something which they did not receive.

This disillusionment regarding unanswered prayers can be traced back to people's lack of knowledge regarding prayer. Prayer is not an automatic machine from which you can get what you want by putting in a coin.

True prayer is in the first place a search for the kingdom of God, His will and His glorification. You can understand the kingdom only when you have met the King and committed yourself to Him. Christ must be the center of your prayer life. Through Him, you enter the presence of the Father.

If you feel that your prayer life is inadequate and leaves you disappointed and disillusioned, it is time for you to do some honest introspection. Do you sincerely seek the will of God in your prayers and in your life? Are you aware of God's holy presence when you pray? Is He precious beyond all else? Or do you use Him as a pawn in your own game of chess?

Sincere and honest answers to these questions may be the point of departure for a new, strong and meaningful life of prayer. Then your prayers will no longer be question marks, but God will straighten them into exclamation marks!

Almighty God, I praise Your Name because You have taught me through the power of the Holy Spirit that effective prayer depends on my relationship with Jesus Christ, my Redeemer. Amen.

Read: Psalm 37:1-11   July 14

Less effort and more faith

Commit your way to the LORD; trust in him and he will do this.
                                        – PSALM 37:5 –

Most of the time we create the problems we experience in our Christian lives ourselves. We build dividing walls where they do not exist; we feel we are far from God while He is close to us; we debate the characteristics of faith, but seldom try to apply them in practice.

It is exciting to prove that faith in God is an attainable proposition. For a while, you may have struggled with a problem. You may have tried every possible solution and as a last resort, you started praying. This prayer was different from all the others. When you prayed before, you were already planning in your mind how to find solutions in your own strength. You prescribed to God how matters should progress. Now you are saying the prayers of a desperate, drowning person. All supports have been removed and you are fully dependent on the Lord.

The action of total surrender to God in complete faith, will give you a feeling of relief and deliverance. You will now have a new spirit of expectation. You will wait on God to act when you have become deeply conscious of your own inability.

To be able to wait during this period – be it long or short – you should joyfully subject yourself to the perfect will of God. Then you will make an exciting discovery. God does act in your best interests in His incomparable way.

The way in which God works and the ease with which He does it, are often amazingly simple. Just let go – and let God!

Savior, I joyfully give my life to You completely. I ask that only Your perfect will be done in my life. Amen.

July 15

Read: John 16:5-16

The Spirit glorifies Christ

"He will bring glory to me by taking from what is mine and making it known to you."

– JOHN 16:14 –

We cannot really understand the work of the Holy Spirit or appreciate it fully before we understand His relationship with Christ correctly and completely. Christ's promise was that the Holy Spirit would comfort His followers after He had left them. The Spirit would reveal Christ in His triumphant, heavenly glory to their hearts. The deepest longing of the disciples was to have Christ with them permanently and continuously. Because He was aware of their innermost desire, He promised them that the Holy Spirit would reveal Him to them in a very special way.

This was a glorious promise of grace, and it still applies to every follower of Jesus Christ. Everything that the Spirit receives from Christ, He makes known to the children of God: His love, joy and peace; every blessing, He will make known to us.

In the life of the committed disciple, the empowering closeness of Christ lies in the work of the Holy Spirit. The Spirit is then used for a purpose: He helps us to remain in fellowship with Jesus; to know and love and serve Him better.

The Holy Spirit does this in our innermost being with dynamic strength. Unnoticed, the fruit of the Spirit grows in our hearts and is revealed in our lives by "love, joy, peace, patience, kindness, goodness, faithfulness, gentleness and self-control" (Gal. 5:22-23).

In this way God is glorified in Jesus Christ through the work of the Holy Spirit in us. For this, we must watch and pray and work.

"Granted is the Savior's prayer,
Sent the gracious Comforter,
Promise of our parting Lord,
Jesus now to heaven restored."

Read: James 2:14-26

July 16

Transform your words into deeds

Suppose a brother or a sister is without clothes and daily food. If one of you says to him, "Go, I wish you well; keep warm and well fed," but does nothing about his physical needs, what good is it?
— JAMES 2:15-16 —

In the times of the Old Testament the religion of people was based on the law of Moses. They lived according to the rules laid down, and a considerable part of their lives consisted of meeting the restrictive demands of the law. The attitudes of people were so rigid because of the demands of the law, that the punishment for transgressions was extremely strict.

In many cases the stipulations of the law could be recommended, since they regulated the worship of God and created discipline that was beneficial for the welfare of both the family and the nation. Nevertheless, this exaggerated and legalistic spirit led people to neglect an absolutely essential aspect of life.

With the coming of Jesus Christ to the world, it was explained to us that we had to practice what we preached. Only then do we become effective witnesses for Him. It is one thing to tell a person how he should live to experience the world in all its fullness. It is something completely different to lead him to that life through your own example.

It is only when you show someone something of the love, compassion and sympathy of Christ, that you become involved in the well-being of your fellow man in a practical way. Then you help him to understand something of the eternal love of God. Then your words and deeds supplement one another and love becomes tangible in the world.

Living Savior, I will glorify Your Name by showing Your love to my fellow man. I confess my love for You anew and this makes it easy for me to keep Your laws. Amen.

July 17

Read: Isaiah 40:1-11, 27-31

Grave and rut – a difference in depth only

But those who hope in the LORD will renew their strength. They will soar on wings like eagles; they will run and not grow weary, they will walk and not be faint.

– ISAIAH 40:31 –

Greek mythology tells of Sisyphus, a king of Corinth who was vain, proud and arrogant. Consequently Zeus punished him severely: he had to push a large block of marble up a steep hill, using his bare hands. He started early one morning. At sunset he was almost at the top when the block inexplicably slipped from his hands and rolled to the valley down below.

The next morning he tried again, with the same frustrating results. It carried on like this every day; he wasted his strength on a meaningless task that could never be completed.

Nothing exciting, adventurous, or unexpected happened anymore. He became the slave of a soul-destroying routine. Every day was a senseless repetition of a monotonous pattern: to rise with effort; go to work sluggishly, go to bed in frustration. Day in and day out; year after dreary year.

How can you prevent routine from becoming boring? How can you solve the constant longing for renewal and excitement? There is only one solution: "Christ!" Those who trust in the Lord will receive new strength.

You must make time to tap into the Divine Power Source so that your life can be recharged with enthusiasm and inspiration every day. We must wait on the Lord so that we can once again have the wings of eagles and walk and run meaningfully without falling into a rut.

Keep me from a life that will decline into a monotonous routine, heavenly Taskmaster. Renew me every day through Your Holy Spirit and make my life a spiritual adventure, in the Name of Jesus. Amen.

Read: John 1:1-13 July 18

Light in the darkness

In him was life, and that life was the light of men. The light shines in the darkness, but the darkness has not understood it.
– JOHN 1:4-5 –

The world can suddenly become pitch-dark when a loved one dies. Then you easily lose your outlook on life. You stumble forward uncertainly like a blind person. It becomes so difficult for you to cope in the darkness, that you cannot even use the aids that God makes available to you. It feels as though everything in your life is contributing to making the night even darker.

There are people who conquer this blindness triumphantly; not because of their intuition, sharpened senses, Braille or a white walking stick, but through Christ who enables them to step out of the darkness and into the light. Jesus is the true Light that gives light to every human being (Jn. 1:9). When the way ahead is uncertain and you must make difficult decisions, Christ leads you step by step from the darkness of sorrow and confusion into His wonderful light.

D. J. Whitmell said, "In the dark there are no choices – it is the light which enables us to see differences. Christ is the Giver of this light." God gives you the eternal light in Christ which reflects His unchangeable love and mercy. The rays of God's love submerge you; He protects you against dangers of which you are unaware. In times of sorrow and grief He lovingly watches over you.

Let us therefore not flee deeper into the darkness in our times of distress, but like the flower that grows in the darkness, turn our faces to the Light. In Christ there is victory and radiant joy. Through Him we can grow rich in blessings in the full sunshine of God's immeasurable love.

Help me, living Christ, to live courageously and wisely in the light that You shine on my path through life. I place my hand confidently in Yours, lead me to Your light. Amen.

July 19

Read: John 3:1-21

The revealing light

"Everyone who does evil hates the light, and will not come into the light for fear that his deeds will be exposed."

– JOHN 3:20 –

There are very few people, if any at all, who do not keep a secret that shames them. Things are said, thoughts enter our minds or we do things that we know are wrong. In our deep realization of guilt we try to keep these things secret not only from others, but also from ourselves. We try to hide them in the darkest and furthest corners of our consciousness.

But it is a useless act that drives you to despair. You allow yourself to become a slave to feelings of guilt. Sooner or later your conscience starts torturing you. The burden of shameful and regrettable secrets will cause you to crack. Eventually you will be robbed of all energy, as the erosion created by your feelings of guilt grows.

In your torment you must remember that the living Christ came to this world specifically to bring light where darkness has enveloped a life. He came so that you would have life in all its fullness. He came as a concrete, tangible symbol of God's love for you.

Instead of trying to carry the unbearable burden of your feelings of guilt on your own, confess your worries in prayer to God. Without holding back pour out everything that's on your mind. Let the light of Christ with its forgiving love shine on your life. In this way, you will find inner healing and experience the peace that only the Light of the world can give.

Light of the worried hearts, Jesus my Lord, You have appeared in the darkness of my night of sin and You have delivered me gloriously and for all eternity. I praise Your great Name. Amen.

Read: John 14:15-31   July 20

Christ's testament

"Peace I leave with you; my peace I give you ... Do not let your hearts be troubled and do not be afraid."

– John 14:27 –

In the merciless pursuit of progress, men and women, boys and girls all over the world are put under terrible pressure. Learned people of our time call it stress. The demands increase all the time, and more and more is expected of the individual. Everywhere people look for deliverance from the unbearable pressure under which they work and play every day. Everyone anxiously seeks peace of mind.

There are, of course, man-made tranquilizers that are used in astonishing quantities. We should undoubtedly thank God for these remedies if they bring relief for some people. For many it is, however, the trapdoor leading to addiction. There are too many hidden dangers and negative side-effects in all man-made remedies used in our search for peace of mind.

Eventually there is only one way that man can be assured of the rest that the body and soul are longing for, "My soul finds rest in God alone; my salvation comes from Him" (Ps. 62:1). Knowing Him and becoming still in His holy presence bring true peace. The Holy Spirit is then able to act as Guide and Teacher.

Our relationship with God should never be just a chance meeting, but a lasting union like that of the branch and the vine. This is brought about by the discipline of prayer, meditation, Bible study and a sensitivity to the working of the Holy Spirit.

That is why Christ could pass the test of His life triumphantly without collapsing under tension and strain. He invites all those who are tired and over-burdened to take on His soft yoke and He will give us the peace of God which surpasses all understanding.

Prince of peace, I accept the peace which You left me as inheritance. Help me to pass Your peace on to others. Amen.

July 21

Read: Job 10:1-7

When your world collapses

I loathe my very life; therefore I will give free rein to my complaint and speak out in the bitterness of my soul.

– Job 10:1 –

You may have once had high ideals and pursued noble principles. While pursuing them you might have experienced adversity and disasters, frustration and disappointments. All hope appeared to be in vain and nothing but ruins and grief remained. The question in your troubled mind is, "Where do I go to now?"

When you feel so overwhelmed and you are in the depths of despair, there is only one direction to go: upwards! It is precisely at this point that you dare not allow self-pity to control your thinking and your emotions. If a storm is threatening, or even if it is raging, look for something uplifting in the ghastly situation.

You may doubt if there is anything uplifting left. Remember that you have the privilege to start anew – even in the darkest moments of your life. There will be a lot of debris to clear up. It may be a painful process. Nevertheless, at this moment you can begin a new life, forgiven, loved and empowered by the Lord, Jesus Christ.

If you are so tired of struggling that you feel like collapsing in despair and if you just want to be left alone in your pain, then your life lacks all meaning.

Give the pieces of your life to the Master Potter. He can fashion a new object that will be acceptable to God and which will deliver and satisfy you. You may be broken, but Christ has come to heal the broken and to give joy where previously there had been despair. Put Him to the test!

When the bottom has been knocked out of my life, Holy Master, I surrender everything into Your omnipotent hands and pray: Let Your will be done in my life, O Lord. Amen.

Read: Ephesians 5:1-14　　　　　　　　　　　　July 22

Love does have a price tag

Live a life of love, just as Christ loved us and gave himself up for us as a fragrant offering and sacrifice to God.

– EPHESIANS 5:2 –

A sensitive awareness of the distress and suffering of others brings its own pain. But it is the primary demand of the household of God that we should care for one another. In addition to our love for God, this is another command of God that we must obey.

A sensitive spirit is often hidden behind a rough appearance because many people think sensitivity is a sign of weakness. However, it is sensitive people in particular who serve their fellow man best, and who bring light to lives where darkness has descended. Sensitivity for the distress of others is the base of true Christian service.

Unfortunately, it is a fact that this sensitivity often brings us pain. When this happens, you should thank Christ that you can identify with Him in this special way. His sensitive Spirit knows the pain and grief that follow when those you love pursue the path of self-destruction. Furthermore, He took our sickness and grief upon Himself. Will He not therefore understand?

The more you become aware of the living presence of Christ in your life, the more you become aware of the distress of others. This is the price of love; and we, who follow His Holy example, should be willing to pay the price. In this way, we can make this broken world a better place to live in, as Christ did. In addition, our lives will become acceptable to God.

O Jesus, Man of grief, help me to develop a sensitive spirit and to care for the distress of others. Give me the will to become involved with the pain of others and to bring sunshine where dark shadows threaten. Amen.

July 23

Read: Acts 4:1-22

You need not feel inferior

When they saw the courage of Peter and John and realized that they were unschooled, ordinary men, they were astonished and they took note that these men had been with Jesus.

– ACTS 4:13 –

So many important contributions to the work of the church of Christ are lost because people see themselves as inferior or unworthy. Many a wise word is left unspoken in the church because of a person's hesitance to participate in a debate with others who are academically better qualified.

There are people who are rich in experience; who are excellent administrators; but who remain silent and in the background for fear of being ridiculed. This is a negative attitude. To do nothing for fear of the opinion of others, is to do a disservice to the work of the kingdom of God on earth.

If you feel that you can play a specific role in any given circumstance at any time, lay it before God in sincere and serious prayer. Then open up your life and mind to the prompting of the Holy Spirit. Allow Him to take full control of your thoughts and your emotions.

Once your faith is strong enough to let the living Christ work through you and in you, you will feel that all the illusions of inferiority and inadequacy disappear like mist before the rising sun. It will no longer be you, but the Master who works and speaks through you. He does it in wisdom, tolerance and understanding.

The love of Christ which radiates from your life, will connect you to Him and the world will see it and know it.

In Your power, almighty Lord, I conquer my self-consciousness while I serve You in faith and love. Amen.

Read: Habakkuk 3:1-19   July 24

Rejoice in the Lord

Yet I will rejoice in the LORD, I will be joyful in God my Savior.
– HABAKKUK 3:18 –

Many people have serious problems when they have to re-concile their Christianity with their joy. Ceremony, dignity and solemnity are all associated with our service to the heavenly Father. Many people think that Paul's call to rejoice in the Lord is somewhat vain.

The Scriptures teach us time and again that there is joy in the presence of our God. In order to experience it, we have to live in complete harmony with Him. This harmony is born from a pure love for the Father; a love which motivates and brings energy and joy to our lives. How we express this Christian joy will depend on every individual's temperament. In the family of God there is room for all types of people.

There are those who celebrate their joy with gestures and the clapping of hands. Others experience the joy and strength of God in silence. However it may be expressed, it is the experience itself that matters and not the way it is revealed.

Do not judge people's inner feelings by appearances. You may shout for joy and bow before God in astonishment because you are His child, or you may experience joy in silent, unspoken gladness. The most important part is that you praise Him in heartfelt grati-tude. May you experience God's joy today and every day.

Jesus, Joy of my heart, I thank You that the love You pour into my heart leads to a joy that is not dependent on my circumstan-ces. I thank You that I can express my joy in songs of praise. Amen.

July 25

Read: Ephesians 4:1-16

Love bridges theological differences

Be completely humble and gentle, be patient, bearing with one another in love.

– Ephesians 4:2 –

Slowly but surely the gap between Christian churches is being narrowed. Old issues and disputes are seen for what they really are – instruments of Satan to divide the body of Christ. Yet there are important differences and they will continue to exist for many years. It may be justified when deep-rooted convictions cannot allow you to accept contentious theological principles.

When two opposing theological viewpoints are maintained by people who are equally convinced of their beliefs, the final test is whether love can rise above the differences to allow the fellowship of believers to take place.

There are cases where spiritual consensus can be achieved, even if there are intellectual differences. The conviction that Christ is gloriously and triumphantly alive and should be praised, is a binding truth of Christianity. Ways of worshiping may differ, but love can rise above variety. Where a human need calls for alleviation, dogmas, credos and structures should take second place. Love then becomes the binding force that finds expression in service.

One of the reasons why churches are moving closer together is because of the urgent need to save a world that is fast declining and falling apart. Existing conditions have made the children of the Lord realize that division is futile and that it is a sin to allow intellectual differences to suppress the Spirit of God.

Where there is Christian love, there is a spirit of underlying unity, despite diverse theological viewpoints.

Holy Lord and Shepherd, keep me from a closed heart which refuses to love. Amen.

Read: Acts 1:1-11

July 26

See past the cloud

He was taken up before their very eyes, and a cloud hid him from their sight.

— ACTS 1:9 —

The experience of the disciples at the time of ascension is definitely not limited to the apostolic period. For us, however, it is the clouds of despair, doubt, disappointment and worry that cause our Master to be hidden from our eyes. When this happens, prayer is essential. We should not lose sight of the fact that the angels might also be asking us, "Why do you stand here looking into the sky?"

When, for some reason or another, you feel that you have lost contact with Jesus and it appears as though He is far removed from you, it is of the utmost importance to remember that He is the living Christ. He is Immanuel; the Lord who is present in every situation and who makes himself known in every facet of life and in every person. It does not matter where you are or what your circumstances are, you can be sure that Jesus Christ is present there.

To break through the clouds that obstruct your view and cause Christ to appear far removed, you should persevere in prayer for strength and guidance. Then look around you. Wherever you may see distress, do what you can to alleviate it. Help those who are less privileged than yourself. Show others your loving compassion and involvement. Support them as far as possible.

As your perfect example, Jesus Christ did, you should also do good to others. While you serve others in His Name, the clouds will vanish and you will find yourself face to face with your Guide and Perfecter. Then you can bathe yourself in the bright sunshine of His presence.

Holy Spirit, give me the ability to look past my own worries and concerns so that I may see the distress of others and help to alleviate their pain. Amen.

July 27   Read: Ephesians 3:14-21

The King is home!

So that Christ may dwell in your hearts through faith. And I pray that you, being rooted and established in love, may have power.
– Ephesians 3:17 –

Christ is the most honored guest in your life. The artist Holman Hunt's portrayal of Christ who stands knocking on the door of our hearts to be let in, is so well-known that there is a risk of it losing the appeal it is supposed to make on our thoughts.

He is always presented as One who will never force open the door. This is entirely true. On the other hand, we should remember that He is not standing there as a beggar, but as the One who, above everyone else, has the right of admission to our lives. Hence, Paul's moving prayer. Christ comes to motivate you and to reform your entire life in all its facets if you will allow Him to do so. The most important thing you can do in your entire life, is to open the doors wide and to invite Christ sincerely into your life.

Accept with cheerfulness the discipline that the admission of the risen Christ into your life will demand of you. What He will do for you can be done in no other way and by no one else in your life. If you invite him to come in, He will rule your heart, and even if you make mistakes and often disappoint Him, He will never leave you. He never leaves the work of His hands.

His healing and restoring power will continue to lead you into a deeper spiritual life. His indwelling presence is our guarantee that we are rooted and established in His love. Then we bear fruit that are appropriate to our conversion.

Wonderful Lord Jesus, enter my life as the most honored Guest I can receive. I thank You for the unspeakable privilege of having You in my life. Make me worthy of it through Your grace and mercy. Amen.

Read: Micah 4:1-7 July 28

To the gold-tinted mountain tops

Come, let us go up to the mountain of the LORD, to the house of the God of Jacob. He will teach us his ways, so that we may walk in his paths.

— MICAH 4:2 —

Some of Christ's most committed disciples experienced dark moments on their spiritual pilgrimage. All of us experience prosperity and adversity in life. The times of prosperity pass like a thought, while the dark moments seem endless. Then the gray clouds of depression and discouragement descend on us. Our view is obstructed and we cannot see the living Christ.

Therefore it is good advice that Micah gives. For every problem in life there is the answer: return to God.

You cannot count all the dark moments in your life as you are too deeply aware of your own. There is no reason why you must stay in the dark. Fix your eyes on the mountain tops, then your road through the dark valley will not seem so long.

Persevere in prayer and meditate on the goodness of God. Strengthen your daily walk with the Master. Perseverance and enthusiasm in the difficult moments of life will lead you from the darkness, and you will see the sun-kissed mountain tops of the Lord's grace.

There is no other path to God and His power than through Jesus Christ, prayer, meditation and Bible study. It will give you courage in the dark and enable you to sing songs of praise, even in the darkest night. God's grace will make you glad again. You then move from the dark depths with a stronger faith and a complete trust in your God.

Light of the world, I thank You that You also shine in the darkness of my life. Even though I go through dark depths, I will not be afraid, because You are with me. Amen.

July 29

Read: John 10:22-29

A message for all seasons

Then came the Feast of Dedication at Jerusalem. It was winter.
— JOHN 10:22 —

Winter has its own charm and brings its own worries. Winter is rich in messages for the children of the Lord. May His Holy Spirit help us to capture these messages in our hearts so that winter will not pass without blessing.

Winter reminds us that summer has gone. The time of growth and fruit-bearing and harvesting is short – and then it is winter. Soon the abundance and the wealth of color of summer disappear and the grayness and cold of winter replace it. Hence the call, *Carpe Diem*! which means "Seize the day!" "Teach us to number our days aright, that we may gain a heart of wisdom" (Ps. 90:12).

Winter reminds us that life is transient and transitory. Every whirlwind has its own quota of falling leaves. Old age will come as surely as winter follows summer. It is wise to keep this in mind.

Winter reminds us that there is a time of rest. We should not become so enslaved by our work that we cannot stop and rest with God. It is essential for us to rest if we want to lead quality lives. That is why God created the night for resting and the day of the Lord to be quiet and still before Him, the Power Source of our lives. Then we will send out new shoots and bear fruit gloriously.

Winter involuntarily reminds us of death, but at the same time also of a triumphant resurrection. We wake up to a new, glorious life of eternal spring in the garden of God.

I thank You, Creator Father, for the message I find in winter. May I rest in You so that I will have strength for new growth and fruit-bearing. Amen.

Read: John 17:1-26

July 30

Glorify the lord!

"I have brought you glory on earth by completing the work you gave me to do."

— JOHN 17:4 —

Do you accept your faith as a matter of course? A large number of people who confess that they are Christians, do exactly that. Over the years their worship has become a matter of routine. They repeat the same old prayers and lifestyle ad nauseam. The great danger of this is the fact that worship takes on a certain pattern and because they are unwilling to change or to do something new, it becomes monotonous and meaningless.

When you worship God, whether in the fellowship of believers, in prayer, in Bible study groups, or in your private quiet time, you should never lose sight of the glorious reality of His holy presence. Your hymn book may inspire you, but the joy of worship can only come from the Source of that inspiration – the living Christ.

Think of the enormous impact the angels had on the shepherds of Bethlehem; or of the imposing figure of Christ preaching with so much authority, healing with so much power and caring with so much love. Meditate on the wonder of the resurrection and ascension. In view of these thoughts, your worship should become a joyous and triumphant experience.

When you worship, you dare not forget that you are in the presence of the King of all kings. He is not tied to the pages of the liturgy, but He lives in your heart. Therefore, give Him the glory and honor His Name deserves. Glorify the Lord!

All praise and thanks to God
the Father now be given,
The Son and He who reigns
with Them in highest heaven:
The one, eternal God
whom heaven and earth adore:
For thus it was, is now,
and shall be evermore.

July 31

Read: Matthew 28:11-20

Do not be dismayed

"Surely I will be with you always, to the very end of the age."
— MATTHEW 28:20 —

Sorrow and grief come into our lives suddenly, unexpectedly and unannounced and change things radically. Where first love was shared, where there was understanding and where experiences of life were shared, there is now only a gaping void that can only be understood fully by those who have been down that path themselves. In such circumstances, the promise of our Savior in the Scripture verse today is a rich comfort for the heart that is torn apart.

Sorrow comes to us in many forms, but the most common form is the sorrow caused by death. For years you have shared your life and love with someone. Now that person is no longer there and you feel completely desolate. You weep for yourself, because your loved one is safely with the Lord. Let it be a comfort and consolation to you.

There are other forms of sorrow that are just as bad as those caused by death. Yes, sometimes even worse. When someone brings great shame to a family we often hear, "Death would have been better!" There can be bitter suffering on account of a physical disability or deformity of a child, or a terminal illness against which we are powerless.

It is in such circumstances that we lift our tearful eyes to the mountains and hear the voice of the God of love saying, "So do not fear, for I am with you; do not be dismayed, for I am your God. I will strengthen you and help you; I will uphold you with My righteous right hand" (Is. 41:10).

Loving Lord Jesus, when my thoughts become too much to bear, Your consolation refreshes my heart. I come to lay my sorrow and grief in faith at the foot of the Cross, in the quiet trust that You will comfort me. I thank You for that. Amen.

AUGUST

August 1

Read: Mark 16:1-8

Go forward with confidence

He is going ahead of you into Galilee. There you will see him, just as he told you.

– MARK 16:7 –

This is the time of the year when many of us need a word of encouragement. To many people, life often seems dark and ominous. People look ahead without any hope or excitement and with a growing sense of fear. You feel uncertain about everything you do. Consequently failure starts to characterize your attempts and you become depressed by the repeated disappointments of your efforts.

If the knowledge of God's lasting presence is uppermost in your thoughts and spirit, it will act as a remedy for depression, fear and failure. Such an experience with God should make you realize that He is not only the Lord of the past and the present, but also of a timeless future. Even if the future is unknown to you and difficult to understand, God is there and He is waiting to lead you onto the road known to Him.

To enter the future by God's side requires a living and practical faith and a willingness to trust Him unconditionally in every situation and every road He may lead you on.

To be aware of His will and to carry it out, may have many facets, but it basically requires two things from you: you must obey the discipline of His laws and you must teach yourself to wait on Him in silence. He gave Himself to you so that you can have fellowship with Him in private; He gave you His law to provide guidance for your life.

In the spirit of obedience to God and in intimate and continuous fellowship with Him, you can enter the future with confidence.

I praise You, faithful Lord, because You make it possible for me to meet the future without fear and with confidence. Amen.

Read: Mark 5:1-20

August 2

A difficult command

"Go home to your family and tell them how much the Lord has done for you, and how he has had mercy on you."

– MARK 5:19 –

An amazing miracle took place. A man who had been demon-possessed was cured. The townspeople could not understand how Jesus had done this miracle. Since they were confronted by something mysterious and unknown to them, they felt threatened and requested Jesus to leave their region.

For the previously demon-possessed man, this was a moment of crisis. His own people rejected the Man who had healed him. It was clear that his loyalty and love were with Jesus. That is why he asked Jesus if he could go with Him. Jesus refused the request with the words, "Go home to your family and tell them ..."

When Jesus left the region of the Gerasenes, He left behind one man who would always be grateful to Him. He would also be a constant reproach to the community which had rejected Christ.

It is a romantic and appealing thought to want to go and work for the Lord far away from home, in a region where the people are receptive to the message of Christ. Your church may appear spiritually dead to you and perhaps you long to be part of a living, dynamic congregation elsewhere. You may be tempted to go and worship there, but what is the will of the Master for you? Possibly He wants you to remain where you are, to be a living witness of His love and power in a depressing and spiritually difficult situation.

Perhaps God's task for you is to light the flame of spiritual life and growth in a dying congregation. Are you obedient enough to accept this challenge?

Loving Master, help me to always remember that Your will for me is more important than the superficial desires of my heart. Guide me through the Holy Spirit to know and do Your will. Amen.

August 3

Read: John 1:1-18

The things that are really important

In him was life, and that life was the light of men.

– JOHN 1:4 –

A person who is intoxicated by self-love misses the whole point of life. Everything he achieves and everything he does is just to glorify himself. Usually such a person thinks scornfully of those who help others. He treats the Christian faith with contempt. There are people who are envious of the self-assurance and possessions of such a person. They are impressed by his apparent success.

To envy such a person shows a lack of understanding of the meaning and purpose of life. To desire the things obtained through selfishness, false pride or disrespect of flawless spiritual qualities, reveals spiritual bankruptcy. In this way an attitude that is in conflict with God's will is accepted.

In order to pursue a noble purpose and to maintain lasting values, it is essential to live in harmony with God's will. It is a privilege that should not be regarded lightly. It requires thorough reflection since it includes all facets of your life: your ambitions; desires; standards of purity and honesty; and the willingness to reject all jealousy, bitterness, conflict, hatred and all destructive influences.

It is when Christ is completely in control and when your commitment stands fast that your life starts taking on the holy pattern and plan of God.

Then you are able to distinguish the things that really matter in life. You will realize once again that it is only God's way that results in a rich and satisfying life.

Heavenly Father, in joy I admit that it is only Your path that brings joy and fulfillment to my life. I praise You for that, through Jesus Christ, my Lord. Amen.

Read: John 11:1-16

August 4

For God it is never too late

Yet when he heard that Lazarus was sick, he stayed where he was two more days.

– John 11:6 –

You have probably also prayed against time. Perhaps something had to be completed before a certain date and because it was so important to you, you spent much time in prayer imploring God to do something before that time, otherwise it would be too late. And then … nothing happened.

If this has been your experience, you have probably learned the hard way that you cannot rush God or subject Him to your personal timetable.

When Jesus learned that His friend Lazarus was dying, He did a strange thing. He stayed where He was for two more days without any attempt to leave straight away to go and support and comfort His friends. When He eventually came to Bethany, He transformed the tragedy of Lazarus' death into an opportunity to glorify God.

There may have been times in your life when God did not act according to your timetable. You prayed fervently but it seemed as if God was too late. God is never too late. His timing is always perfect.

Your life is bound and regulated by earthly time but God views your life in terms of eternity. You think you know what would be the best for you at a given time. However, God sees your entire life and acts according to His omniscience for your own good.

If you love Him and trust Him, He will let all things work out for your good, in His own perfect time. Instead of demanding from God to act within a certain time frame, you should allow Him to form and polish you according to His perfect will. Then you will live in harmony with Him and have peace of mind.

Forgive me, O Lord, for my selfishness and ignorance. I place my life and my wishes in Your hands and accept Your perfect timing. Amen.

August 5

Read: Matthew 26:36-46

Let Your will be done

"Yet not as I will, but as you will."

– MATTHEW 26:39 –

When we walk in the sunshine, it is easy to say, "Let Your will be done." But in the shadows of Gethsemane it is an entirely different matter. The victory of Gethsemane is about preferring God's will to our own desires. It is a blessing and not a disaster when things unfold according to God's omniscient will and not according to my will. Then I will never be defeated, but always victorious.

However, there are different ways that one can say, "Let Your will be done."

We can be fatalistic about it, in a spineless and helpless way. With a shrug of the shoulders we can say, "We are in the hands of blind fate and there is nothing we can do about it." Hope dies and we passively resist. We act like slaves who have been chastised into submission. This means that we keep quiet while on the inside we curse, because we feel it does not help to argue with God. This is total defeat.

We can become frustrated just like someone who has had a dream and then suddenly realizes it can never come true. He experiences regret and bitter anger about what could have been. He leads a life of hopeless defeat.

We can, however, say this with a firm belief and complete faith – like Jesus! He speaks to His Father whose arms are supporting Him. He subjects Himself to a love that will never forsake Him. He accepts what He cannot change or understand. This is love that's stronger than death and that has the power to triumph in every situation in life.

Loving Father, I thank You for being in control of my unsteady life boat. Direct it according to Your compass and itinerary and direct it to the Harbor where there is peace of mind. Amen.

Read: Ecclesiastes 1:12-18 August 6

Help those in need

I devoted myself to study and to explore by wisdom all that is done under heaven.

— ECCLESIASTES 1:13 —

The principle of determining a need and then satisfying it, forms the basic philosophy behind many fortunes. Businessmen have built their empires in this way. People can do exactly that if they first determine a need and then do everything in their power to provide for that need.

Everywhere in the world there are needs waiting to be relieved. God may ask you to do precisely that. The need you will have to satisfy will possibly not bring you a fortune or enable you to establish an empire, but it may be more important than both of these in the eyes of God.

Can you look around and honestly tell God that you do not see any need? That difficult person whom no one understands and whom everyone tries to avoid may have an urgent need for a sympathetic ear and an understanding heart. That widow, or divorcée who has been shut out from the community in a subtle way through no fault of their own, would certainly react to the offer of sincere friendship. There is probably a need in the life of the next person you will meet. You only need to be sensitive enough to the prompting of the Holy Spirit to notice it.

You may ask why you should tire yourself with the needs or distress of others while you have enough problems of your own. The answer is simple: you belong to Christ! As His follower, dare you neglect relieving someone's need to the best of your ability? He said that if we do it for the least important of His brothers, we do it for Him!

Teach me daily, O Holy Spirit, to be sensitive towards my fellow man. Amen.

August 7

Read: Exodus 15:22-27

A recipe for conquering bitterness

When they came to Marah, they could not drink its water because it was bitter.

— Exodus 15:23 –

Bitterness can subtly steal into your heart and influence your entire life negatively. Accommodating bitterness is to harbor a negative force that can eventually destroy you and put those you love at a disadvantage.

Embittered people are never happy people. Their bitterness gnaws at their insides like a cancer and the end product is never pleasant to see.

The only really effective remedy for bitterness is to be purified by the love of Jesus Christ. If His example and attitude control your life, it is impossible to instigate bitterness and hatred. His closeness and love will neutralize these destructive forces. It will enable you to rise above the long nurtured bitterness and to choose a life of reconciliation. Then the miracle of God's grace and mercy takes place: "And the water became sweet" (Ex. 15:25).

Some people turn their backs on the love of Jesus Christ and cling to their bitterness. They exclude the light of love and stubbornly stumble forward in the darkness of hatred. Eventually they pay the painful price: they become lonely people.

To triumph over bitterness, you need to surrender your life to Jesus Christ so that all the wrong attitudes in your life can be changed and healed. Then the cross has "sweetened" your life as you live in harmony with the will of God.

The deliverance that love brings, will make you kneel before God with songs of praise and thanksgiving.

Help me, O Savior, to experience Your presence in such a real way that all bitterness will disappear from my life. Give me still more of Your heavenliness and love in my fellowship with my fellow man. Amen.

Read: Proverbs 16:20-33

August 8

Happiness is an achievable goal

Blessed is he who trusts in the LORD.

– PROVERBS 16:20 –

Happiness is the one thing that all people anxiously seek. Yet, it seems as though it constantly escapes most people. That is why someone said, "Happiness is like a butterfly: if you hunt it, it will evade you; if you sit down quietly, it will come and sit on your shoulder."

We find it difficult because we forget that happiness is something that comes from deep inside when our spirit is in harmony with God. With God in the center of our lives, it is possible to find lasting happiness, even in the most trying circumstances.

Many people seek happiness in material things. To put your trust in earthly possessions is to elevate things that are destroyed by moth and rust to the highest level. Such people often find out too late that they do not own their possessions, but that their possessions own them. "What good will it be for man if he gains the whole world, yet forfeits his soul?" (Mt. 16:26).

Others think that freedom from all restricting laws brings happiness. Then they lead a wild life, only to discover that this leads to tragic degeneration. One should guard against confusing freedom with immorality.

You can also seek happiness by isolating yourself from the world and living for yourself only; never taking note of your fellow man and his needs. Then you come to a point where you are lonely and unfulfilled beyond measure. Love finds its highest fulfillment in service to others and this service is a requirement for happiness.

A life where God has complete control, is a life of happiness and inner peace. This is, through what Jesus Christ did for me, an achievable goal.

I seek You with all my heart, O Lord, because I know that with You alone can I find true happiness. I thank You that Your love found me when I strayed, and that Jesus Christ is the guarantee of my happiness. Amen.

August 9

Read: 1 Peter 1:13-16, Leviticus 20:1-9

Guide to sanctification

"Be holy, because I am holy."

– 1 PETER 1:16 –

Consecrate yourselves and be holy, because I am the LORD your God.

– LEVITICUS 20:7 –

"Holy" is not a very popular word in the vocabulary of modern man. To some people this word personifies those who are "holier-than-thou", who look down on others, are spiritually arrogant and whom one suspects of hypocrisy. But in its purest form, this word defines a meaningful experience.

"Holy" means "being set apart" and implies surrender and an intimate fellowship with God. Every Christian should strive towards the achievement of this superior goal. Many people don't want to surrender and this is detrimental to their faith and their relationship with the living Christ.

Some people reject it as impractical due to its requirements, because it is totally impossible to lead a holy life if your commitment is lukewarm. Someone truly holy, has surrendered to God completely and is steadfastly obedient to Him.

To live a holy life demands constant awareness of your attitude, your actions and your motives. As follower of the Master, there is no excuse to persist in the sin that you secretly nurture. You cannot have one foot in the world and the other foot planted waveringly in God's kingdom without being torn apart.

The guidelines for a holy life are found in the Word of God. Christ is our perfect example of holy conduct. He gave us the Holy Spirit to guide us in the truth of sanctification. The more we listen to the prompting of the Holy Spirit, the more progress we will make on the path of sanctification.

Give me a new, a perfect heart,
From doubt, and fear and sorrow free:
The mind which was in Christ impart
And let my spirit cleave to Thee.

Read: Luke 21:7-19

August 10

Be careful with your testimony

"This will result in your being witnesses to them."
— LUKE 21:13 —

The advertising industry has discovered the amazing value of personal testimony. Housewives become excited about a consumer product they have used and found excellent. Radiant celebrities tell about the advantages of investing with a certain financial institution due to increased interest rates.

The success of this type of advertisement lies in the personal recommendation. However, if this is not completely true, the fastidious and selective observers will soon see it as hypocritical and non-effective.

The Christian church grew on the basis of personal testimony. The early disciples knew the resurrected Savior personally and shared this experience with others. The theme was unmistakably: "May I introduce my Redeemer and Savior to you?"

Through the ages, personal testimony has been a powerful and effective method of Christian witness. However, caution should be taken when applying this method. It is possible that your personal testimony may sound so repetitive that it has little impact. Then the testimony becomes self-centered and it glorifies the speaker instead of the Master.

Many committed Christians try to testify without asking for the guidance of the Holy Spirit. Then the testimony not only loses its power, but also creates intense antagonism. Testifying necessarily means close and intimate cooperation with the Holy Spirit.

If you desire sharing your Christian testimony with others, allow the Holy Spirit to create the opportunity so that you can be a useful witness through His wisdom, to the glory of Your Redeemer.

Holy Spirit, make me Your obedient instrument when I testify about the reality and the glory of my Redeemer – Jesus Christ. Amen.

August 11

Read: 1 Peter 5:1-11

A caring God

Cast all your anxiety on him because he cares for you.
— 1 Peter 5:7 —

Corrie ten Boom said, "Worrying does not empty tomorrow of its grief; it only deprives today of its power." In this regard William Inge said, "Worry is the interest paid on trouble before the expiry date." There are few things in life that are more destructive than worry. It is amazing to see the harmful effect of worry on a person.

To worry deprives you of your physical and intellectual abilities. It causes so much tension that you are often left in a state of complete helplessness and despair. The vitality vanishes from your life and your actions.

At times Jesus must have experienced anxiety about His safety and the safety of His disciples. He had to struggle with this alone, since His disciples did not have the faintest idea of the full extent of His mission. Nevertheless, Christ's peace of mind and calm spirit amazed people time and again. This was not because He wasn't aware of the seriousness of the situation. On the contrary, He knew too well what the price was that He would have to pay. His life had been completely and unconditionally surrendered to the care of His heavenly Father.

If we want to experience peace of mind in this rapidly changing world with all its temptations and enticements, we should follow the example of the Master. Through the firmness of our relationship with Him, we must place our lives with its burdens, problems and worries, entirely in God's hands. Then we can face life with strength and peace of mind.

Lord Jesus, I worship You as the true vine. I draw my strength from You like a branch does from the vine. Being dependent on You gives me strength to do what You expect from me. Amen.

Read: Exodus 3:1-14   August 12

Who, me?

Who am I, that I should go to Pharaoh and bring the Israelites out of Egypt?

— Exodus 3:11 —

Through the ages people have been called to undertake tasks they thought they were not equipped for. These tasks may have varied from undertaking huge projects to normal domestic duties. So often the person involved doubted and questioned his own ability to cope with the situation.

It is very unfortunate that many people have allowed big opportunities to slip through their fingers, merely because they had convinced themselves that they were inadequate to do the task. Their weak excuse is then that they are not equipped to confront the problem.

Some of the greatest people in history had no qualifications for their tasks. Jesus was a simple carpenter's son from Nazareth and He is the reason we are Christians today. Great people take the opportunities God gives them to accomplish much in His strength.

It may be possible that you are facing such a challenge in your life right now. Perhaps you doubt your own ability to carry out a big assignment. Take your problems and worries to God in prayer, and if it is His will that you should act, do it in complete dependence on Him. Be convinced that Christ would not call you to a task that He will not equip you to accomplish.

Help me, heavenly Father, never to let an opportunity to serve You pass by unused because I only saw my own limitations. Amen.

August 13

Read: Malachi 1:1-14

Second best is not good enough

"When you bring injured, crippled or diseased animals and offer them as sacrifices, should I accept them from your hands?" says the LORD.

– MALACHI 1:13 –

We dare not think of giving God our second best. God gave His best, His most precious to us, "For God so loved the world that He gave His one and only Son" (Jn. 3:16).

If we place God at the bottom of our list of priorities, we should not be surprised if our lives turn out to be pointless and superficial. God uses only what we give to Him in trust. If we give Him the worthless things of our lives, what's left of our love, time, possessions and strength, we should not complain if our blessings are equal to our offerings.

Giving less than your best to God implies that there are more important things to you than God. This means that you prefer the temporary, to eternity; that you are desperately attached to the here and now; that you refuse to store up treasures in heaven where moth and rust cannot destroy them. You try to appeal to the world while you forfeit your soul. When God only gets a negligible spot on your agenda, you will later find that the quality of your life has lost its value because God has only received your second best. Your values are distorted because your life is not built on the Rock.

When you give God the place of honor that He deserves as King of your life, when you offer Him the best you have, there will be unparalleled growth in your spiritual life. Only the Holy Spirit and a pure love for the Lord can guide you there.

Take my very best every day, O Lord. Only Your best was good enough for me, my Savior. Purify what I bring You and use it to Your greater glorification. Amen.

Read: 2 Corinthians 4:7-15   August 14

There are indeed dark days

We are hard pressed on every side, but not crushed; perplexed, but not in despair; persecuted, but not abandoned; struck down, but not destroyed.

– 2 Corinthians 4:8-9 –

Sometimes the course of our lives is cruelly disturbed as problems arise. Not one of us is safeguarded against difficulties and Christ never promised that the Christian's voyage through life would be smooth sailing on a calm ocean.

If we approach our problems with a positive attitude, God can even use them to motivate us to serve Him more effectively and to approach our fellow man with greater compassion. This is the positive approach about which Paul speaks to us today.

When you are going through difficult times, wait in silence, trust God and find out through prayer if He is not trying to teach you something. Do not allow problems to control your life. Guard in particular against panic, however great your dismay may be. God is greater than any problems you may experience.

Every problem has its own way of attacking your spirit. Some problems appear dramatically out of nowhere. While others enter your thoughts and life quietly and subtly.

Without a sincere and living faith that enables you to triumph over your problems, the way ahead will be impossible. Faith in the goodness of God and in the sure knowledge that He has a purpose for your life will enable you to face the future with confidence. Nothing can separate you from the love of God that is in Christ Jesus our Lord (Rom. 8:39).

Heavenly Supporter, grant me that special mercy which will enable me to not collapse under my problems. Let me take to heart those lessons You teach me in times of great anxiety. I worship You as the God who can transform darkness into light. Amen.

August 15

Read: 2 Chronicles 20:18-30

When religion becomes confusing

Have faith in the LORD your God and you will be upheld.
– 2 CHRONICLES 20:20 –

We live in a period of spiritual awakening and the Spirit of God is working across the entire world. Although this does not always seem to be true, humankind is becoming increasingly aware of spiritual values. There is a search for God and for truth as seldom observed in previous generations.

This desire for spiritual values has resulted in various interpretations of the doctrines of Christ. There are many sectarian teachings that create confusion in non-Christian communities and even among Christians of established churches.

What you say in defense of your faith is important. But still more important, is the place you give to Christ Himself in your life. You should love Him more than the doctrines and theories on Him. The core of our Christian belief is after all based on the love we have for Christ.

Outraged propagandists may argue and perhaps confuse you about what you should believe. Unless their testimony is inspired by the love of Christ, He is not the center of their focus. They should then be distrusted.

When you are confused by strange and new doctrines, keep your spiritual eye on Jesus, your Guide. Allow Him to renew and strengthen your faith through the Holy Spirit. You'll have the wealth of a noble tradition and a life filled with joy and tolerance through the working of the Holy Spirit .

Your faith then rests in Christ and His Spirit will protect you against confusion in your spiritual life.

Savior and Friend, You captured me through love and You are the foundation of my faith. I praise Your glorious Name. Amen.

Read: Philippians 4:2-8   August 16

Notice the beauty

Finally, brothers ... whatever is lovely ... think about such things.
                                        – PHILIPPIANS 4:8 –

Many people realize that the world around them is becoming sordid and polluted. This is no surprise in the light of the shocking headlines in newspapers, sickening revelations in the media and the lack of elegance and grace in our society.

Shocking fashions and lifestyles which are reprehensible and tasteless are taking the limelight. It seems as if decency has been replaced by rudeness and arrogance to such a degree that everything civilized and lovely is under the threat of being destroyed. The kind heart finds this sorrowful and disconcerting.

If you feel like this, you should guard against being overcome by negative tendencies and yielding to the temptation of believing, although hesitantly, that this degradation of values has become the norm and standard of modern society.

You should rather try to look past the filth and sordidness of the world. Look around you and search for the beautiful things in life.

Seek the glory of our Creator God in the song of birds; in the breathtaking miracle of sunrise and sunset; the mountains and fields; the ebb and flow of the tides and the abounding wildlife and the inspiring beauty of flowers.

Listen to soothing music and concentrate on the good things that are still present in the world. Then you will experience the peace of God that surpasses all understanding.

By paying attention to beauty, holy Master, I want to take away the sordidness of this world through the help of the Holy Spirit, and replace it with beauty and goodness. Amen.

August 17

Read: Exodus 15:22-27

God heals

"For I am the LORD, who heals you."

– EXODUS 15:26 –

Many of the diseases in the world can be traced to spiritual instability. More and more people are seeking professional help to deal with the intellectual and emotional stress of life. Uncertainty is more evident than ever before. In many cases it has become fashionable to try to evade responsibilities. Consequently family life is suffering and personal integrity is seriously threatened.

There is no doubt that the only safe lifestyle is that which is firmly based on the Rock of Ages, Jesus Christ. Without Him as the anchor in your life, you will find yourself being tossed about by the storms of life that descend on your life quite suddenly and violently.

Whatever help you may then get will be of a temporary nature and quite soon you will fall into your previously unhappy and unsteady circumstances – unless your solution has Christ at the center.

On your pilgrimage through life, and while you are handling unavoidable problems, make sure that you are holding on to Christ and His glorious promises. Put your trust in Him and live strictly and obediently according to His commands.

Then you will find that the healing balm of His great peace will enable you to triumph over all opposition. Your life will reflect all the necessary qualities of trust and firm faith. Then you will experience inner healing from the great Healer.

Father and Healer, I thank You for the assurance that my spirit will be healed through my faith in You. I praise and glorify Your great Name. Amen.

Read: Luke 4:16-30 August 18

How are you affected by Jesus' words?

All the people in the synagogue were furious when they heard this. They got up, drove him out of town, and took him to the brow of the hill.

– LUKE 4:28-29 –

Jesus never flattered people by telling them what they wanted to hear. He persisted in telling them what they needed to hear. Because His words penetrated their spiritual stubbornness and arrogance, it made them react in different ways.

Many accepted the challenge His words posed and started pursuing justice, paying the price for discipleship, putting their everything on the altar and following Him. Others again, felt hurt by what He had said, because He revealed their hidden sins and weaknesses, and they were afraid when they saw how well He knew them.

The words of Christ still have the same penetrating power today and cause the same basic reaction. Some people react with joyful willingness and obey His commands. They have seen a vision of what life can be if it is in harmony with His will. Their love for Him is revealed in their willing obedience.

There are few people who reject the words of the living Christ on purpose and forthrightly. They sidestep His invitation to a new and meaningful life rather skillfully.

The time is not right, discipleship would cause embarrassment at work and among friends, and many other similar weak excuses for disobedience to His call, "You must follow Me!" are used.

If Christ sets a challenge, He speaks to the heart and not to the mind. His words have a healing quality and when applied to your life, they bring peace which surpasses all understanding. Out of this peace, you can live to His glory every day.

My Guide and Redeemer, grant me the courage to purposefully accept Your challenge for my life. Amen.

August 19

Read: Psalm 30:1-12

For dark days of the spirit

Weeping may remain for a night, but rejoicing comes in the morning.

— PSALM 30:5 —

Some Christians always appear cheerful and happy, while others go through dark times. Some people live sparkling and joyous lives without letting depression and dejection touch them. Many admire their ability to thrive on adversity, while others are almost paralyzed by discouragement when they move through a dark valley. Yet, there is hope and rich heavenly comfort for them as well.

Some of God's most sensitive children also had this experience. Many, like Elijah, almost fell into the depths of despair and they wished that God would end their lives. Even our Savior was sometimes dismayed; such was the case in the dark shadows of Gethsemane. Spiritual depression or dismay is not necessarily synonymous with spiritual failure. It becomes an embarrassment only when you stop trying to move from the darkness to the light.

Rectify your relationship with God. Eliminate all those things from your life that separate you from Him. Do not consider your own desires above your duty to obey His will and to follow His path. And if there are sins that leave you speechless before God, walk the path of repentance and confession of guilt, and taste the deliverance of forgiveness in Jesus Christ.

Then the dark shadows will disappear and you will walk in the bright sunshine of God's mercy. A song of praise and thanksgiving will resound from your heart. Then you will know without a doubt that these dark times are just the path to a place of bright light and a deeper love for your Lord and Master.

Loving Lord, be merciful unto me so that I can use the dark times in my life meaningfully. Let Your friendly light lead me in these times, especially to a pure and clear appreciation of Your infinite love. Amen.

Read: Luke 6:20-26

August 20

Popularity can be dangerous

"Woe to you when all men speak well of you."

– LUKE 6:26 –

All of us would like to be loved and to be popular. However, unless we are very careful, popularity can cost us dearly. When principles are sacrificed, purity soiled and our spiritual lives suppressed in an attempt to win other people's approval, the price we pay becomes too high.

One thing is certain: you can never please everybody. If you try to do this, you will eventually discover that you are pleasing no one. No responsible person will take you seriously after a while.

When you regard principles as more important than popularity, it is possible that you will be misunderstood, that you will be called a spoilsport and that people will speak badly of you and taunt you. But remember that this will only be done by those who live according to worldly standards.

There are values in life which last much longer than popularity. True popularity cannot be separated from sound principles. These principles must be maintained, even if they antagonize some people. Maintaining a strong conviction while remaining friendly and peaceful will only strengthen that conviction.

As a Christian you should not try as much to satisfy other people. You should live in such a way that you earn the approval of the Master. His principles will become your principles if you try to live according to them. You will become aware of an inner strength developing in you that is part of everyone who trusts in Him and who lives according to His standards.

Enable me, loving Shepherd, through the strength of the Holy Spirit, never to compromise principles for cheap popularity. Amen.

August 21

Read: 1 Thessalonians 4:13-18

Peace replaces grief

Brothers, we do not want you ... to grieve like the rest of men, who have no hope.

— 1 Thessalonians 4:13 —

If we are absolutely certain that we are children of God, it is our sure guarantee that we can break through the barrier of grief and pain. We can then come to quiet waters where there is peace, no matter how stormy the way might have been.

This does not mean that we are called to welcome grief. On the contrary, our Master Himself prayed for the bitter cup to be taken away from Him. However, He accepted it in the knowledge that it was the will of His Father to lead him to Golgotha. It is not God's will for us to remain unemotional and untouched when the shadows of grief darken our paths. It is no sin to grieve. Christ Himself cried at the grave of Lazarus. The Lord doesn't want our grief to deprive us of our peace.

There is a liberating joy in the knowledge that our faith and trust in God have withstood the test of personal grief and loss.

Let us be clear on this: never in our earthly existence will we be guaranteed freedom from grief. God Himself never promises this to His children. What He does promise us is His peace.

Time heals all wounds. God leads His faithful children to new levels of acceptance and a greater understanding of their grief. The greatest peace in life is not born out of superficial experiences, but in the hour of pain and sorrow.

It is as though we see God better through a veil of tears. Grief can then serve a holy purpose in our lives, "I consider that our present sufferings are not worth comparing with the glory that will be revealed in us" (Rom. 8:18).

I thank You, Word that has become flesh, for Your assurance that, "Whosoever sows in tears, will bring in the harvest with rejoicing!" I exult in Your peace. Amen.

Read: 2 Corinthians 12:1-10   **August 22**

Unanswered prayers

"My Father, if it is possible, may this cup be taken from me."
— MATTHEW 26:39 —

What indescribable tragedy would it have been for this sinful world, if Christ's prayer in Gethsemane had not been left unanswered? Because this prayer of despair went unanswered, Jesus Christ became the Redeemer of the world.

Another classic example of such a prayer is that of Paul, who prayed for the thorn to be removed from his flesh. The thorn continued to cause him pain, but he tasted the fullness of God's glorious promise, "My grace is sufficient for you." This enabled Paul to say triumphantly, "Therefore I will boast all the more gladly about my weaknesses, so that Christ's power may rest on me" (2 Cor. 12:9).

Sometimes God does not answer us, because He has something better in store for us. Moses prayed fervently to God to allow him to proceed into Canaan. God refused to listen to him because he had been disobedient at Kadesh. Yet, God gave him the heavenly Canaan, which was infinitely more than he could have prayed for or thought possible (Deut. 32:48-52).

David pleaded with God in prayer for the life of his child, but God took the child away. Through this, David came to a true confession of his sin. As fruit of this, David wrote the unforgettable fifty-first Psalm.

Eventually God answers *all* faithful prayers. Not always according to our own desires; sometimes in such a way that we do not recognize the answer, but somewhere along the line, through God's loving actions, we do get the answers.

When we look back on the journey traveled, we will be grateful that the answers were according to His holy will and not according to our own desires. The prayer of him who gets up from his knees feeling a better person, has already been answered.

Jesus of Gethsemane, teach me to say after You in obedience, "Yet not as I will, but as You will." Amen.

August 23

Read: Philippians 4:1-9

Joyful Christians

Rejoice in the Lord always. I will say it again: Rejoice! Let your gentleness be evident to all.

– PHILIPPIANS 4:4-5 –

Let us enter this new day with joy in our hearts. Come, let us share the glory of this joy with everyone we meet today, because joy is an important virtue for Christians and one of the fruit of the Spirit (see Gal. 5:22).

If your faith is making you a happy person, you will not be able to keep this experience to yourself. If what you believe in does not increase your joy, you should earnestly ask yourself where the fault lies and pray for the Holy Spirit to guide you in truth. Thomas à Kempis said, "If there is joy in the world, then the person with a pure heart undoubtedly has it."

To share your joy with others is an outstanding privilege. An expression of appreciation; a friendly gesture; a word of encouragement for spending time with someone who is experiencing intense grief: these are all evidence of a deep and sincere joy that lives in people's hearts. He who brings sunshine to the lives of others, cannot keep the reflection of that joy from his own life.

To generously hand out friendliness is a way of life that makes our existence worthwhile. It builds friendships and makes us sensitive to the needs of others. You act positively because you see the positive things in life. Happiness and joy are things which come from deep in your heart. It is a gift of God to His faithful children. God is, after all, the Source of all true and lasting happiness.

Robert Louis Stevenson claimed, "When a cheerful person comes into a room, it is as though a light has been switched on." Christ said, "You are the light of the world!"

Redeemer and Friend, help me through Your love and mercy to always be a cheerful person. Give me the desire to share my joy generously with others. Amen.

Read: John 15:1-8

August 24

Over-sensitivity

"Remain in me, and I will remain in you. No branch can bear fruit by itself; it must remain in the vine. Neither can you bear fruit unless you remain in me."

– JOHN 15:4 –

This is Christ's prescription for the disease of over-sensitivity. There are people who are easily hurt by life. Maybe you are one of them. Perhaps you are so sensitive about what others might say or think about you, that your life has become an awful nightmare.

You know in your heart that if you allow this situation to continue, it will negatively affect your body, soul and mind. It is challenging to think that it is your own responsibility to decide whether or not this condition will continue.

God gave you the responsibility and privilege to choose: you can decide whether you will remain on the mountain top of hope, or whether you will descend into the valley of despair. It is not so much external circumstances that influence your spiritual condition, but your thoughts that make you what you are.

If you place every aspect of your life under the rule of Christ, He will necessarily control your thoughts as well. Suddenly you will discover that petty remarks that caused so much pain in the past no longer hurt you, because God's comfort is greater than any sorrow the world can cause you.

In Him you are protected against the onslaughts of your easily hurt, over-sensitive heart. The only requirement is that you remain in Him, the Vine.

My Lord and God, I want to remain in You always so that I can gain the victory in Your Name over all the evil and negative forces I have to face. Help me by the strength of the Holy Spirit. Amen.

August 25

Read: Zechariah 2:1-13

Being quiet before the Lord

Be still before the LORD, all mankind, because he has roused himself from his holy dwelling.

– ZECHARIAH 2:13 –

One of the most important lessons that we have to learn in God's household is to become still before God and be deeply aware of His Holiness.

Silence takes on many forms: it can be without sound or it can be resounding; it can be sensitive or insensitive; it can be active or passive. There is the unhappy and destructive silence when people in one house do not talk to one another anymore; when nothing remains to be said and the communication channels have finally been blocked. This type of silence becomes all the more bitter as time goes by. That is why it should be dealt with right at the beginning before it spreads like a ghastly and destructive cancer.

There is also the enriching silence of resignation and satisfaction. It is the stillness between life-partners who have found such peace in each other's presence that words are often unnecessary.

There are people who fear silence. Perhaps they are afraid of the voice of their conscience in the stillness. Or maybe memories from the past overwhelm them in the silence.

The most glorious and fruitful stillness any person could experience, is to become quiet before the splendor of God. It requires time and concentration, but when you personally experience it, the silence in God's presence is your guarantee of peace in this world of chaos and noise.

Teach me, O Holy Spirit, to be still before God, so that I will hear His voice, know His will and experience His peace at all times; in the Name of Jesus and with thanksgiving. Amen.

Read: Isaiah 43:1-9 August 26

Are you afraid?

"Do not be afraid , for I am with you."

– Isaiah 43:5 –

Fear is a paralyzing and destructive phenomenon in our lives. It is no wonder God made so many glorious promises regarding victory over fear in His Scriptures. God's call of love, "Do not be afraid," echoes constantly.

Behind these words lies a world of comfort and strength. It leaves us ashamed to think that our fear is the consequence of our unbelief and inability to believe in God's Word.

Sometimes problems come rushing into our lives like waves. They create a situation that seems overpowering and unmanageable. Then the fear either paralyzes or clouds our thinking so that it is difficult to consider matters clearly and to remember the omnipotence of God.

Fear is the illusion that rules the lives of many people and threatens to let them fall apart. It is carried into our lives and thoughts in a subtle way by the Evil One.

Faith is the unbreakable cable which keeps our lives from falling apart. God urges us repeatedly in the Bible not to be afraid, because fear destroys everything that is worthwhile. The basic cause of fear is sin. Adam confessed in Paradise that he had sinned, "I heard you in the garden and I was afraid."

How can you effectively fight fear? By realizing that your Father is the Almighty who is bigger than anything that can happen to you. Place your trust in Him; place your fear, in whichever form, at His feet before it starts ruling your life. A living faith in God is a sure antidote for fear.

Heavenly Father, through Jesus Christ I place my full trust in You and face the future without fear. Amen.

August 27

Read: Matthew 5:3-12

Through tears to comfort

"Blessed are those who mourn, for they will be comforted."
– MATTHEW 5:4 –

Tears offer deliverance and purify a grieving heart. Shakespeare said, "To weep is to make less the depth of grief." Tears are a natural way of unloading sorrow and grief. Crying prevents grief from changing into despair. If you never cry, you cannot experience inner healing. Christ Himself emphasized the advantage of discharging your grief in this way, "Blessed are those who mourn, for they will be comforted" (Mt. 5:4).

Tears are not only shed by weaklings, but also by the strong, because they originated from love, tenderness and compassion. Washington Irving said, "There is a sacredness in tears. They are not the marks of weakness but of power. They speak more eloquently than ten thousand tongues. They are the messengers of overwhelming grief, of deep contrition and of unspeakable love."

Through the tears of Jesus Christ our tears have also been made holy. He was divine enough to resurrect Lazarus from death and human enough to weep with those who were mourning. He was sufficiently almighty to stop their tears and sufficiently human to shed tears Himself.

Thank God for the healing, delivering and purifying power of tears. They soften sorrow, bring acceptance and eventually lead to joy. The soul would not see any rainbow if it did not know tears.

In addition, we have God's promise that there will be an end to all tears. When John speaks of the new heaven and the new earth, he says, "He will wipe every tear from their eyes. There will be no more death or mourning or crying or pain, for the old order of things has passed away" (Rev. 21:4).

C. J. Langenhoven once said, "If you have to shed tears, may they shine like drops of dew to introduce the days of joy."

O Holy Comforter, I thank You that my tears comfort me; that they make my grief bearable and bring me closer to You. Amen.

Read: Hebrews 11:1-10

August 28

Victorious through faith

"Now faith is being sure of what we hope for and certain of what we do not see."

– HEBREWS 11:1 –

To many people faith is a mystic, almost foggy belief that is totally removed from practical everyday life. People desire more faith, yet they are sadly lacking the ability to believe everyday spiritual things. They beg God continuously for more faith but their testimony remains ineffective.

We must realize that faith is an integral part of humankind's make-up. Every person practices some kind of faith. The tragedy is that so many people experience it wrongly. They have faith in their inability to lead dignified and dedicated lives; they believe in their fear which obstructs their view; and strangely enough, they believe in defeat, not in success or victory. It is not a question of more faith, but of correctly using what we already have.

When Jesus commands His disciples to have faith in God, He is educating them to a positive and constructive way of life. Everyone can believe in someone or something, but without faith in Christ, no person can be a Christian or please God.

Faith is essential for victory in our spiritual lives. Without it, we can have no fellowship with God; we cannot tackle the struggles of life; we cannot work through our own grief and problems. Faith is to trust God and His actions in our lives. Faith flourishes on what it brings forth.

The glorious fruit of Christian faith is the certainty of God's presence and the unshakable knowledge that He loves you unconditionally. With this, everything that happens in your life falls into place in a meaningful way.

Thank You, Father, for knowing that the Holy Spirit works in my heart and assures me of Your love for me. Amen.

August 29

Read: Joel 2:18-27

Compensation for damages

"I will repay you for the years the locusts have eaten – the great locust and the young locust, the other locusts and the locust swarm."
– JOEL 2:25 –

Through the years we have to forgo many things, and sometimes we are forced to make drastic changes and adjustments. Our inborn fear of change and our stubborn reluctance to make adjustments in a rapidly changing world become a cruel reality when the inevitable is forced upon us.

In this painful and disillusioning experience, God's words to Joel comfort us. Wisdom is to accept the realities of life and see them in the perspective of eternity without sacrificing our principles.

The adjustment after the death of a loved one is a traumatic experience. The uprooting from a familiar environment and the renewed adjustments to the presence of strangers, require courage and perseverance. Exchanging the space and comfort of one's own home for a flat or an old age home, brings tears and hours of worry and sleeplessness.

Trusting God and His master plan for my life means not becoming rebellious, but accepting the challenge of change in praise to the glorification of God.

As the years pass, our physical strength decreases, the voids in our lives become more painful, and it is more and more difficult to leave a known environment and to make changes. But trusting in God and submitting to His will, bring unparalleled peace and you realize that God has an answer for every want and every joy that life takes away from us.

What a wonderful God we worship! He compensates for damage that we have suffered, even when we have suffered through our own shortsighted digression and disobedience.

God of yesterday, today and tomorrow, we are so earthbound that we cannot think in terms of eternity. Help me to be courageous and obedient when You call for change and adjustment, in the strength that Jesus Christ gives me. Amen.

Read: Philippians 3:1-14

August 30

The ability to forget

*But one thing I do: Forgetting what is behind and straining toward
what is ahead, I press on toward the goal to win the prize for which
God has called me heavenward in Christ Jesus.*

– PHILIPPIANS 3:13-14 –

A person's memory is a wonderful gift from God. There are people who are exceptionally gifted in this area. The Bible reminds us to remember the day of the Lord and to think of our Creator in the days of our youth. If we want to have peace of mind, we should, however, learn to forget certain things in life.

We must forget about the sins we have already confessed. Satan will always try to remind us of them, but if we have confessed our sins in sincerity and with repentance, God will acquit us through Jesus Christ and treat us as though we have never sinned.

We must forget about our mistakes and failures. Fretting about mistakes of the past is counter-productive. The best approach is to learn from your mistakes and to act with more caution and wisdom in future.

We must forget the petty quarrels and misunderstandings of the past. We are all fallible and human and we should not nurse the mistakes others made.

We must forget the good deeds we do, because we do them in gratitude to Christ, for our undeserved salvation and only to His glorification. We must forget our sorrow. We must guard against staying in the dark valley for too long. We should prayerfully and obediently allow the comfort of Christ to lead us to the light. It is out of grace from above that we can forget certain things in life. That is why we should continuously remain in prayer before Him. He is, after all, the God who rules our thoughts.

Help me, Lord Jesus, to forget those things which not only obstruct my spiritual growth, but could also stop it completely. Amen.

August 31

Read: Psalm 146:1-10

Faith that sings songs of praise

I will praise the LORD all my life; I will sing praise to my God as long as I live.

– PSALM 146:2 –

The purpose of all of creation is to proclaim the glory of God. The most uplifting thing you can do is to contribute to that praise. It is a sad fact that we give an inferior place to praising God in all areas of life – even in the practice of our religion.

When someone mentions praising and worshiping God, the average person involuntarily thinks of a formal church service: hymns in church; the reading of Scripture verses; communal prayers and sermons. A faith that brings praise to God is, however, much more than formal religious ceremonies. It is an attitude towards life inspired by our faith in Christ Jesus. To praise God is to gain the power of faith which sanctifies our everyday lives, because then God is in the center of our lives and all other things are arranged around Him.

There are many things that small children or very old people cannot do. But one thing we can all do with all our hearts, right from the beginning of our lives to the very end, is to praise the Lord.

Honoring and praising God happens with every simple, noble deed we do in His Name, and with every uplifting thought in our minds. Let us then leave this month behind with rejoicing in our hearts and enter the new month with the motto, "Praise the Lord!"

Praise the LORD, O my soul; all my inmost being, praise His holy name. Praise the LORD, O my soul and forget not all His benefits" (Ps. 103:1-2). Amen.

SEPTEMBER

September 1

Read: 2 Corinthians 5:11-21

Love and growth

Therefore, if anyone is in Christ, he is a new creation; the old has gone, the new has come! All this is from God, who reconciled us to himself through Christ and gave us the ministry of reconciliation.
– 2 CORINTHIANS 5:17-18 –

During this month we are going to explore the concepts of love and growth.

May God in this time open your heart to His love; your mind to His wonders; your ears to His voice and your entire life to His holy and loving presence.

May you receive from His hand His peace for your unease, His forgiveness for your guilt, His presence in your loneliness, His light when your way becomes dark, His guidance on your pilgrimage and His love for every day. Many people fervently wish they could start their lives anew. They are tortured by feelings of guilt from the past, or by failures and missed opportunities. They want to erase these and other negative things.

The living Christ offers you just such an opportunity! Despite what you are or what you have done, He asks you to allow Him to come into your life and to take control of your life. He does not break down doors – He waits for you to open them (see Rev. 3:20).

While you are reading, simply ask God to take control of your life and to fill it with His Holy Spirit. Surrender your life unconditionally and confess to Him everything that depresses you and causes you sorrow. Do it boldly, because you know that He understands; He cares for you and loves you deeply. Then accept the "new life" in faith. He erases the past completely and never thinks of it again. Follow Him while He guides you out into the light of a new life of love and spiritual growth. He is waiting for you at the point of departure to a new, meaningful and joyful life. Praise His Name!

Holy Lord Jesus, I open my life to Your Holy Spirit. I thank You that my life has found new purpose, sense and meaning. Amen.

Read: Proverbs 27:1-10 September 2

Today – your most precious possession

Do not boast about tomorrow, for you do not know what a day may bring forth.

— PROVERBS 27:1 —

Every responsible person plans thoroughly for the future. If you fail to plan, you plan to fail.

This does not make today less important. On the contrary: the past is history and the future is an unborn dream. All that we actually have is today! If we boast about tomorrow and neglect today, we are foolish and living in a fool's paradise.

Alexander the Great usually laid siege to a city in order to force it to surrender. Then he lit a great fire which burned outside the city for an entire day. If people surrendered before the fire went out, everything would go well. If they refused to surrender, he used battering rams to destroy the city walls mercilessly.

The only thing we have to do to ensure our safety today is to surrender ourselves to Christ. We surrender our hearts, our lives and desires unconditionally and without delay to our King and Conqueror, Christ. He is keeping a light burning – the light of the gospel which has been lit with the wood of the Cross and which is flaming brightly in the dark night of our sin and distress. When this light has gone out there is no hope for salvation. Failing to surrender because you are hoping for a better future, is foolish.

As a child I once saw a dog sleeping peacefully while the sparks off the village blacksmith's anvil were raining down on him. Similarly we calmly continue with our old lives ignoring the challenges of the gospel.

Do not delay what you have to do today. Tomorrow may never come. Procrastination is the thief of time, and in view of eternity, this is a fatal mistake.

Loving Savior, I thank You that I may receive the gift of redemption from Your hand. Grant me mercy that I may use it wisely today. Amen.

September 3

Read: Psalm 102:13-28

Use time wisely

But you remain the same, and your years will never end.
– PSALM 102:27 –

There are people who determine the quality of a life according to the number of years a person has lived. They say that a person had a long innings and then forget that it is not the duration of the innings that counts but the number of runs he made.

It is the content of a life that determines its length. A long life, empty of good deeds, surrender to God and service to one's fellow man, can be very short if God measures it. Then again, a short life, filled with love, godliness and love for your fellow man can be very long in the eyes of God.

Sometimes a promising life is cut short and you wonder why God allowed it. Just remember, God never makes mistakes. We are bound by time and a concept of earthly promises. God, however, is omniscient: He knows whether a task has been completed on earth and whether a life can be promoted to higher service.

There are many people who have reached the evening of their lives. It can be said that they have achieved much and have enjoyed the love and respect of their fellow man. Others again, never reached their peak, but their influence is clearly visible for generations.

The Master Himself was in His early thirties when He was crucified. Many of those who stood at the foot of the cross probably mourned the fact that He had to die before His work of redemption was completed. Precisely that – and infinitely more – was achieved by His death. The full extent of His redemption would be difficult to determine.

Our consolation is that amidst our changing and uncertain lives, God remains the same. Do not judge the value of a life according to its duration, but according to what was achieved in that life through the power and mercy of God.

Give me, O heavenly Father, a clear view of eternity, so that I can make a true evaluation of time. Amen.

Read: 2 Peter 3:1-18

September 4

Ensure that you are growing spiritually

Grow in the grace and knowledge of our Lord and Savior Jesus Christ.

– 2 PETER 3:18 –

The point of departure for our spiritual lives is unconditional surrender to the love of Christ. However, afterwards it is essential that we grow. Growth is the goal and purpose for most people. Children wish to become adults; short people want to be taller; a weak person longs for a powerful and muscled body. Gardeners and farmers sow seeds so that flowers, vegetables and fruit will grow. The best methods are accurately followed to ensure maximum growth.

This is similar to our spiritual lives. If we do not work at it in a dedicated, committed way, no spiritual growth will occur. A life starving for spiritual food will never develop to its full potential. It will be handicapped in its development and lack spiritual quality.

Just as you would care for your body or a cherished plant, you should care for your spiritual life conscientiously by nourishing it with the Word of God. Thus, you create a sturdy foundation for spiritual growth. In addition you should be aware of the presence of the living Christ. This must happen every day so that He can accompany and guide your growth. His Holy Spirit must reveal to you the true meaning of His eternal Word.

Pay serious attention to it and you will be surprised to discover that you are developing your full spiritual potential.

Master, help me through Your good Spirit to nourish my spiritual life so that I will grow to reveal Your nature in my life. Amen.

September 5

Read: Ephesians 4:1-16

Growth in Christ

Instead, speaking the truth in love, we will in all things grow up into him who is the Head, that is, Christ.

– Ephesians 4:15 –

It is thrilling to see new life bursting forth all around us in spring, and to become aware of the shades of green. Christianity without spiritual growth can never bring deep and true joy and satisfaction. You did not only accept Christ with your mind when you invited Him into your life. It was more than just doctrines and beliefs. You promised eternal faithfulness to Christ. The strength or weakness of that faith depends on your relationship with the risen Savior.

The strength of any human relationship depends on the growing intimacy of communication between the two parties. Through the interaction of shared hope, fear and ideals, people develop a clearer knowledge of each other. Without communication, friendship will die.

In the Christian life the Master knows you better than you know yourself. You, however, can only understand Him better if you share your life with Him unconditionally.

You will grow in Christ only when you no longer focus your attention on yourself. Your own interests, ambitions and desires will be moved to the background for the sake of those people you rub shoulders with every day: those who experience distress; those who are unattractive; the lonely and the underprivileged who stagger along in the darkness of life.

Growing in Christ is not meant as an exercise to create a comfortable religious feeling which is far removed from the hard realities of life. It is supposed to motivate the spirit to positive action. Renew your life of prayer and rediscover the Spirit of Christ in the Scriptures. Discover that growth in Christ leads to new dimensions of life.

Lord Jesus, make my faith a dynamic power through the renewal of my prayer life and Bible study. Do this through the work of the Holy Spirit and give me abundant spiritual growth. Amen.

Read: Psalm 18:17-35

September 6

With God today

With your help I can advance against a troop; with my God I can scale a wall.

— PSALM 18:29 —

It is essential that we live according to this motto every day in a practical way.

When you wake up in the morning, confirm it. Be aware of the presence of God, of His omnipresence and of your unity with Him. Thank Him for His guidance and safekeeping and His almighty love every day.

Trust God today. Develop a constant sense of trust in Him for every situation that life may bring. Do it especially when danger and fear threaten your life.

Control your thoughts. Nip every worry in the bud. Relax and turn your thoughts towards God. Put your problem at His feet and leave it with Him in faith. Trust the Lord with all your heart.

Guard against criticizing, judging, hating, ridiculing and envy. Remember that it is more detrimental to you than to the object of your feelings. Forgive completely. Remove all old grievances from your system. Remember that Christ has forgiven you completely. Forgive yourself, in particular for mistakes and misdemeanors of the past – Christ did this a long time ago.

Try to be fully aware of the presence of God. Always remember that you live, move and exist in Him. Discover His living presence through His Spirit in your heart.

Ensure that you are alone with God at least once a day in prayer, meditation and contemplation of the Scriptures. Relax, let go and let God, until you become aware of His holy presence. Let the Spirit work in and through you, and recognize the omnipotence of God in everything you undertake.

I thank You, merciful Father, for all the spiritual aids You have made available to me so that I can see Your omnipotence and loving presence. In the Name of Jesus and with thanksgiving I pray. Amen.

September 7   Read: James 1:1-11

Misfortune as a means of growth

Consider it pure joy, my brothers, whenever you face trials of many kinds, because you know that the testing of your faith develops perseverance.

– JAMES 1:2-3 –

If the Christian faith could have guaranteed deliverance from all temptations and suffering from the moment it was accepted, everyone would want to be a Christian. However, Christ never makes this promise in His pronouncements. On the contrary, although Christ offers His followers a new relationship with God, He guarantees them that they will be tempted and will experience times of suffering and problems.

One of the inspiring themes of the New Testament is that by carrying a burden, a disciple will grow in grace and to a deeper understanding of and identification with his Master. The Christian is urged to rejoice when the road becomes difficult, because in every misfortune it is possible to prove that God is all-sufficient and that faith in Him can carry us through.

Handling every situation without self-pity requires a positive faith in the eventual purpose of God and in His goodness and love. This again requires faith in the risen Christ, a faith which rises above fear for the unknown. It enables the followers of Christ to experience that inner joy which is the portion of everyone who lives in harmony with Christ.

It is definitely true that you can grow as a Christian through suffering and temptations. If you deal with your misfortune in a positive and constructive way, you will gradually develop a deeper understanding and love for your Father and Lord. It is an important component of spiritual growth.

In Your power and strength, holy Master, I can transform defeat into victory. I praise Your holy Name with thanksgiving. Amen.

Read: Revelation 21:1-8   September 8

Do it in a new way

He who was seated on the throne said, "I am making everything new!"

— REVELATION 21:5 —

Monotony creeps into our lives subtly. Perhaps you have done the same thing in the same way for years, until you are convinced that it could not be done in any other way. You have become so familiar with the well-known routine, that you regard change with suspicion and horror. You just cannot believe that there might be a more effective method. Then you plod along in a monotonous way because you are too scared or lazy to try a new approach to an old problem or situation.

It will be worthwhile to do some self-examination and to determine whether you have become the victim of a habit which requires no conscious thought or action from you. Many people live without thinking: they go to work in exactly the same way every day; their actions are automatic and they have created a way of life that requires no conscious effort or original thought from them. The days become months and the months become years with a monotonous regularity that destroys the soul and the personality.

Try to be different. Be original in your attitudes, thoughts and actions. You will then discover new interests which will give you energy and inspiration for your daily life.

Just as monotony can destroy your interest in everyday things, it can also destroy your spiritual life. Old, familiar prayers are mumbled or rattled off without emotion. It prevents you from becoming fully aware of Christ. Pray in unexpected places, at different times and with different people, and you will approach your faith in a new way. It will become sparkling and challenging and will lead to unparalleled growth and joy.

Guide and Lord, a new freshness, originality and beauty enter my life when I am close to You. Guide me further on my path through Your Holy Spirit. Amen.

September 9

Read: 1 Corinthians 3:1-9

Spiritual growth is a process

You are still worldly. For since there is jealousy and quarreling among you, are you not worldly? Are you not acting like mere men?

— 1 CORINTHIANS 3:3 —

There are many people who believe that God is great, yet they view life narrow-mindedly. They accept the basic Christian principle that God is love, but they do not want Him to touch their lives with kindness. They know that He promises His strength to all who serve Him sincerely, and yet they remain weak. They say that they believe in God, but they have never experienced His transforming presence in their lives.

Tragically these people remain spiritually immature. They might perhaps be active in rendering Christian and religious service, but as soon as matters go against their wishes, they refuse to cooperate. If they cannot be the leaders, they refuse to follow. Their characters reveal their spiritual immaturity.

The example of Christ and His actions is a source of enrichment to His followers. It broadens their view on life and their understanding of the actions of other people. While the process of growth and maturity continues in their lives, they develop a greater understanding of their fellow man and an increasing love is reflected in their lives.

If the love of Jesus Christ controls your life through His indwelling Spirit, there will be no room for jealousy, struggle or bitterness. These immature emotions and attitudes will fall like dry leaves from branches when spring arrives. Only God's immeasurable love can enable this.

Through the power of Your indwelling Spirit, Holy Lord, I want to become spiritually mature. Make me a channel of Your love and an instrument of Your peace. Amen.

Read: Ephesians 4:17-24

September 10

Challenge to a new life

You were taught to be made new in the attitude of your minds; and to put on the new self, created to be like God in true righteousness and holiness.

– EPHESIANS 4:22-24 –

It is when our Christianity becomes trapped in the quicksand of abstract theories and pointless speculation that it loses its enthusiasm and joy. When it is accepted for what God intended it to be – a new lifestyle – the full glory can be seen and appreciated.

People experienced the impact Jesus' life had when He was on earth. They saw the confirmation of divine love in the way He touched their lives and healed them. They listened to God's truth from His lips. When they were with Him, they knew unmistakably that they were in the presence of God.

Many would claim that He breathed new life into an old and respected religion. They would, of course, be correct, but, and this is even more important: He gave this new life to everyone who came to Him and confessed the sovereignty of Christ in their lives.

The risen Christ still offers true life today to everyone who comes to Him. When He takes control of a life, false values are rejected, sins are forgiven, new goals are set, twisted human relationships are corrected through forgiveness and love, self-interest becomes of secondary importance and the obedience to God's will becomes of paramount importance.

The revolution that takes place in the life of a Christian is beneficial and constructive. At the same time it is demanding, because it demands the surrender of your heart and life to your Savior. Then a new life awaits you under the loving guidance of the Spirit of Christ.

I thank You, Lord Jesus, for the new life You have given me out of love. Amen.

September 11

Read: 2 Corinthians 8:1-15

The art of surrender

They did not do as we expected, but they gave themselves first to the Lord and then to us in keeping with God's will.

– 2 Corinthians 8:5 –

You can only experience a full and satisfying life if you are prepared to give your best. You have a definite contribution to make in determining the quality and joy in your life as well as in the lives of others.

Initially you may distrust this pronouncement, because you may think that you have no contribution to make at all. If you limit your concept of "giving" to money or possessions, prestige or social standing, it may be true.

If someone experiences strong opposition and stands alone in a struggle for justice, and you firmly stand by him, it will be enormously encouraging to him. Perhaps there is someone in your family who feels that you are taking him for granted. By showing your love, you will convey joy and inspiration to his life.

True love, understanding, loyal friendship and other influences which bring about reconciliation and healing are yours to give freely.

While you are giving these treasures to others, your own life will be enriched beyond your wildest dreams. It is impossible to be a source of blessing to others without being richly blessed yourself. Stagnant areas of your life will be regenerated and will bear fruit and infertile areas will become productive.

You must however first give yourself joyfully and unconditionally to God and then to your fellow man. It is an enriching experience of exciting spiritual growth.

Holy God and Father, I thank You for the blessings I receive from Your treasury so that I may also be a blessing to others. Amen.

Read: Proverbs 3:1-18 September 12

Do you feel like you've reached a dead end?

In all your ways acknowledge him, and he will make your paths straight.

– PROVERBS 3:6 –

You may experience a time in your life when it feels as though everything has come to a standstill. Your daily routine continues, but everything seems futile. It feels as though you have come to a dead end and you start wondering whether life is worthwhile at all.

Honestly ask yourself why you have reached this dead end. Have you lost sight of the vision of what life holds for you? Is your self-confidence vanishing at a disconcerting tempo? And, most important of all, has your spiritual enthusiasm decreased to such an extent that God is no longer the most important aspect of your life? The fact of the matter is that no one who has placed God in the center of his life, who loves Him and whose life is arranged according to Christian principles, ever asks the question, "Does life have meaning?" Neither do you reach a point of extreme frustration and despair.

Introspection under the guidance of the Holy Spirit is essential. If you are honest and truly get to know yourself, you can control your attitude towards life and you will not allow circumstances or problems to control you. Worry, fear, tension, pressure, hurt, suffering and grief are factors that contribute to creating an immature and frustrated life.

These diseases of the spirit can only be rooted from your life by the power of the indwelling Christ. When you have given your life to Him unconditionally and live being fully aware of His presence, a new life will start for you, and every God-given day will have meaning and purpose.

I thank You, heavenly Guide, that You give direction and meaning to my life. Make me obedient to Your will through the guidance of Your Holy Spirit. Amen.

September 13   Read: 1 Chronicles 11:1-9

Tell me who your friends are ...

David became more and more powerful, because the LORD Almighty was with him.

– 1 CHRONICLES 11:9 –

There is truth in the saying, "Tell me who your friends are and I will tell you who you are." It is inevitable that one eventually becomes like one's friends. Some people still associate with their old worldly friends after they have given their lives to Christ. They think that since the quality of their lives has changed, their friends' lives will also change. This seldom happens.

What is more likely to happen is that a new Christian will gradually revert to his old friends and old standards and eventually to his old way of life. The company you keep uplifts you or pulls you down to its level.

When you have accepted Christ as the Lord and King of your life, and you have committed and dedicated yourself to Him, you should seek and maintain fellowship with Him on a daily basis. You should do everything in your power to strengthen your relationship with Him. This happens through prayer, contemplation, Bible Study, obedience to His will and service to Him and your fellow man. Strive to make your walk with God a wonderful reality.

Maintaining a meaningful relationship with Him from day to day will have an amazing effect on your lifestyle. Your insight will broaden and you will have a greater understanding of other people. You should be able to have a life of joy and fulfillment, which will attract the type of friends who will also have a living relationship with Jesus Christ.

In this way, together you become instruments in His hands. While you seek Him in your fellowship with other believers, He will enrich your life with His lovely presence.

Lord, my Lord, inspired by Your Holy Spirit and in fellowship with Your faithful children, I want to grow in strength, grace and maturity. Amen.

Read: John 3:1-21

September 14

We belong to one another

"For God so loved the world that he gave his one and only Son."
— JOHN 3:16 —

It is a glorious and overwhelming truth that you belong to God. Undeserving and unworthy as you may be, the eternal Father has called you and made you His child. The love that He has poured out on you reassures your innermost being and frees your spirit, so that you unmistakably know that you belong to Him.

You might not be able to explain this experience, but you know to your own joyous satisfaction that you are God's child and that you belong to Him. Yet, there is a still greater and more glorious truth born out of God's love: not only do you belong to God, but He belongs to you. God, in His immeasurable love, has made Himself available so that you can own Him to the extent in which you accept Him. Once you have accepted Him and made this truth your own, you enter a new dimension of life.

God gives you wisdom so that you can deal with your problems in a calm and constructive way. You become aware of a dynamic inner strength that is not your own or from yourself. This strength helps you to resist temptations and to live victoriously. God becomes a living reality as He starts to flow through you to others.

To be owned by Him and to own Him, are the two greatest experiences of the Christian faith. They bring the reality of God back to the everyday life.

Lord God, I rejoice in the fact that I belong to You and that I experience inner strength and power when I realize that You belong to me. Amen.

September 15

Read: Jude 1-25

The responsibility is yours

Keep yourselves in God's love as you wait for the mercy of our Lord Jesus Christ to bring you to eternal life.

– Jude 21 –

Salvation, God's free and undeserved gift to man, is one of the cardinal principles of the Christian faith. Nothing you can do can earn you God's love, but He gives it freely to everyone who wants to accept it.

It is often said that what you receive for free is not appreciated as much as something you earn through effort and exertion. Who can ever earn the love of God? God's love for you is complete and perfect. The only obstruction that may prevent you from experiencing a deeper awareness of His love is your inability to receive it to a greater degree. The necessity to deepen and enrich your spiritual life is a holy responsibility which you will have to accept if you want to experience a meaningful relationship with God through Jesus Christ. The Father has already given you His love and nothing can detract from that. Whether you utilize this gift or not depends entirely on you.

Remaining aware of God's love requires prayer, Bible study, meditation and a quiet waiting on the Lord's presence. A Christian is just as strong and steady as his quiet time. Your quiet fellowship with God should cause Christ's presence to submerge your whole life. Your sanctuary and quiet time become your power station, which enables you to cope with the demands of life.

The Master is with you all the time. It is your responsibility to admit and confess His presence in every situation in life.

God of love, praise and thanksgiving flow spontaneously from my inner being when I rejoice in Your undeserved love. May Your love flow through me to the world through the working of Your Holy Spirit. Amen.

Read: Malachi 1:1-14   September 16

Immortal love

"I have loved you," says the Lord. *But you ask, "How have you loved us?"*

— Malachi 1:2 —

Through the centuries people have questioned the love of God. The Old and the New Testaments make this clear. It is noted in the secular history. It has also undoubtedly happened in your life or in the lives of people you know. There are times when everything seems hopeless and lost, when hope is destroyed by despair. People then ask, "How can a God of love allow something like this to happen?"

The greatness of God's love for us can never be determined or measured. His love is too staggeringly great for that. We find it essentially inconceivable.

Who else but a loving God and Father will persist in loving humankind, who have been so disobedient and rebellious? Who else but a loving God and Father would have left the glory of heaven and come to earth in the person of Jesus Christ, taking on the human body of a servant to live and suffer among people?

Who else but a loving Redeemer God, would have sacrificed His life to save the people who despised and humiliated Him; a world which cruelly crucified Him?

Who else but a loving God, through the Spirit, would have given mortal people the power to do great deeds? Christ is the loving God who will come again, to gather those who belong to Him so that they can live in eternal happiness with Him.

This is the love of God our Father, our Lord and King! Praise the Lord, O my soul, and forget not His mercies!

God of love and mercy, when I consider what You have done for me, I dare not doubt Your overwhelming love. Amen.

September 17   Read: Philippians 3:1-13

Christ first

I want to know Christ and the power of his resurrection and the fellowship of sharing in his sufferings, becoming like him in his death.
– PHILIPPIANS 3:10 –

Many of God's servants are so busy working for Him that they do not have time to spend a few quiet moments alone with Him. Christian service without prayer is not deliberate. Few people dare say, "I work for God and therefore I do not need to pray!" They are so busy working for His Kingdom that their activities cancel the necessity for solitude and quiet time. They are working for God without experiencing the presence and power of the living Christ.

Trying to serve Christ without the inspiring strength of the Holy Spirit leads to frustration, and eventually to spiritual suicide. When the ideal of what you are trying to do for Him fades away, when your spiritual reserves are not supplemented by prayer and meditation, when you try to maintain a Christian testimony without experiencing Christ as most important in your life; then your service will become powerless, without any effect or impact on the world.

Wherever in life you want to serve the Master, you must put Him first in everything you do. He must be placed first on the agenda of your life. The service you offer Him must be the result of experiencing Him firsthand and not the result of hearsay.

Only if you put Him first in everything, can you determine your goal in life according to His will. If you place Christ first in your life, it makes you a more effective and acceptable servant.

Lord, my Lord, I place You first in my life. You are my inspiration and my motivating strength in the service that I offer You. Amen.

Read: 1 John 3:11-24

September 18

Love transforms

Dear children, let us not love with words or tongue but with actions and in truth.

– 1 JOHN 3:18 –

So many people think love is only an emotion which changes according to the circumstances we find ourselves in. The popular song, "I'm in the mood for love", expresses the transience people associate with this dynamic power.

Love is far more than a theory or passing emotion. It is the expression of the character of God and should never be taken for granted. It surrounds you continuously, and even though it is often abused by greed and lust, it is the way in which God has revealed Himself to mankind. God is love. Divine love should first be accepted intellectually before it can become visible in man's life. It can never be taken for granted, but has to be accepted consciously. When this happens, it transforms your character and your personality. You are in a complete new relationship to God.

The knowledge that God loves you makes you humble but at the same time gives you self-confidence. You are humbled because He calls you His child, despite yourself. You develop self-confidence, because you can live victoriously through the spiritual strength that He gives you.

When you start experiencing His love in your daily life, you will find that you do not have a vague, pious desire to do good. It means carrying His love into every aspect of your life. It is often difficult and demanding. It is only when you allow God to love you that such a love is possible.

God of love, when I find it difficult to love, I plead with You to continue Your love in my life, despite myself. Amen.

September 19

Read: 1 Corinthians 13:1-13

Work on your love

It always protects, always trusts, always hopes, always perseveres.
– 1 CORINTHIANS 13:7 –

True love never gives up hope. It is a great tragedy when love is taken for granted and left unanswered by mutual love. Love reacts to love, but it can fade away and eventually die when it is exposed to neglect, ridicule or indifference.

The truth that love is like a delicate flower is often ignored. A couple who court each other express their love by doing things for each other. Nothing is seen as too much trouble to satisfy the loved one. Many people regard the marital promise as the ultimate expression of this love. Soon afterwards, the spirit of loving concern starts fading, and selfish demands take the place of sacrificial love.

If after the wedding, people would just show the same concern for one another's interests as before the wedding, there would be fewer divorces. Love finds expression in many ways. It often means that you should give yourself in sacrificing service without thinking of a reward. You often experience pain when you watch a loved one destroying himself deliberately. There are times when you cannot do anything but observe and pray.

Love is a positive force that should be applied practically otherwise it will wane. Therefore, we should work on our love at all times. God's Holy Spirit is always willing to assist us.

Source of all true love, enable me daily and throughout my life to appreciate love and to work at it all the time. Amen.

Read: 1 Corinthians 13:1-13

September 20

The wonder of love

Love is patient, love is kind. It does not envy, it does not boast, it is not proud. It is not rude, it is not self-seeking, it is not easily angered, it keeps no record of wrongs. Love does not delight in evil but rejoices with the truth.

– 1 CORINTHIANS 13:4-6 –

In everyday language this means: when I felt weak and worthless, you had time to listen to me and your love picked me up again. When I could not pray, you prayed with me. When I was afraid, you were tender with me; your love was patient and kind. When I searched for the will of God, you searched with me. I came to you with my problems and you helped me.

When I was successful, you also rejoiced. Because you accepted your limitations, I learnt to accept mine. When I needed a sounding board for my thoughts, you listened objectively. When I had to make a choice, you did not place me under pressure, but you prayed with me. When you knew that I was hurt, you came and said, "I am sorry!" When I had to speak about myself, you gave me your undivided attention.

I made mistakes and failed, but you accepted me. When I behaved badly, you continued to love me, hoping that I would realize my mistakes. When I hurt you, you forgave me. When I was eager to accept responsibility, you did not remind me of my previous mistakes.

When I was envious of other people's gifts, you taught me to appreciate my own. When I saw only the negative, you pointed out the positive. When I was lonely, when I doubted and strayed, your faith supported me. When I took life too seriously, you taught me to laugh. If I speak, you understand, even if I do not understand myself. When you had authority over my life, you used it for service and not for your own profit. Due to your presence in my life, I grew in my commitment to and love for Christ. In this your love has become immortal.

I thank You, Lord God, for people who love me and make me understand something of Your unfathomable love for me. Amen.

September 21

Read: 1 Corinthians 13:1-13

Love is eternal

Love never fails.

– 1 Corinthians 13:8 –

God is love! God is immortal and indestructible and so is His love for us. Love does not only link us to one another, but also to the almighty, eternal God. Because of that our love can also be indestructible.

That is why I will love you today, tomorrow and forever. I will love you during all the tomorrows God may grant me; for as long as a love song lives in the hearts of people, and for as long as there is only a single shining star in the heavens.

I will love you in springtime when the breeze is but a soft stirring among the tender branches. I will love you in the rain when deep red roses appear; in summer, when the sun's golden rays scorch. Even in the loneliness that autumn brings despite its wealth of richly shaded color and copper leaves.

I will love you in the night when the field is white, enfolded in the icy shawl of frost and snow. As long as the mountains are standing firm, and as long as the eternal swell of the deep ocean continues, I will love you!

I will love you to the end of time, as much as a heart can love, and after death, in God's glory, our love will still continue. Wherever you may be, as long as a word of love may be said, and as long as God's love can ignite human hearts, that long will I love you.

True love is as immortal as God Himself: God *is* love. God guided us to each other so that we can understand something of love – something of God Himself.

I thank You for the wonderful gift of love, O Father. Let me handle it with care and in prayer under the guidance of the Holy Spirit. Amen.

Read: 1 John 4:7-21   September 22

Love has many facets

Dear friends, let us love one another, for love comes from God. Everyone who loves has been born of God and knows God. Whoever does not love does not know God, because God is love.
                                                    – 1 John 4:7-8 –

There is no substitute for love. It is the most precious gift of God to us. A piece of heaven itself – no, of God Himself – that He has put in our hearts. Nothing can take the place of love: not the languages of people or the tongues of angels; not the gift of prophecy; not knowledge. Not the giving of all my possessions or the surrendering of my body as a sacrifice – not even the faith that can move mountains. Without love I am nothing.

Love, like God's love, is indestructible. It is our guarantee that every true love relationship in our life will last. So indestructible is love that it is all we will take on our journey to eternity. Hope will cease, because everything we hope for we will receive from God; faith will cease, because we will see Jesus. But love will remain.

Love, like God, is unselfish. Love does not ask, "What can I get from this relationship?" Love asks, "What can I give of my best, my most precious, my most noble?" That is why God gave His one and only Son: because He is love. Love gives of itself, above all!

Love is not afraid. John, the apostle of love, says that love drives out fear. Love is not afraid of yesterday, today, or tomorrow, because God is there. Love believes in God, believes in the future and believes in the object of its love. That is why love trusts at all times, in all circumstances and without words.

Distrust undermines a relationship, but love creates trust and fearlessness.

I thank You, Lord and Master, that You have come to teach us how to love. May love triumph in us. Amen.

September 23

Read: John 21:15-19

Tell Him about your love

"Yes Lord," he said, "you know that I love you."

– JOHN 21:15 –

It can happen so easily that spiritual truths become mere platitudes to us. Since they have been known to us for such a long time, they no longer have any impact on our thoughts. They no longer excite our spirit. The truths remain unchanged, but our attitude towards them varies according to our moods.

Great and holy values need to find expression all the time so that they can remain alive. You may believe with your whole being that God is love, but unless His love is expressed through your life, this faith remains ineffective, without warmth and commitment. A noble faith without practical application has little essential value.

You may say that you love God, but have you ever expressed that love in words? You may argue that God knows you love Him and that it is therefore unnecessary for you to say it. Love should never be taken for granted. If your love is not expressed in words, it will eventually cease. God does not take your love for Him for granted!

When you can say in all sincerity "God, I love You!" and it involves your heart and mind completely, you strengthen the bond you have with the Lord. When you fearlessly spell out your love, you will experience the inspiration that only the presence of the Master can bring. Rejoice in the truth that God loves you and that He rejoices in your mutual love.

Do not remain silent, but tell Him that you love Him. It enriches your spiritual life.

I love You sincerely, O Lord. You know everything. You know that I love You. I praise Your Name. Amen.

Read: 1 John 3:11-24

September 24

A challenge to our love

Those who obey his commands live in him, and he in them. And this is how we know that he lives in us: We know it by the Spirit he gave us.

– 1 JOHN 3:24 –

However great your love for Christ may be, you will always feel that it is inadequate when you compare it with His love for you. No one can ever love you as He loves you. It should not, however, keep you from striving to increase and deepen your love for Him.

The Christian who does not feel inspired to love the Master increasingly, runs the risk of becoming shallow and diminished. Without love there can be no spiritual growth or deepening of the Spirit.

In order to accept the challenge of your love, you should often meet Jesus in private. You cannot love Him unless your thoughts are turned to Him in prayer, Bible study and contemplation. It puts your spirit in harmony with the Holy Spirit.

You know undoubtedly from the Scriptures and the testimony of many of His disciples, that the Master gives Himself to those who love Him and serve Him. You dare not decline His offer. Allow Him to do His will freely in your life. Allow Him to let your love grow to maturity and bring it to Him as a sacrifice that will be pleasing and acceptable to Him.

Through your love for Him, you can never sabotage His love for you. But if you open your life to the tender influence of the Holy Spirit, and allow His love to work in and through you, your imperfect love is touched and sanctified by His holiness. He accepts the sacrifice of your dedicated life and your love. This is joy born from accepting the challenge of your imperfect love.

Source of love, I thank You that I may remain in You like the branch remains in the vine, and that my imperfect love can be nurtured by Your perfect love. Amen.

September 25

Read: Mark 12:28-34

Love cultivates understanding

To love him with all your heart, with all your understanding and with all your strength, and to love your neighbor as yourself is more important than all burnt offerings and sacrifices.

– MARK 12:33 –

To love Christ means to be freed from a condemnatory attitude. You are so aware of your own sins which He has forgiven in love, that you not only hesitate, but refuse to judge the shortcomings of others. Such deliverance creates a totally new approach and understanding of your fellow man and is born out of Christian love.

To love and understand in this way, does not mean that you are blind to the mistakes and thoughtlessness of others. When you accept these two basic approaches in your human relationships, you understand the intention as well as the result of someone's actions. Whether the saying "to know all is to forgive all" is true or not, it is an irrefutable fact that a deeper knowledge and understanding enable you to look past the sin and to have compassion with the sinner.

If the Spirit of God lives in you, you see the shortcomings of the transgressor, but you also understand what he can become through the redeeming power and love of the indwelling Christ. Although man has to accept the final responsibility for his sin, God lovingly sees the sinner separate from his sin.

When you see someone as God sees him, you'll realize that behind the rough and often unattractive exterior, a spirit is waiting to be freed and delivered to the fullness of a new life in Jesus Christ. You then develop an understanding and compassion that pleases God. Finally the love of Christ has been given free reign in your life.

Holy God and Father, You have looked at me with so much love and understanding. Help me, through Your Spirit, to love and to understand, so that the world around me will become a better place. Amen.

Read: John 2:1-12

September 26

Christ works miracles

His mother said to the servants, "Do whatever he tells you."
— JOHN 2:5 —

The first miracle Jesus Christ performed while He was on earth, happened at a wedding. In the same way, He wants to make a miracle of love out of every marriage today. He is intensely interested in our personal happiness – it is such a simple and yet breathtaking truth. He guides us to each other; He ignites the love in our hearts. He knows that "it is not good for man to be alone". And, wonder of wonders, He does not only undertake to accompany us during the wedding ceremony, but also for the whole of our wedded lives. He remains the Good Shepherd for the entire path of life.

Jesus was invited to a wedding in Cana. He never forces Himself on us. He does not randomly intervene in relationships. He does not force open doors. It is essential for us to invite Him in and say with Joshua, "But as for me and my household, we will serve the LORD" (Josh. 24:15). It is true, especially in a marital relationship that "unless the LORD builds the house, its builders labor in vain" (Ps. 127:1).

Like He did at the wedding feast, Christ gives a new sparkle and effervescence to ordinary, everyday things. Water becomes "good wine" in His hands. We so easily fall into a soul-destroying rut in our marriage. Christ rekindles the spark of true love and adventure to a relationship. The definite and irrefutable condition for this divine miracle lies in the words of the mother of Jesus to His disciples, "Do whatever He tells you." Obedience to His will as revealed in His Word, assures us that every marriage can become a miracle in His loving hands.

I thank You repeatedly, living Master, for the continuous miracle of love that You work in my life every day. Amen.

September 27   Read: 2 Corinthians 1:1-11

The wonder of God's love

Praise be to the God and Father of our Lord Jesus Christ, the Father of compassion and the God of all comfort, who comforts us in all our troubles.

– 2 Corinthians 1:3-4 –

We can so easily lose sight of the greatness and goodness of God. We become depressed so easily, and consequently we lose courage. When it seems as if things are going wrong for us, we give up all hope and fall into despair. We allow pessimism to rule our lives, and this obstructs our view of the future. Our plans and prospects are affected negatively. This happens because we have underestimated the omnipotence and love of God.

Secular and biblical history have confirmed that God miraculously intervened in the lives of people. Weakness was transformed into strength; grief was changed into joy and misfortune and apparent failure were transformed into triumphant victory. The greatest example of the omnipotence of God is the wonder of Golgotha. There Christ died and rose victoriously from the dead. The pitch-dark hopelessness of Golgotha gloriously grew into the shining hope and love of the blessed Easter festival!

When the prospects seem dark and you are depressed by anxiety and concern, remember the wonder of God's omnipotence and love. Surrender yourself and your circumstances unconditionally and trust Him. "Commit your way to the Lord; trust in Him and He will do this" (Ps. 37:5).

His immeasurable love will support and carry you through every crisis and at all times. This is how wonderful the love of our God is!

Lord Jesus, You know the days when everything is dark. I thank You that the omnipotence and love of God are available to me through You. I rejoice in Your comfort and power. Amen.

Read: Luke 4:1-13

September 28

Spiritual poverty

"Man does not live on bread alone."

– LUKE 4:4 –

When we speak of someone who is "poor" or "bankrupt", we usually refer to a person who lacks financial means or who is destitute. These undesirable circumstances can be the result of reckless extravagance or of circumstances that the individual had no control over.

Financial poverty is something which should be avoided at all costs. However, there are other forms of poverty and bankruptcy that are far worse. You may be rich in material possessions, yet be mean and nasty which is detrimental to your character and personality. You may suppress every urge to be generous because you fear that your generosity will be exploited or abused.

You may be spiritually destitute because you refused to give yourself to Christ unconditionally. Perhaps your prejudice deprived you of the full and satisfying life which could only be yours through Jesus Christ. A poor spirit and outlook deprives you of the pursuit of your God-willed purpose in life. It creates a negative attitude towards life.

Be determined to lead a full and rich spiritual life under the guidance of God your Father and the Holy Spirit, your Guide and Teacher. Put aside a few minutes every day, and break away from everyday duties. Concentrate your thoughts on the Lord. Let this time of reflection restore the balance in your life.

You will discover inner resources in your heart and soul that have been lying latent for a long period. Use them for your spiritual growth and enrichment. It will automatically result in a rich and satisfying spiritual life.

Father of mercy, give me a true appreciation for the things that are truly important in life. Let these be my wealth, through Jesus Christ and the Holy Spirit. Amen.

September 29   Read: Romans 5:1-11

Holy Spirit – cultivator of love

God has poured out his love into our hearts by the Holy Spirit, whom he has given us.

– Romans 5:5 –

The knowledge that Christ lives in you can cause a breathtaking spiritual revolution in your life. It inspires your thinking, broadens your outlook, gives you new confidence, creates enthusiasm, and gives a purpose and meaning to your daily existence. This is the work of the Holy Spirit, who assures you of your link with the Source of all true love.

However powerful and inspirational you may find this mutual love between you and your God, it should remain firmly anchored in the foundation of reality and faith.

Saying that you love Christ, yet refusing to alleviate the burden of an oppressed fellow man is a blatant renouncement of that love. If you love Him truly through the Holy Spirit, it makes you painfully aware of the need and distress of others and it creates in you the urge to do something about it.

If you say that you have the love of God in your heart, it will find expression in your words, in your attitude towards others and your willingness to serve others through His Spirit and in His strength. God expresses Himself through the love His Spirit works in your life. Then you accept the full responsibility of your faith in love through the Holy Spirit, your Teacher.

This love enables us to seek the highest good in our fellow man despite insults, injuries or humiliation done to you. It is a deliberate effort to seek nothing but the best for others with the help of the Holy Spirit. The foundation of this love is God Himself, and it was shown to us by Jesus Christ and revealed to us by His Holy Spirit.

O Spirit of Love, light up my mind and let Your love burn brightly in me. I am still weak; fill me with the power of Your love, in the Name of Jesus. Amen.

Read: Matthew 28:11-20   September 30

The invisible partner

"Surely I am with you always, to the very end of the age."
— MATTHEW 28:20 —

Let us end this month with joy and let us meet the future with this maxim: "Immanuel – God with us!"

Christ is the inspiration and source of a positive, faithful, Christian approach to life. Whatever your interpretation of the gospel may be, if it neglects making Christ a living reality and the center of your life, you will not achieve the highest and best for your spiritual life.

It is only possible to be aware of the living presence of Christ if He occupies the place of honor in your life. If He occupies an inferior position, you will never experience the wonder and joy that His presence can bring. You should spend quality time with Him if you want to know Him.

Although you cannot see Him, you can place yourself in His presence through faith. Speak to Him as you would speak to a trusted and loved friend. If you pour out your spirit and mind to Him, you will not only experience peace and deliverance, but also a stronger bond of love between you.

Talking to the living Christ before the bustle of the day starts creates a relationship which will have an immense and unparalleled influence on your thoughts and actions throughout the day. The wisdom and strength you find in quiet time with Him can be strengthened if you focus positively on His holy and blessed presence. Even brief prayers during the day can keep you in touch with Him.

Then He becomes a living reality in your life and you develop a balanced and self-assured spiritual life. Then you do not only exist, then you live actively and victoriously in His holy presence.

Companion of my life, Jesus my Lord, draw me to You continuously, so that I will be aware of Your living presence at all times. Amen.

OCTOBER

Read: Isaiah 30:19-26

October 1

Where to from here?

Whether you turn to the right or to the left, your ears will hear a voice behind you, saying, "This is the way; walk in it."
— Isaiah 30:21 —

Ralph Waldo Emerson said, "There is guidance for every one of us. And by listening humbly we will hear the right word." Children of the Lord are pilgrims on their way to eternity. We are not travelers without addresses on their way to nowhere. We are not seekers who never find what we are looking for.

Jesus Christ Himself has promised that they who seek, will find. Many people, however, live in continuous fear; fear of the past and fear of the future. We are often like children who are lost in a great and frightening jungle. We hear ominous sounds in the dark. We fear the terrible monsters with their flaming eyes who will charge at us. We cannot go back because we are scared. We cannot go forward because we are uncertain. We continue wandering in circles in dark woods.

We are often too scared to make choices. Should I go forward or backwards? Left or right? What shall I do? Who will advise me? How reassuring it is to hear a loving and confident voice behind you say, "This is the way; walk in it."

Sometimes we no longer hear the voices of people because we are not capable of listening or hearing. Our distress is too great. But God can reach us; His love says that there is a way out of every problematic situation. That way is Jesus Christ, He who said, "I am the way" (Jn. 14:6).

You need not be concerned about the end of this way. Abraham, Moses, the murderer on the cross, Paul and many others, ventured this way and reached their destination victoriously.

"Show me Your ways, O Lord, teach me Your paths; guide me in Your truth and teach me, for You are God my Savior" (Ps. 25:4-5). Amen.

October 2

Read: Psalm 37:1-11

Assured of God's guidance

Commit your way to the LORD; *trust in him and he will do this.*
— PSALM 37:5 —

The lives of scores of people prove that God does guide people. Every person sometimes experiences a bleak day when you want to question God's guidance. You should not think this way, because God does not ever stop guiding those who have entrusted their lives to Him unconditionally.

Guidance assumes an intimate and personal relationship. To enjoy God's guidance, you should live in close fellowship with Him. You must make time to be quiet in His presence so that you can hear His voice and be aware of the direction He wants you to take. You should lay your problems, your confusion and your wishes before Him in prayer regularly and faithfully. When you place God's will above your desires, you are practicing your faith. Face life with this type of faith every day and be sensitive and obedient in every step that God wants you to take.

"In all your ways acknowledge Him, and He will make your paths straight" (Prov. 3:6). Initially, it will be difficult to adjust your will to God's will and your progress on His way will be slow. But gradually you will experience the inner conviction that you want to do the will of the Father and walk in His way joyfully. In this way you learn that it is God who gives you guidance.

You will walk in His way without fear, in obedience, and in the knowledge that He is the Guide and the Finisher of your faith.

Doing Your will is the highest joy of my life. Thank You, O Master, that You make me willing every day to follow obediently where You may lead. Amen.

Read: Acts 1:1-11

October 3

Faith and practice

"Men of Galilee," they said, "why do you stand here looking into the sky?"

– Acts 1:11 –

There are pious, sensitive Christians who are inclined to overspiritualize. They have an interest only in spiritual matters. They would like to have wings to fly from this life straight into heaven. Forgetting the earthly because of the heavenly is just as wrong as forgetting heaven because of earth. There is a golden middle way between idolizing the world and feeling contempt for the world.

The indispensable and the perfect is above! But there are also things here below that may claim the dedication of our hearts and the strength of our hands. Our faith must not turn us into impractical dreamers – people who continuously stare up at heaven and neglect obvious responsibilities.

The life of labor on earth is an apprenticeship for eternal life. The Bible calls us time and again to perform our daily tasks faithfully. The light of our divine calling should however shine on it. We dare not exalt ourselves spiritually and stuff ourselves with heavenly pleasures, while neglecting our daily duty.

It is not a true divine fruit if it leaves you beyond the boundaries of this world, simply because you cannot escape the evil world inside you. Even if we are not of this world, we are living in the world.

There are rich blessings in looking up at heaven. Mount of Olives hours are essential. They empower you for the good struggle. But you should return to reality, your hand more firmly on the plough. The results of a Mount of Olives experience must become visible in your service to the Master. He will return as He left. May He find you ready when He comes, whether it is on the Mount of Olives, or while you are laboring in the field.

I thank You that Your Holy Spirit enables me to maintain a true balance between faith and speech, my Redeemer and Lord. Amen.

October 4

Read: Ephesians 5:6-20

Spiritual lethargy

Wake up, O sleeper, rise from the dead, and Christ will shine on you.

– EPHESIANS 5:14 –

The dictionary explains the meaning of "lethargic" as "a lack of energy and enthusiasm". If your spiritual life can be described in this way, you are facing an enormous challenge.

It is easy to become lethargic in spiritual things, since the demands and pressures of life are continuously influencing your mind. Before you realize what is happening, your prayer life has suffered and you are left with only a pretence of faith, robbed of life and vitality.

It requires courage to admit that your faith is ineffective. Excuses are readily available and you can convince yourself easily that they are true. When prayer loses its charm and when Bible study becomes an unbearable burden, you have to realize that something is radically wrong with your spiritual life.

God created you in His image and gave you His Holy Spirit. Identifying with you in this way He gave you the responsibility to live within His holy presence. He is with you always, but it is up to you to decide whether you want to be aware of His living presence in your life.

The closeness of Christ, the risen Lord, through the power of His indwelling Spirit, brings a glorious awareness of the reality of the Master. All lethargy, laziness and coldness will disappear before His radiance. Then you will live fully and with great expectations.

Lord Jesus, I praise Your Name. Through the inspiration and strength of Your good Spirit my faith is kept alive. Amen.

Read: Genesis 1:14-31

October 5

Being joyful in your labor

God saw all that he had made, and it was very good.
— GENESIS 1:31 —

God is the source of all creativity. He is the Creator who creates through labor. Divine approval rests on the nobility of labor. Creativity and work both have deep biblical roots. The command to work comes directly from God: "Six days you shall labor and do all your work" (Ex. 20:9). When man obeys this command he is filled with pride and joy. True creativity can now develop.

Honest work is noble; it enriches your soul because you are achieving God's purpose. That is why it requires sustained effort, applying your best and most noble in dedication and in faithfulness. Even if no one notices your hard work, God knows. This knowledge should determine the quality of your work.

Laboring and creating require sacrifice. It has a price tag, but not one involving money. It requires your time, your strength, your energy, your talents – your whole self. True creative work can never be slave labor. Your labor should justify sacrificing yourself.

Labor and creativity also require idealism and vision. You must be able to see the end result: a fantasy of labor! You have to believe in it. You must pursue your dream zealously. Do not remain an idle dreamer. Place a sword in the hands of your dreams.

To labor and to create require self-respect. You can labor and create because of God's grace. There is something somewhere that you can do. You dare not simply loaf. Even of your one talent you will have to give account. Always remember: God does not call the competent, but He empowers those He calls. It is exciting to labor and create in His strength, to His honor and glory.

Heavenly Father, I kneel in humble thanksgiving before You. I thank You for being able to labor and create and for the mercy of experiencing joy and pride in my labor. Amen.

October 6

Read: Job 1:1-22

Godliness

In the land of Uz there lived a man whose name was Job. This man was blameless and upright; he feared God and shunned evil.

– Job 1:1 –

Testimonials have lost their trustworthiness for various reasons. Like all things, they have been influenced by human weaknesses. Should God write a testimonial for a man, it is a completely different matter. Then we would pay attention, because it is absolutely trustworthy.

Through the Holy Spirit God gives Job's testimonial. The primary thing said of Job is that he was blameless. When people judge one another, they always place other qualities first: money; position; knowledge; beauty; achievement; influence and status. As an afterthought we might add, "Oh, yes, and he was something of a churchgoer." "Godly" is not a term we hear much these days. In our modern society godliness or piety seldom plays a role when judging character.

God's judgment is different. Yes, Job was definitely more than blameless. In the first three verses beautiful things are said about Job. But his godliness comes first in God's judgment of his personality. It is the most important quality in his life. It is the aspect on which all the others are based and from which they originate and develop. Without it, the other qualities are left hanging in the air – without roots, without purpose or sense.

Above all, God judges the heart of man. It forms the core of your life and personality. Godliness concerns the heart. It directs and focuses your heart on God. Godliness implies that your heart lives for heaven and from it. The heart can only be judged by God. And about Job, God Himself said, "He was blameless." May God also say it of you and me, by the grace of God.

Let me live united with You, the true Vine. Only then will I have a testimony that pleases You. Amen.

Read: John 13:1-17   October 7

Not now ... Later!

Jesus replied, "You do not realize now what I am doing, but later you will understand."

— JOHN 13:7 —

Sometimes confusing things happen in life and we find them so hard to believe that we want to blame God in our ignorance and confusion.

From the cradle to the grave, we are engaged in a struggle. However, what often worsens the situation is the fact that we sometimes do not understand what is happening to us at all. This is what happened to Peter.

Peter could not and did not want to understand: "No, You shall never wash my feet" (Jn. 13:8). He had to realize that he had to share in the cleansing grace of the Redeemer, Jesus Christ; he also had to learn the lesson of absolute humility. It was necessary to prepare him for the great task that he had to perform.

God can make every misfortune and puzzling situation in your life work out for your benefit. He can change your grief into gladness. Paul states it strikingly, "No discipline seems pleasant at the time, but painful. Later on, however, it produces a harvest of righteousness and peace for those who have been trained by it" (Heb. 12:11).

Perhaps something occurred in your life that left you bewildered. The Master has something to tell you, "If you do not understand now, believe and trust to the end. Do not fear, only believe. Later you will understand everything" (1 Cor. 13:12-13).

Your ways are so different from our ways, Lord Jesus, and Your thoughts are so much higher than ours. I do not always understand You, but I would like to follow You in faith and in trust. Grant me Your peace. Amen.

October 8

Read: Psalm 31:15-24

Take heart

Be strong and take heart, all you who hope in the LORD.
— PSALM 31:24 —

At no point in our lives is our courage threatened more severely than when a loved one dies. It is then that we need courage the most: courage to look ahead when we would rather look back; to be strong when we are deeply aware of our weakness; courage to reach out to others when we want to draw back into seclusion; courage to make decisions when we are broken and still dealing with yesterday.

Death has already deprived you of so many precious things; do not allow it to steal your courage! Courage is built on two pillars – faith in the purity of your goals and trust in your abilities. God provides the purpose as well as the strength for these two components. That is why we should take courage, persistently and steadfastly.

Fear and surrender without a struggle nourish cowardice but faith and endurance give us the victory. In faith, we should look past the temporary to the eternal. Then we will realize that death is just a landmark on the road to our loved ones who have gone ahead. While holding on to God's promises, our courage will grow and flourish. Jesus Christ said, "I will also keep you from the hour of trial that is going to come upon the whole world" (Rev. 3:10).

The deepest experiences of life are not found in superficial pleasure, but in the hour of our most painful grief. Grief can serve a holy purpose in our lives, if we receive the grace to take courage and have faith.

Almighty and loving God and Father, renew my courage every day through Your infallible promises. Allay my fears and make me courageous in imitating my Lord and Master, Jesus Christ. Amen.

Read: Psalm 27:1-14

October 9

The Christian's self-image

Though an army besiege me, my heart will not fear.

– PSALM 27:3 –

Nurturing feelings of inferiority and incompetence can paralyze you spiritually. You know that these negative feelings are contrary to the wishes of the indwelling Spirit of God for your life, but you feel incompetent to do anything about them. The only antidote for a poor self-image, insecurity and feeling inferior, is a positive attitude towards God, "The LORD is my light and my salvation – whom shall I fear?" (Ps. 27:1).

To achieve and maintain religious confidence, you must allow Christ into your life and dedicate yourself to Him completely. Then He will live in you and His power will be expressed through you. Prayer and meditation will strengthen your self-confidence and your faith in God.

You can rid your life of these negative and detrimental attitudes if God works in you through Christ, enabling you to lead a life of faith, trust and victory. The more you cultivate an awareness of the presence and omnipotence of Christ in your life, the stronger your faith and trust in Him will become.

Through this, you will conquer your feelings of insecurity and inferiority, and you will be able to lead a fruitful and satisfying life. Nothing is impossible if we are anchored in the power of Jesus Christ: "If you remain in Me and My words remain in you, ask whatever you wish, and it will be given you" (Jn. 15:7).

The treasury of God is wide open to those who want to enter into a life of fruitfulness and victory through Jesus Christ.

Eternal God and Father, dwell in me through Your Holy Spirit so that I will never be saddled with feelings of insecurity and inferiority. I praise You that I can do all things through Christ who gives me strength. Amen.

October 10

Read: Psalm 4:1-8

Share your joy

You have filled my heart with greater joy than when their grain and new wine abound.

— PSALM 4:7 —

Legend has it that when Lucifer was cast from heaven, he was asked what he missed most of his previous life. His sad answer was, "The joy, the trumpets, the song of angels in the morning, afternoon and evening. I miss the joy!"

If your Christianity makes you a happy person, you will want to share it with others. If it does not increase your joy, it is time for an honest self-examination in the light of the Holy Spirit.

Sharing your joy with others is a privilege. Your joy is enriched by unexpected actions of goodness to other people who do not expect it and cannot repay you for them – a word of encouragement to someone who is depressed or time spent with someone who is grieving. It reveals a spirit in harmony with God and in possession of a quiet inner joy that cannot be hidden.

Conveying joy to others is a way of life that will make your existence worthwhile. It builds friendships and creates sensitivity for the suffering of others. It enables you to think and act positively. You see the best of life and help others to see it as well. If your life and thoughts are filled with God, your joy is infinite.

When you live in joyful harmony with God, you show a spirit of consideration towards others, you are concerned about their well-being and you spread the virtue of practical joy that only God can bring into a life.

I thank You, Lord my God, that I can be a joyful person through Your love and grace and the merit of Jesus, my Lord. Amen.

Read: 1 Timothy 6:11-21   October 11

Success in perspective

Fight the good fight of the faith. Take hold of the eternal life to which you were called when you made your good confession in the presence of many witnesses.

                                        – 1 TIMOTHY 6:12 –

Success means different things to different people. The universal question is: What is success? How can one achieve it? The answers will vary from person to person. Yet, there are certain basic characteristics that have crystallized over the centuries.

Success is utilizing every day to the full; not postponing until tomorrow what has to be done today. We should plan for tomorrow, but only if we do our duty properly today. "Do not boast about tomorrow, for you do not know what a day may bring forth" (Prov. 27:1). Success is being aware of your limitations and seeing them as challenges rather than as stumbling blocks. There are things that others can do better than you. God's gifts to people differ, and He expects you only to give your best. Your limitations should only inspire you to give more of yourself in whatever you do; to do more than just the minimum of what is expected of you. It is a challenge to contribute your very best.

Success means hard work. There are no shortcuts to success. Someone once said, "The elevator to success is out of order; you must use the stairs." You should not try to get away with as little sacrifice as possible, but you should see how much of your most noble characteristics you can put into it.

Success is to place God first in your life. "But seek first His kingdom and His righteousness and all these things will be given to you as well" (Mt. 6:33). If God has the place of honor in your life and you approach life from His perspective, success is sure to follow.

Living Lord Jesus, I thank You that I am capable of doing everything through You who gives me strength. Grant me mercy and grace to put You in the center of my life and my plans, always. Amen.

October 12

Read: Proverbs 16:24-33

The glory of maturity

Gray hair is a crown of splendor; it is attained by a righteous life.
— PROVERBS 16:31 —

There is an idiom that states, "We all want to live forever, but none of us wants to grow old!" However, old age is an important component of God's plan for our lives. God intended our lives to be beautiful from the beginning to the end. Like a mighty chorus it rolls towards the breathtaking climax when the creature meets his Creator.

The charm of a newborn baby; the bubbling anticipation of the world-conquering youth; the strength of adulthood; the calmness, wisdom and peace of old age; these are all part of the stirring chorus we call "life".

Life has seasons, just like a year. One glides gradually and often unnoticed from one into another. Suddenly one day, it is winter and you are gray and old. But even this mature part of life has its own meaning and purpose. God wants us, within the restrictions that He imposes, to utilize and enjoy this period of our lives.

The challenge is exciting and rewarding. Encouraged by a goldmine of life experience, you can continue to live in faith and trust that the Lord will lead you to quiet waters where there is peace and to green pastures that offer rest.

The condition, according to the author of Proverbs, is that we should live righteously. For this we need the guidance of the Holy Spirit and an intimate and personal relationship with the Lord Jesus Christ. How beautiful is the crown that life then places on the head of the maturing person.

Teach me, O Lord, to receive every day with the right attitude, as a gift from Your loving hand and to live in such a way that it pleases You. I thank You for the wonder of a complete life through Jesus Christ. Amen.

Read: Psalm 127:1-5

October 13

Prayer relieves tension

In vain you rise early and stay up late, toiling for food to eat – for he grants sleep to those he loves.

– PSALM 127:2 –

Life increasingly makes demands on all of us. If we try to control the circumstances and problems that threaten to overwhelm us, tension starts building up in our minds and hearts. Insomnia, touchiness and depression are the external symptoms. People close to us see how our personalities change. We act unpredictably, but we are incapable of doing anything about it.

Preventing tension is easier than healing it. In order to do this, it is necessary to develop a meaningful life of prayer. Time spent quietly with God lifts the lid off the pressure cooker and brings calmness and balance. His holy· presence enriches your life and you are blessed.

Unnoticed, the tension disappears and you are your old self again. The Lord leads you to oases of peace and calm. You'll find rest and renewal in prayer. From the eddying whirlpool of life which threatens to rob you of your peace of mind, God brings you to the quiet of His holy fellowship. There you will find deliverance and healing.

Do not neglect this experience simply because you believe in action and drama. Time spent in prayer and meditation is not a luxury but a definite necessity. It heals the wounds of your heart through the tender touch of His Spirit.

Then you will deal with tension like a mature disciple of Jesus Christ. Then you will understand how the Lord God gives a good restful night to His loved ones.

I thank You, heavenly Father, that there is a place of peace and quiet in the eye of the storm. May I always find my strength and peace with You by being quiet and trusting in You. I thank You for the privilege of prayer. Amen.

October 14

Read: James 1:1-18

Faith and temptation

You know that the testing of your faith develops perseverance.
– JAMES 1:3 –

Defeat in our struggle against sin and temptation could have a very negative effect on our spiritual lives. Some of the Lord's children find it so discouraging that they fall into despair and have no confidence in their ability to be what God intended them to be. They doubt whether victory could ever be theirs because of what they regard as their inherent weakness.

Here is glorious encouragement for those people: Christ can help you! "Because He Himself suffered when He was tempted, He is able to help those who are being tempted" (Heb. 2:18).

Perhaps you have been struggling with a sin or moral weakness in your spiritual life for longer than you care to remember. You are sincere and honest in your efforts to break from this dominance, but many times your promises to God have been broken and you have been disheartened and defeated.

You may give up, but God would never give up on you. Christ assures you that you can be saved. He understands the force of temptation in your life, a force which causes you to hurt yourself. He was tempted just like you; yes, far worse! He resisted the temptation and won the victory, and He expects you to do the same through His power.

Because He understands and cares, it does not mean that He is condoning your weakness, but that He grieves over the power it has in your life. However, He makes power available to you to ensure that you can overcome your weakness to live triumphantly. "No temptation has seized you except what is common to man. And God is faithful; He will not let you be tempted beyond what you can bear" (1 Cor. 10:13).

You can triumph in His name by persevering steadfastly in your struggle!

Perfect Example, I thank You that You strengthen my faith and support me when I'm tempted. Amen.

Read: Job 30:16-31

October 15

Why do bad things happen to good people?

Yet when I hoped for good, evil came; when I looked for light, then came darkness.

– Job 30:26 –

We are sometimes confused by the injustice of the world. "Why?" is a timeless and universal question: as old as the first tear and as fresh as today's newspaper headlines.

We can understand it more easily when criminals die young, but why do committed children of God die untimely deaths? We can justify it when a villain is struck by a deadly disease, but why do innocent little children suffer? Misfortune in the life of an unbeliever can be understood, but why is there misfortune in the life of a believer?

The Word of the Lord answers these questions. Good people suffer because God does not make distinctions in His mercy: "He causes His sun to rise on the evil and the good, and sends rain on the righteous and the unrighteous" (Mt. 5:45).

We are subjected to law and order. Diseases strike down the good and the bad. However, good people have a faith that keeps them standing in the face of misfortune and disaster.

Suffering sometimes brings forth our best qualities. Paul says that when he is weak then he is strong. Love, patience, compassion and empathy are often born from suffering. Suffering inspires the search for solutions to improve situations.

Crucified Savior, I thank You that I have obtained redemption through Your suffering. Amen.

October 16

Read: Matthew 9:32-38

Compassion

When he saw the crowds, he had compassion on them, because they were harassed and helpless, like sheep without a shepherd.
— MATTHEW 9:36 —

Compassion and pity were the outstanding characteristics of the unique personality of Jesus Christ. These were signs of His greatness and not an indication of any form of weakness. These characteristics formed the core of His message and His life.

Scripture tells us that ordinary people enjoyed listening to Him and that they traveled great distances on foot to hear Him speak. His words reveal the depth of His wisdom and knowledge of human nature and the particular way in which He revealed God to humankind.

Nevertheless, the way in which He spoke these words did not only touch the minds of people, but also their hearts. They could feel His love for them and responded to that with mutual love.

Because the eternal Christ is alive, His compassion for people is just as real today as it was when He walked the roads in Palestine. While we are reading the gospel and rejoicing in the undying truths of what He told us, love for Him is generated in our hearts because of His love for us.

If life has disappointed you, or if you have failed somewhere and have been overwhelmed by despair, if you do not know where to turn for courage, strength and inspiration, then remember the compassion and empathy of the living Christ. He is with you in your distress by the power of His undying love. Get up and purposefully start building a new life for yourself. Christ cares for you; He understands and can give you courage and strength. He is the Lord who has sympathy with us in our distress.

I thank You, Lord Jesus, for the joyful knowledge that I have not been left to myself, but that I am an object of Your compassion and sympathy. Amen.

Read: Matthew 18:21-35   October 17

Get rid of your grievances

Peter came to Jesus and asked, "Lord, how many times shall I forgive my brother when he sins against me? Up to seven times?" Jesus answered, "I tell you, not seven times, but seventy-seven times."
– MATTHEW 18:21-22 –

It is very difficult to forgive, or to refrain from nurturing ill-feelings when you have been wronged or treated unfairly. When someone berated you, or ridiculed you, especially in the presence of others, it is almost impossible to even think of forgiveness. When you have been treated unjustly, you instinctively feel hostile. Your anger almost reaches boiling point and if it boils over, you just create more and greater problems. If you suppress ill-feelings, they become like an evil, festering sore in your heart, which will gradually poison your entire being and your thoughts.

Guard against collecting grievances and complaints. Eventually you yourself will become the helpless victim. However difficult it may appear, there is only one way to handle such a situation. In your prayers and in your heart, you should continuously confirm that you have forgiven the person who hurt you or caused you grief. Ask God for grace and strength so that you, through the Holy Spirit, can forgive as Jesus forgave.

Your forgiveness must not be restricted to your place of prayer. Jesus' command is, "Leave your gift there in front of the altar. First go and be reconciled to your brother; then come and offer your gift" (Mt. 5:24). Tell the other person that you forgive him, even if he has trespassed against you. Only then do you obtain deliverance.

Discipline yourself to forgive them who cause your suffering. The peace of mind you will experience as a result of this, will enable you to conquer your grievances and to live in peace with God, with him who trespasses against you and with yourself.

God of Love, give me the ability to forgive, as You forgave me in Jesus Christ. Amen.

October 18

Read: 2 Corinthians 12:1-10

Unsteady faith

"My grace is sufficient for you, for my power is made perfect in weakness."

– 2 CORINTHIANS 12:9 –

Perhaps there is some aspect of faith that you feel disappointed or insecure about. Someone you greatly respected because of his or her Christian principles came to a fall through some misconceptions, and this shook your faith. Perhaps some new religious doctrine started dominating your thinking and now you feel dissatisfied and discontented with your traditional beliefs. Suddenly you are uncertain about where you stand and what you must do.

In such an unhappy situation it is necessary that you recapture the certainty and enthusiasm of your faith. Do you remember the time when faith saturated every aspect of your life? Now coldness and aloofness have descended onto your spirit and your faith is unsteady. Why has this happened?

Through the neglect of prayer and spiritual discipline you have lost your awareness of the presence of the living Savior in your life and your faith diminished proportionally.

The amazing truth is that even when you feel far removed from the Master, He is as close to you as He has always been. He is only a prayer away. He is waiting to fill you with His Spirit and to heal your faith until it regains its previous strength and power.

What He requires of you is a renewed action of surrender and commitment. This will rekindle the flame of your love for Him and the flame of faith will lighten up your entire life.

I kneel in gratitude merciful Redeemer, because You still love me and still have confidence in me, even when my faith is unsteady. Strengthen my faith anew through Your Holy Spirit. I put myself on the altar before You. Amen.

Read: 1 Kings 19:1-13

October 19

You are never alone

I am the only one left, and now they are trying to kill me too.
– 1 KINGS 19:10 –

Feeling lonely can be a destructive experience. You need not necessarily be in a secluded or isolated place, since you can experience the excruciating pain of loneliness amidst the bustling crowds of a city or in a meeting.

You should first ask yourself why you are feeling lonely. A friendly person is never lonely for long. You may perhaps have experienced a few setbacks in your efforts to be friendly. But if you have offered or received friendship, you know the joy of companionship. If you are lonely, go out and offer your friendship to someone who experiences the same loneliness that you know so well.

When you are threatened by the searing pain of loneliness, strictly guard against self-pity. In your unhappy condition you are easily inclined to accuse others, or to accept the "poor-me" attitude and wonder angrily why it happened to you.

If you examine your own actions instead of accusing others, you may discover a spiritual shortcoming in yourself. Perhaps God is no longer a living reality to you and it feels as though you are roaming in a spiritual desert. It is a simple, yet deeply meaningful truth that your loneliness will be under control if you have a living faith.

The best antidote for loneliness is the awareness of Christ's living presence. It is God's gift of love to you although it may take some time to obtain. Prayer, meditation, Bible study and a single-mindedness to know Him, will allow Him to become a still greater reality for you. Then you will never be alone again. He promised you, "surely I am with you always, to the very end of the age" (Mt. 28:20).

With You in my life, Redeemer and Friend, I can never be alone.
I thank You for this with all of my heart and soul. Amen.

October 20

Read: Galatians 5:13-26

Walk in the Spirit

So I say, live by the Spirit, and you will not gratify the desires of the sinful nature ... Since we live by the Spirit, let us keep in step with the Spirit.

– GALATIANS 5:16, 25 –

Being controlled by the Spirit means having a daily and steady fellowship with the Spirit. In your daily conduct, in your struggle and striving, you follow the guidance of the Holy Spirit loyally. It is the essential characteristic of a person filled with the Spirit to serve God in sincerity and not to trust his own sinful flesh.

The guidance of the Holy Spirit is not something abstract or separate from life. It is not a watertight compartment of our lives that we unlock on Sundays or only on certain occasions. This is an error that impoverishes us and destroys our spiritual life. It forces us to live below the level of our spiritual breadline.

The Lord gives us His Spirit in His fullness to guide us every day, the whole day long. The attractions of the world are so vast that we desperately need the guidance of the Spirit, especially outside the church.

We should plead every day to be filled with the Spirit of God, since the world is consistently trying to deprive us thereof. Once again, read Galatians 5:19-21 where we find a catalogue of the sinful practices of man that the Spirit must protect us from. That is why it is good to assure ourselves throughout the entire day that the Holy Spirit remains with us and controls our lives if we would only make ourselves available to Him.

Outside the Holy Spirit's circle of influence, the sinful flesh gains the upper hand and we become victims of our enemy, Satan, who goes around looking to devour believers. If we are guided by the Spirit, we reveal the rich fruit of the Spirit: love, joy, peace, patience, kindness, goodness, faithfulness, gentleness and self-control. That is why it is essential to walk in the Spirit.

O Spirit of God, Giver of life and Comforter, I thank You that You came into my life and act as my guide to Christ. Amen.

Read: Hebrews 13:7-25   October 21

Lasting center

Jesus Christ is the same yesterday and today and forever.
                                    – HEBREWS 13:8 –

In this time of rapid change, as well as the accompanying challenges and demands made on our personal lives, we search for a
lasting center to which we can join our lives. This we find pre-emi-
nently in Jesus Christ: He is eternal and unchanging.

Here on earth everything changes – change and decay take place
around us everywhere. Circumstances change quickly and relentlessly: quiet and storm; sunshine and clouds; health and illness; life
and death. Only Jesus Christ never changes. From the moment that
we are born, until we enter the valley of death, He is our Companion and Partner.

In Him we have a Rock that remains solid, unshaken and firm.
Because of the dramatic changes in our lives, we might have suffered much damage and pain. If our losses and pain brought us to
Him, stripped of all superficialities, then we have gained far more
than we have lost.

When we feel alone and desolate, He is there to whisper to us, "It
is I, do not fear!" He is Immanuel, God with us! But He is more: He
is God in us! God is always ready to help us through Jesus Christ.

Sometimes God allows a tempest in our lives to force us to relinquish all worldly help and to take refuge in Him. If we are anchored
in Him for eternity, we will remain standing strong in a changing
world.

*My Lord and my God, I thank You that I can say: You are my
refuge; You surround me with joyful songs of deliverance; You
are a resting place for my heart, through Jesus Christ, the Anchor
in my life. Amen.*

October 22

Read: Matthew 6:25-34

Pray *and* work

"But seek first his kingdom and his righteousness, and all these things will be given to you as well."
— MATTHEW 6:33 —

We should ensure that we understand clearly what Jesus prohibits, and what he demands. He prohibits worry resulting from unbelief. He is not a supporter of a lazy, reckless, irresponsible or shortsighted attitude towards life. He prohibits nagging and distrustful fear, which removes all joy and faith from life.

We are called to do our duty faithfully and joyfully; confident in our faith. We should take all the necessary steps to organize our lives and to provide for our needs. At the same time we may not fear or worry about the day of tomorrow.

We should not nurse worry, as God gave us life, the greatest gift of all. We can indeed trust Him to give us the things which support life.

Jesus does not tell us in this passage that the birds do not toil. Scientists claim that birds work harder than any other creatures to find their food. But while they are laboring, they are not worried about tomorrow. God will take care of that. If God cares for the transient beauty of lilies, will He forget His children? Worry shows that you distrust God.

It is possible to conquer fear if we focus our thoughts and work on the kingdom of God. There are greater sins than worry, but there is truly no greater paralyzing sin. We dare not stop laboring, and we dare not stop trusting. Charles Spurgeon said, "We should pray in the storm, but we may not stop rowing!" We must pray as though no work would help; and we should work as if no prayer would help.

Holy God, You commanded man to labor, but You also created within us a yearning for You. Give us the grace to maintain a true balance between prayer and labor. Amen.

Read: Revelation 2:8-11   October 23

Faithful until death

Be faithful, even to the point of death, and I will give you the crown of life.

— REVELATION 2:10 —

Any testimonial is incomplete when faithfulness is not mentioned. Faithfulness is one of the most important Christian virtues. Nothing in life can be substituted for it and lacking it is a serious shortcoming in dealing with life.

Christ demands an unwavering faithfulness from His followers, even if death is the price they have to pay for it. He did not only demand it; He demonstrated it when He sacrificed His life in faithfulness. When Christ demands faithfulness, He also adds the promise of a royal reward: eternal life.

You must not only be faithful when exciting things happen and you are in the spotlight; but also in the monotony of your ordinary, everyday duties when it feels as though the routine is getting too much to handle.

It is taken for granted that people will be faithful in more important matters and moments of life. But the acid test for faithfulness lies in the small, apparently unimportant things and events in life. It is easy to be faithful when people are watching you, but you should also be faithful when no one but God sees you. You must be faithful to your team, your group, your people, since a chain is only as strong as its weakest link.

You should also be faithful to yourself. In Shakespeare's Hamlet, Polonius gives his son Laertes the following advice: "To thine own self be true and it must follow as the day the night, thou canst not then be false to any man."

Above all, be faithful to God. Polycarpus, a father of the church, died on the stake because he remained faithful to his God. In your life, God is the principle from which all other principles in your life flow. Without Him, life itself loses its meaning.

God of grace and mercy, enable me through Your Holy Spirit to be faithful in life and if it must – until death. Amen.

October 24

Read: John 15:9-17

Chosen to bear fruit

"I chose you and appointed you to go and bear fruit – fruit that will last."

– John 15:16 –

God's people are new people. They experienced a one hundred and eighty degree turn-about in their lives. And it did not happen because of hearsay, but through firsthand personal experience of the living Christ. All of this is the result of God's love for us. Augustine said, "God loves each of His children as though he is His only child." This love we cannot earn; it is pure undeserved mercy and grace. God's grace, together with our surrender to His love, transforms us into fruit-bearing disciples. Our faith and belief must also result in deeds.

We were chosen to serve with joy, however difficult the task, otherwise our service becomes mere slave labor. We may never create the impression that we find our work for the Master burdensome. Our lives should radiate joy, because we are His children and do His work. R. L. Stevenson said, "When a joyous person enters a room, it is as though a candle is lit."

We were chosen to serve in love. Without love, we cannot be ambassadors of the Source of all true love. Love gives us a passion for souls and keeps us from competing with one another for petty honor and status.

Since Christ is willing to call us His friends, we must guard against becoming like slaves in our service to Him. We may never become like the elder brother in the parable of the lost son. This attitude easily creeps into our prayer life, Bible study, worship and relationships. We are fellow workers of Christ. We accompany Him on His triumphant journey through the centuries. That is why our service and fruit-bearing should be of the highest, most noble quality in our lives. The world should be able to see in our lives that we are workers of His vineyard.

I want to stay close to You, beloved Guide. I want to trust You always and remain faithful to You so that I can bear Your fruit in the world. Amen.

Read: James 3:1-12   October 25

Taming the tongue

Set a guard over my mouth O LORD; keep watch over the door of my lips.

— PSALM 141:3 —

It is easy to destroy and demolish: a tree that took a hundred years to grow can be chopped down within minutes; a priceless vase, painstakingly created by an artist can be shattered in anger or someone can start a devastating fire by carelessly throwing a burning match into dry grass.

People are far more sensitive than plants or vases and can be destroyed much easier. Our tongues can become weapons if we do not control them. Words uttered in a moment of anger can destroy a person or a relationship. The words of a smooth talker might trap a spouse who feels uncared for. This could cause a strained marital relationship to fall apart and innocent parties could suffer heartache.

A blatant lie or a half-truth can start a smear campaign that could leave many casualties in its wake.

A negative word can cause a promising young life to go awry and eventually end in tragic failure. An unfounded accusation can cause a worker to lose his job and a misunderstanding can end friendships.

Christ came to mend broken things and to renew everything. He alone enables us to prevent the potential harm the tongue can cause or to heal the wounds caused by words. We should confess it to Him and ask forgiveness. We need His help to control our tongues. Scripture tells us that the person who controls his tongue is far stronger than the man who conquers a city.

Almighty Lord, set a guard over my mouth and keep watch over what I say. Amen.

October 26   Read: John 13:1-17

Wash one another's feet

"Now that I, your Lord and Teacher, have washed your feet, you also should wash one another's feet."

– JOHN 13:14 –

The episode where Jesus washes the disciples feet is used as a practical demonstration to teach all arrogant followers humility and service.

In the kingdom of God the path to victory requires willingness to serve others. The road to the top will force you to bend low; the prerequisite for receiving is giving. You should be humble before being promoted and the "self" has to die on the road to eternal life.

The apostles on the road to Jerusalem, arrogantly argued amongst themselves about who would be the greatest in the kingdom of heaven. Christ taught them that the question of hierarchy or rank may not even be mentioned among His followers. They should guard against the attitude of the Pharisee who bragged about his own virtues but looked down on his fellow man.

Jesus wanted to emphasize the fact that His followers had to be servants. It does not imply that we should literally wash the feet of others, but that we should serve, help and comfort one another: the lonely widow; the fallen young person; the childless parents; the hungry and thirsty whom we encounter. These are little things we should do for one another – all we need is a towel and a basin of water.

"Having loved His own who were in the world, He now showed them the full extent of His love" (Jn. 13:1). This verse holds the key to humble service. We must be stripped of our elegant clothing and descend from our thrones if we want to wash and dry feet.

It is only when we have been cleansed by the blood of the Lamb Himself that we can do this. He, the King of kings, stands before us in the figure of a servant. Dare we do less?

Perfect Lord and Master, help me to become a washer of feet for You in this world, through the power and strength of Your Holy Spirit. Amen.

Read: Matthew 16:24-28   October 27

Discipleship demands discipline

"If anyone would come after me, he must deny himself and take up his cross and follow me."

– MATTHEW 16:24 –

Trying to avoid discipline in life is to choose a path which leads to weakness and inefficiency. The apprentice should accept the discipline of training in order to master his trade. Discipline helps both the student and the soldier in their training. Without discipline you accomplish very little in life.

The Christian is no exception. Without discipline, faith becomes powerless and dependent on emotion. You can only become spiritually fit if you want to be fit – if you do not want to exercise, you will always have something else to do as an excuse. When spiritual discipline relaxes and flags, faith is undermined.

It is so wonderful that you can turn to God in prayer at any time and in any place, and that is why you start thinking that a fixed time and place for prayer and meditation are unnecessary. This is a restricting way of thinking which deprives you of the life-giving strength that can be appreciated only by those who have actually experienced it.

If you spend a little time with your Lord amidst your busy life, the value of this will strike you dramatically. Such times are precious and valuable and should therefore be cherished. But they may not take the place of those enriching times when you are alone with the Master and your whole being and thoughts are focused on Him.

It may be difficult and demanding, but it is more than worthwhile to develop the discipline of a fruitful quiet time. He meets you there to encourage you and to strengthen you.

Lord and Master, I dedicate myself to You again and I ask Your Holy Spirit to teach me the discipline of a quiet time with You. Amen.

October 28

Read: Psalm 84:1-12

Fountains in the desert

Blessed are those whose strength is in you, who have set their hearts on pilgrimage. As they pass through the Valley of Baca, they make it a place of springs; the autumn rains also cover it with pools.
— PSALM 84:5-6 —

Fountains, wells and early rains are of vital importance to the desert dwellers of the Middle East. For his spiritual growth the believer is also dependent on the fresh water of a fountain, especially if he has to travel through the dry valleys of problems, suffering and grief. In the valley of adversity, fountains of comfort and hope rise up by the grace of God. It is important that we turn to God for help and strength in such times. The psalmist testifies that time after time you will receive new strength.

Jesus Christ became the Fountain of living water to us. The Samaritan woman at the Jacob's well becomes a witness thereof: "Indeed, the water I give him will become in him a spring of water welling up to eternal life" (Jn. 4:14). Jesus puts an end to all thirst and we will never have to travel across the dry plains without His comfort.

When we journey through the valley of suffering, we are given the opportunity to discover these wells and to drink from these fountains. The more we trust in Jesus, the more we experience the relief and refreshment of the comfort and strength He offers.

No one wants to remain in the desert of suffering and grief of his own free will, but we don't have control over grief or its cause. In order to triumph, we must put our hope in Christ.

During His life Jesus was an example to us; in His death He became a sacrifice and offer; in His ascension to heaven He was a king; and in His intercession with God, a high priest. He is the gushing Fountain that provides everything we need in the desert of life.

Fountain of living water, I long for You as the deer pants for water. I thank You that I can drink from Your fountain of mercy and grace so that I will never thirst again. Amen.

Read: Luke 11:1-13   October 29

A cry of distress

"Lord, teach us to pray."

– Luke 11:1 –

Man has an inborn urge to pray. Certain emotions can only be expressed in fellowship with the eternal God. If this longing is not satisfied, we become bitter and dissatisfied.

When man in his distress says, "Lord, teach me to pray," he asks God to open the door to a fuller, richer and more noble life. You cannot utter this cry of distress and remain embittered or small-minded. The desire for prayer is the desire to reach out and find the hand of God, and to continue life with Him as your Companion and Guide. He shows you the way to a meaningful existence. He will place your feet on the path which leads to your destination, if you prayerfully remain dependent on Him.

There will be times when you are exhausted and will have little desire to pray. Guard against your emotions then and do not think that you do not have to pray because you do not feel like it. On the contrary, this is precisely when you should be praying with greater effort.

Do not allow the devil to deceive you into believing that you would be false to pray when you do not feel like it. When your spiritual life is barren, you must persevere in prayer until the sunshine of God's love is visible in your life again.

Your own prayer journal will help you on such days. Write down all the beautiful things that occur in your life: inspiring thoughts; striking poetry and prose and beautiful natural scenes which lift your spirit to God. Make a note of prayers that have been answered. When you find praying difficult, page through this book and you will find courage, strength and inspiration to pray.

Pray at all times, since this is the only way you can develop a continuous and productive life of prayer. That is why the burning desire in our hearts should be, "Lord, teach us to pray."

O Lord, who answers prayers, every man has to come to You. I beg that Your Spirit will enable me to pray genuinely, for the sake of Jesus Christ. Amen.

October 30

Read: Habakkuk 3:1-19

Yet I will rejoice

Though the fig tree does not bud and there are no grapes on the vines, though the olive crop fails and the fields produce no food, though there are no sheep in the pen and no cattle in the stalls, yet I will rejoice in the LORD, I will be joyful in God my Savior.
                                                    – HABAKKUK 3:17-18 –

"It's easy enough to be pleasant when life flows along like a song; but the man worthwhile is the man who can smile when everything goes dead wrong."

The anonymous author of this verse stresses the fact that it is easy to praise God when the sun shines. When threatening storm clouds gather and your prayers remain unanswered; when you are convinced that no one understands your problems, then it is easy to believe that God is not interested in you any longer. Then praise appears to be impossible and life becomes a burden.

True praise is more than an emotional lifting of your heart to God. Figuratively it means looking up into the face of God and sincerely asking, "Lord, what do You want me to do?" When you ask this of God, the answer may be surprising.

He may reveal to you truths about yourself that have been hidden from you for a long time: an unforgiving spirit; arrogance; bitter antagonism against a fellow man or some other pet sins that you refuse to let go.

When your life has been cleansed by the grace of God and the blood of Christ, you will experience a cheerfulness that will make it easy for you to praise God, even in misfortune and disaster. Then you will experience new spiritual growth and maturity as well as an unknown joy which will call forth songs of praise from your heart.

Redeemer, Jesus Christ, I thank and praise You for Your cleansing power that enables me to praise You even in times of misfortune and disaster. Amen.

Read: 2 Samuel 24:11-25 October 31

The responsibility of leadership

"I am the one who has sinned and done wrong. These are but sheep. What have they done? Let your hand fall upon me and my family."
– 2 SAMUEL 24:17 –

With authority comes a lot of responsibility. Those who are subjected to authority look up to and respect those who are placed in positions of authority over them. They usually follow these persons blindly. This can be seen clearly in the relationship between parent and child, master and servant, pastor and congregation. In many cases it also happens between a ruler and a subject.

If you are in a position of authority, it is necessary to realize that you are privileged. You have the authority to control and influence the lives of other people. This can have far-reaching consequences.

It is therefore necessary for you to use your authority justly. You will need great wisdom. You will have to organize your own life in such a way that you set an example to those who have been placed under your authority. They will have to be guided and led wisely so that they can follow the right way and be protected against evil influences and temptations.

In order to achieve this, you will have to follow Christ's example as a model for your life and actions. No one has ever exercised more authority, guided, led and influenced more people than the Master. He did it perfectly. Let Christ be your example and draw your strength and inspiration from Him. Then you will have the reassuring knowledge that those placed under your authority are safe in your care.

This will protect you against self-reproach and bitter remorse. Walk in Christ's footsteps and continue to learn from Him.

Grant me, holy Master, a spirit of humble dependence on You in my actions and dealings with those You have entrusted to my care. Amen.

NOVEMBER

Read: Hebrews 13:1-6   November 1

Facing the future without fear

So we say with confidence, "The Lord is my helper; I will not be afraid. What can man do to me?"

– HEBREWS 13:6 –

Here is a verse that you can take with you as you enter the most demanding month of all. During this month the social activities for the year will be concluded and functions peculiar to this time of the year will multiply. Our strength will be drained by the demands of the year that is almost at an end, and spiritually we might have reached a low-water mark. This is reason enough to be anxious. But these words of faith lay to rest all fear as we place our trust where it's supposed to be: with the Almighty!

Christ is the answer to all our fears. He takes the judgment of God away from us. Since the Fall, man has lost so much that nearly nothing but fear remains. Sin is the main source of all our fear. But Christ has paid the price to reconcile us with God and in this way He took away the cause of our deepest fear. He conquered sin, Satan and death.

He also takes away His children's exaggerated fear of the future. For the child, the young person, the adult and the elderly, the unknown future is fearsome and intimidating. We fear the demands of life and we fear the certainty of death. Then Jesus comes along and says reassuringly, "Do not be terrified; do not be discouraged for the LORD your God will be with you wherever you go" (Josh. 1:9).

When we become scared in the storms of life, Jesus tells us as He told His disciples during the storm, "Why are you so afraid? Do you still have no faith?" (Mk. 4:40). Whether it be in the examination room, in the conclusion of a phase of life, or in old age, Christ and our love for Him is the answer to all our fears. "The one who fears is not made perfect in love" (1 Jn. 4:18). Face the future with confidence, since God, the Almighty, is in our future through His Son, Jesus Christ.

Almighty Lord, I thank You that I can rejoice: Immanuel – I will not fear! Amen.

November 2

Read: Isaiah 6:1-8

Broken, cleansed and commissioned

I said, "Here am I. Send me!"

— Isaiah 6:8 —

We often hear people ask, "What must I do?" It is good and right because it is very important to know what God expects of you. But first we have to deal with another question before we are equipped to be sent out: "Lord, what must I *be*?"

I must be saved. Even though Isaiah was a prophet who did the work of the Lord, his life changed drastically when he met God. Filled with remorse, he fell down at the feet of his Lord and cried, "Woe to me! I am ruined!" Nicodemus, a Pharisee, was seeking God when Christ told him, "You must be born again!" Job was a pious man, yet he struggled relentlessly with God in forty-one chapters until he met Him in a storm. Then he confessed, "My ears had heard of You but now my eyes have seen You. Therefore I despise myself and repent in dust and ashes" (Job 42:5-6).

God never leaves His child shattered and broken-hearted if his repentance is sincere. God cleanses us from our sin. A glowing coal from the altar must touch my life to cleanse it. The Holy Spirit must purify my life completely, as gold is purified in the furnace. I must be purified and cleansed of lovelessness, wrong attitudes, spiritual bankruptcy and every other error of my heart. The Holy Spirit must purify my thoughts, life and actions. For this, conscientious and persistent fellowship with God is necessary. Neesima said, "Let us advance on our knees."

Only then can the Lord send me. Then I will answer joyfully, "Here I am, Lord! Send me!" Then I will do His work faithfully and enthusiastically since I believe in the power of prayer; in the cleansing power of the Holy Spirit; in the preciousness of souls and in the Word of God.

That is why you and I should reach out to God with our tattered and sin-torn lives. Then the Holy Spirit can do His cleansing so that we can become competent witnesses of His love.

Here I am, Lord! Send me. Amen.

Read: Psalm 51:8-19

November 3

Exhaustion and renewal

Restore to me the joy of your salvation and grant me a willing spirit, to sustain me.

– Psalm 51:12 –

It is a fact of life that man ages and this ageing often has its hidden cause deep within us: self-reproach about lost opportunities; guilt about neglect and sin and the nagging thought that time wasted can never be regained. We have feelings of guilt about neglect towards ourselves and towards our fellow man. We have neglected God through living a superficial life that wasted time and energy.

It is then that we can pray like David, asking God to renew our spirit. A positive attitude to life and a cheerful and merry heart is what we desire from God. Be enthusiastic about your life. Let every day be a song of praise for what God gives you, especially for His wonderful gift of life and health.

Obviously, ageing does occur and there is a darker side of life, but do not dwell on it. God intended each one of us to have a good and beautiful life. From your disappointments and failures, take the good things that God wants to teach you and then forget about the past. God's healing and renewing strength can neutralize all damaging and negative attitudes. He created us to live positively and cheerfully in every phase of our lives: from our early youth to ripe old age.

Let us therefore grasp every moment of every day with gratitude and enter each new day, like the psalmist, with this prayer in our hearts:

Satisfy us in the morning with Your unfailing love, that we may sing for joy and be glad all our days. Make us glad for as many days as You have afflicted us, for as many years as we have seen trouble (Ps. 90:14-15). Amen.

November 4

Read: Isaiah 55:1-13

God has a better plan

"For my thoughts are not your thoughts, neither are your ways my ways," declares the LORD.

— ISAIAH 55:8 —

Do you live in a world of shattered dreams where everything has collapsed like a house of cards? Possibly you pursued success over a long period of time. You had a goal which inspired you in times of boredom and depression. Now everything has gone wrong and nothing remains, not even your dreams.

How you react to this situation is important for your future spiritual well-being. You can lapse into self-pity and relate your sad tale to everyone who wants to listen. You can convince yourself that you are a loser and will now never again attain success. You accept your failure or defeat as inevitable. You can possibly become embittered in your outlook on life and withdraw from people.

If your dreams have been shattered, there are a few heart-searching questions you should ask yourself. Why did you experience failure? Were you too ambitious and did you over-estimate your abilities? Did someone you trust leave you in the lurch and disappoint you? Ask questions that will reveal the truth to you. Show courage to accept the truth about yourself and do something positive about it.

Find encouragement in the knowledge that the world is full of people who initially failed, but who experienced triumphant success after a second or third attempt. You fail only if you accept failure as a fact.

Remember that failure or disappointment is possibly God's method of blocking your way so that He can guide you onto a better path. If you trust Him steadfastly, you may experience some setbacks because you misunderstood His plan for your life. But if you persevere in trusting Him, you will burst through the barrier of failure and experience true success.

Guide and Father, make me sensitive to Your plan for my life and make me willing to follow You unconditionally without reservation. Amen.

Read: John 4:27-42

November 5

What is the purpose of life?

"My food," said Jesus, "is to do the will of him who sent me and to finish his work."

– JOHN 4:34 –

All of us have asked this vitally important question at one time or another. Does life have a purpose, or is it a meaningless struggle from birth to death? Is it necessary to have a goal? These and other similar questions haunt ordinary people.

There are people who set goals for themselves which require all their energy and concentration. They look forward to a time when they will achieve success and will enjoy a position of prestige and authority over others. Others again, who are perhaps more open-minded, do not see success in worldly, secular terms, but as a service to their fellow man.

We all seek our own goals in life. Inevitably, we search for our own happiness and satisfaction. In this way we believe there is a goal which brings satisfaction.

As a dedicated and committed Christian, your highest pursuit should be to please God and not yourself. To the uninitiated, this may sound very prosaic, but it is the key to a purposeful and satisfying way of life.

There is no greater goal in life than to do the will of God and to pursue the purpose you were born to fulfill. By deviating from it, you are choosing second best. It only leads to frustration and dissatisfaction.

Living to carry out God's will is a way of life that requires a high standard of commitment. However, it is not an unbearable burden which deprives life of its joy. Then you live with the Source of joy and you experience the wealth which belongs to those who love and serve Christ.

Master, I commit myself to You anew, so that I can taste the joy of a purposeful life. Amen.

November 6

Read: Psalm 111:1-10

The healing power of joy

Praise the LORD. *I will extol the* LORD *with all my heart.*
— PSALM 111:1 —

People are inclined to concentrate on all the negative features of old age while there is still so much to rejoice about. Fortunately ageing is a process and not something that occurs suddenly. With the right attitude towards old age, it can be a joyful period in our lives.

There is the joy of friendships that have matured and in which we can find joy. There is time to visit at leisure, to travel, to meet people and to broaden our horizons. There is the happiness of enjoying a hobby for which we never had enough time before.

Then there is the pure joy of seeing younger people take over the torch from us with enthusiasm, and seeing them carry it with new vision into the future. Then you joyfully know that your labor is greater than yourself, and that mercifully, you have been allowed to do work for eternity.

In the spiritual field you have more time for prayer and fellowship with the Word of God. In the hurried life of earlier times, this was not always possible. Now you can enjoy devoting attention to your soul. There is now time to wait on the Lord, to talk to the Lord and to listen to the Lord. Due to physical weakness some elderly people can do nothing else but intercede in prayer for their children, relatives, friends and acquaintances.

You can find happiness in nature. You can hear the rejoicing and exultation in creation and feel how your heart and life come into harmony with the Almighty. A song of praise to His glory and honor rises from your heart. How great is God in His love to give so much joy and meaning to our autumn years, "I will extol the Lord with all my heart."

We praise You, O Lord, that Your children may bear fruit until their old age by bringing blessings and joy to others. Amen.

Read: Matthew 27:11-31

November 7

The question you cannot avoid

"What shall I do, then, with Jesus who is called Christ?"
– MATTHEW 27:22 –

If one should ask what the most important question of our time is, you would obtain very different answers. Some would say, "The environment – what will we do about the pollution of planet earth?" Others would say, "Inflation – how will we deal with the ever-rising costs and the devaluation of our money?" There are those who would answer, "The elderly – how are we to care for the ever-increasing number of old people?" Yet others would say, "The youth – how are we to channel the explosive energy of the youth into the right direction?"

All these questions are of great importance, but the cardinal question of life is the "Pilate question". "What shall I do with Jesus who is called Christ?" The right answer would mean that you gain everything for time and eternity; the wrong answer could mean that you will lose everything.

There are those who prefer ignoring Jesus. Like Pilate they wash their hands in innocence and then announce theatrically that they will have nothing to do with the entire business. However, it is not that easy to wash your hands of Christ. Your destination is inextricably bound to Jesus Christ.

Then there are people who choose to oppose Christ. They shout, "Away with Him. Crucify Him!" until they are hoarse. They want to shout Christ out of their lives. It is futile and self-destructive and can end only in defeat.

There are those who accept Him. They accept Him as Redeemer and Savior. He rules over their lives. Delivered of sin, they obtain peace of mind, joy and eternal life.

Life with Christ is endless hope; life without Christ is a hopeless end.

Yes, my heart chooses You as its eternal King! Rule in me, Lord Jesus, and fill me with Your strength. Amen.

November 8

Read: Luke 19:28-44

Lost opportunities

"If you, even you, had only known on this day what would bring you peace – but now it is hidden from your eyes."

– LUKE 19:42 –

There are certainly few people who can say in all sincerity that they have no self-reproach about letting opportunities for doing a friendly deed or speaking a word of encouragement slip past. A day seldom passes without the opportunity to cheer up someone who is depressed; to help someone who is going through a hard time; or to speak a friendly word to someone whom the struggles of life are threatening to overwhelm.

To be sensitive to the distress of others, and to do your utmost to relieve that distress is a definite way of preventing regret, when it is too late to do anything about it. To be offered the opportunity of doing a kind deed for someone, and then to turn away instead, will impoverish you more than the other person. It is a basic rule of life that it is impossible to enrich other people's lives through love and good deeds without enriching your own life at the same time. Giving yourself in love and service to others is the privilege of everyone who loves and serves Christ with a sincere heart. It is a certain way to spiritual growth.

Find God's purpose for your life while you serve others in His glorious Name. Do not look over your shoulder all the time or brood on lost opportunities. It is a total waste of time. Be determined to do better today and tomorrow. Throw yourself enthusiastically into the service of your fellow man as a product of your sparkling joy about God's goodness to you. Use every opportunity in His strength, and the future will hold no self-reproach for you.

Spirit of the living Christ, make me sensitive to the distress of others and help me not to let any opportunity for service go past unused. Amen.

Read: 1 Corinthians 13:1-13　　　　November 9

From fantasy to reality

When I was a child, I talked like a child, I thought like a child, I reasoned like a child. When I became a man, I put childish ways behind me.

– 1 CORINTHIANS 13:11 –

When we were children we played games of make-believe and we lived in a world of fantasy in which only children could feel at home. When we became adults, our childish ideas were replaced by dreams. Some dreams inspire us to make them come true. Yet others remain illusions since they lack driving force. They deprive life of the joy born from real achievement.

For most people there is a time of awakening. They begin to distinguish between fantasy and reality. The idle and unrealistic dreams are discarded and they concentrate on the art of living. Some people never awake from their dreams and remain in a world of fantasy and make-believe until the end of their lives.

When you accept Christ's challenge, you come face to face with the realities of life. With Him, you have no illusions about vain greatness, since you see yourself as God sees you and that is a humbling experience. Meeting reality drives away all fantasy and enables you to struggle with life under the guidance and strength of the Holy Spirit.

As unreal and damaging dreams are driven away by the light of reality you actually realize what God expects from you. God's reality is a greater inspiration than all the games of make-believe that were present in your life. God reveals to you what you can become and He gives you the inner strength to achieve it. Then you become mature in Christ and children's games are forever a thing of the past.

Lord Jesus, I thank You that Your Holy Spirit guides me from a make-believe world to the reality of a new, dynamic life in You. Amen.

November 10   Read: Genesis 48:1-22

The generation gap bridged

Then Israel said, "Bring them to me so that I may bless them."
— GENESIS 48:9 —

The poignant picture painted by the author of Hebrews is almost like a painting by Rembrandt, "By faith Jacob, when he was dying, blessed each of Joseph's sons, and worshiped as he leaned on the top of his staff" (Heb. 11:21).

Eternity will one day reveal how many blessings flowed over generations from the loving prayers of grandparents for their children. Three generations are brought together here.

Jacob, the gray old man, over a hundred years old, is the binding factor. He lives at peace in the land Goshen. His son and grandsons live in the city. But he does not write them off. He trusts them and believes in them. The power of his prayers reaches out to include them in its blessing. We should never underestimate the impact of the prayer service of the elderly.

Joseph is Jacob's son, but he is also the governor of Egypt. He is a busy man with great responsibilities. He is summoned to his old father's tent. He offers no excuses. He does not forget his father. He comes and brings the children with him to preserve the bond between the generations. Joseph is great before man, but small before his parents and before his God.

Ephraim and Manasseh are Jacob's two grandsons and they are in their prime years. They are the promise of a future for the generation. Despite their youth they feel the wonder of what is happening in Jacob's tent. Because they have become part of the events they are richly blessed and they will have a big influence on the further history of their people. They chose God as their share and their future. In the simple tent of Jacob, they were ensured of descendants and of an eternal blessing, because the God of their fathers also became their God.

Holy God and in Jesus Christ our heavenly Father, we praise You for the wonder of family ties and the power of elderly people's prayers. I thank You for the blessings that flow from their prayers to generations of descendants. Amen.

Read: Galatians 5:13-26

November 11

Wonder fruit!

But the fruit of the Spirit is ... kindness.

– GALATIANS 5:22 –

Kindness is not something we can wear on the outside. It is an inner quality which originates in the attitude of our hearts. This attitude is born from our relationship with God. It enables us to be kind towards friends and enemies, acquaintances and strangers, children and old people, believers and unbelievers. It is the fruit of a new life in Jesus Christ.

Jesus' kindness is renounced when we are intolerant or when we believe our own interpretation of an issue – even religion – is the only correct one. Religion without kindness can be cold and without feeling. Religion which tells about love and forgiveness is often the battlefield of intolerance and a spirit of persecution.

We also renounce the fruit of kindness when we neglect to perform a good and grateful action. There is a crucial moment when we feel the impulse, but through neglect the moment passes irrevocably: a note of thanks for a deed of love; a handshake of sympathy or a word of comfort. How easily do we not forsake the elementary Christian virtue of hospitality.

We often try to accomplish with violence that which we could more easily do with kindness. There is the story of the wind and the sun debating who would be the first to make a man on a bench remove his coat. The wind stormed, howled, pulled and tugged, but the man clung to his coat all the more. The sun shone down on him in a friendly and comforting way. The man enjoyed the good warmth and gratefully took off his coat.

Kindness always brings us to Jesus and the Spirit that He gives us; which makes all things new and calls forth the fruit of kindness.

Holy Spirit of God, I thank You for the miracle fruit of kindness which You brought into my life. I praise You, Jesus my Lord, for the example You have set me in this area. Amen.

November 12

Read: Revelation 3:14-22

Half-hearted Christians

"I know your deeds, that you are neither cold nor hot. I wish you were either one or the other!"

— REVELATION 3:15 —

There are people who expect more from Christianity than they deserve. When they pray, they expect an immediate answer. They expect guidance without any intention of obeying God. They are disappointed when they do not experience the presence of God in their quiet time, even when they neglect becoming quiet before God.

God gives His gifts of mercy and grace to those disciples who are sincere in their commitment and dedication to Him. They are people who are willing to sacrifice time for the sake of their spiritual growth and development: people who are disciplined in prayer and serious Bible study; people who worship in spirit and in truth, and whose faith is reflected in sound human relationships.

A fulfilling relationship can only be experienced when you have surrendered to God totally; when you have cheerfully given to Him everything you are and everything you have. It is only through such commitment that the glory, power and beauty of Christ will develop in your life. If you sacrifice anything less to Christ, you limit His influence in your life and you deprive yourself of the reward of true Christian discipleship that can be yours.

One of the tragedies in Christianity is the large number of followers who are completely satisfied with half-hearted commitment to Christ. They love Him, but they are not willing to accept the challenges of that love. They are willing to serve Him, if His demands do not clash with their own plans, or do not require any personal sacrifice. Placing the living Christ first and in the center of your life means complete surrender to Him. It deserves your highest commitment and best effort. The rewards will be breathtaking.

Living Lord and Savior, I commit myself to You again. Make my faith and love dynamic and alive through Your Holy Spirit. Amen.

Read: Exodus 23:1-9   November 13

The lost individual

Do not follow the crowd in doing wrong. When you give testimony in a lawsuit, do not pervert justice by siding with the crowd.
                                        – Exodus 23:2 –

We live in an age where the mentality of the masses is the norm. Man has been reduced to a number, a statistic, an insignificant cog in the enormous machine of society. This was not God's intention at all. Every person is a unique creation of God and He doesn't make doubles. No two leaves on any tree are the same, scientists say. Would God make the crown of His creation like bullets from the same mould? We should maintain a healthy respect for our individuality and integrity and that has nothing to do with pride.

The majority is not necessarily always right. However, it is easier to follow than to lead. Civilization owes much to people who dared to be true to themselves: Galileo, Columbus, Madame Curie, Martin Luther and Albert Schweitzer just to name a few.

One important aspect of the doctrine of Christ is the emphasis He placed on the importance of the individual. You are invaluable in God's eyes. You should appreciate and develop this individuality.

As the Holy Spirit reveals to you your own unique personality, you will find that the ties of habit and convenience which bound you to the thoughts and actions of the masses will loosen. You no longer desire to drift with the masses at all costs, and you seek a more intimate relationship with your Lord and Redeemer.

As your relationship with Christ grows, and as your thoughts become attuned to His way of thinking, He will become your Leader and Guide. The influence of His Spirit enables you to make true evaluations and to identify your priorities. Then you will regain your individuality.

Loving Lord Jesus, I place You in the center of my love and my trust. Bless me with the gift of being myself within the boundaries of my limitations and strengths. Amen.

November 14

Read: Psalm 42:1-11

Handling stress

Why are you downcast, O my soul? Why so disturbed within me? Put your hope in God, for I will yet praise him, my Savior and my God.

– PSALM 42:11 –

Stress is the extra demand made on your body in a dangerous or tense situation. Depending on the amount of danger or tension you experience, your autonomic nervous system releases hormones which cause chemical changes. Your heart starts beating faster, your breathing speeds up and blood flows to your brain. In different people this leads to different reactions: they either fight it, or they want to escape the situation.

How can I find peace in the eye of this hurricane? I must accept responsibility for my own life by discovering my limitations and my possibilities; my strengths and my weaknesses. I must then accept myself, plan my life and determine my goals. I should also firmly handle the past. I must identify the obstacles which hamper growth and increase stress: feelings of guilt; bitterness; anger; self-reproach and disappointments. Do not carry the burden of the past with you. Do not pamper your grievances. Grant yourself inner healing by forgiving yourself as God forgave you.

Do not repress your feelings. Discuss your problems with parents, friends or a trusted adviser. Obtain professional help if necessary. If you seal a pot with water in it and place it on a hot plate you have all the elements for a volcanic explosion.

Learn to relax in the refuge of: friendships, sport, poetry, music, art or nature. Do not live on a battlefield; create your own paradise. Do not lapse into passive dejection. Serve others with your talents and guard against self-pity. Work continuously on your relationship with the living Christ. He grants the grace to handle stress. Spend time in relaxed meditation with Him. The reward of peace of mind will not be withheld.

Good Shepherd, I praise and extol You because You make me lie down in green pastures and bring me to quiet waters where there is peace. Amen.

Read: Ephesians 4:25-32

November 15

Heal that breach

"In your anger do not sin": Do not let the sun go down while you are still angry.

— EPHESIANS 4:26 —

Anger is a destructive emotion. When bitterness wells up and causes physical violence or painful, cutting remarks, the effect can be devastating. Marriages are broken up; friendships come to an end; business relationships are twisted – and all because someone succumbed to the temptation of expressing hurt feelings or irritations, that had mounted into fuming anger.

When you consider the consequences of angry words, think about the negative effect they have on your own life. If you allow your feelings to run riot, you will pay the price in your spiritual, moral, emotional and physical well-being.

In the heat of your anger your outlook and judgment are clouded. Decisions which were very simple before, now become enormous problems. Even your health is affected negatively when you harbor feelings of rage, bitterness and guilt. Your spiritual life will especially suffer. The words of John are true: it is impossible to love God, yet hate your brother (1 Jn. 4:20).

If you revealed anger in your relationship with someone else, then remember the humility of Jesus Christ. Follow His command and with the help of the Holy Spirit, be courageous enough to take the first step on the path of reconciliation. The peace of mind you will then experience will make the effort worthwhile. Only Jesus Christ's attitude will enable you not to let the sun go down on your anger.

Redeemer and Savior, keep me from being too proud to take the first step on the path of reconciliation. Amen.

November 16

Read: Matthew 28:1-20

The Christ of today

"Surely I am with you always, to the very end of the age."
— MATTHEW 28:20 —

We can never thank God enough for the Bible. In it we see how He guides His followers; how He admonishes and inspires them who love Him; and above all, how He sent His beloved Son to save a world torn apart by sin. The Bible is the revealed will of God for His children. Secular books describe the historical Christ, but in the Bible His true divinity and omnipotence are revealed.

While the Bible and secular history confirm that Christ did live on earth, we find the greatest proof of His existence in the lives of His followers and those whose lives have been renewed by the Holy Spirit. It is an encouraging thought to know that Christ is still active today in the life of man. Christ's presence can be observed only where there are followers of His who have surrendered and committed themselves completely to Him.

There are certain obligations to meet if you want to experience the living Christ in your life. He gave Himself for you and the degree of your efficiency in His service depends on the quality of your commitment and dedication to Him.

If you neglect or refuse to spend time with Him in private so that you can learn His will for your life, you will not be able to find this knowledge anywhere else. If your faith depends solely on the written Word, you will never know the power that His living presence releases in your life.

The Holy Spirit is God's gift to all His believing children. If you accept this wonderful gift in your life, Christ's presence becomes a glorious reality. Then Christ becomes "Immanuel": the Christ of the here and now; the Christ of "today" and every day, until the fullness of time.

O living Redeemer, I open my life completely to Your Holy Spirit so that You can be a wonderful and glorious reality to me. Amen.

Read: Proverbs 25:11-20

November 17

Give your friends space

Seldom set foot in your neighbor's house – too much of you, and he will hate you.

– PROVERBS 25:17 –

Friendship is one of God's most precious gifts and it should be nurtured and developed; it should not be taken for granted and should not be placed under unnecessary strain. It can quickly wither under too much familiarity.

Do not ever make the mistake of thinking that because you know people well, you can allow yourself liberties which will restrict their freedom. You dare not claim them for yourself. They are entitled to times of privacy when they can be alone to lead their own lives.

Man is very gregarious and he finds joy in the company of his fellow man. However, he is also a spiritual being and he needs space to develop in spirit and thought. Wise friends respect this principle and have appreciation for the privacy of their friends. However welcome you may be, you should never overstay your welcome and make a burden of yourself. Being considerate is the hallmark of a healthy friendship.

Even within the intimacy of the family and marriage, where mutual understanding and love exist, respect for the individual is of the utmost importance. No person may be too possessive and try to dominate or control another person. Then the happiness and security of the family becomes threatened.

If someone, be it a family member, neighbor or friend, wishes to be alone, it should not be seen as anti-social behavior. This person may be seriously trying to discover God, or to understand himself.

Understanding Lord Jesus, help me to understand my friends and family and to have respect for their need for privacy and time spent alone with You. Amen.

November 18

Read: Proverbs 11:1-20

Think before yielding

The truly righteous man attains life, but he who pursues evil goes to his death.

— Proverbs 11:19 —

No one has the ambition to become an alcoholic, a criminal or a failure. Every alcoholic was a moderate drinker at some stage; every criminal thought that he could lie and steal and not be affected; people who commit injustices against society think they can cover it up without being caught and without being seen as failures.

Unhealthy and ultimately destructive habits do not enter your life suddenly and in full force. That is why they are not immediately rejected. They start with an insignificant and apparently harmless gesture which seems to be pleasant and innocent. While the enjoyment increases, you delude yourself that you are still in control. One day you suddenly realize that you cannot resist the temptation in your own strength.

It is important that you recognize the potential addictive power of an experience or habit. For this the indwelling strength of the living Christ is invaluable. He gives you the Spirit of awareness, which makes you mindful of those habits which can have a binding power over you. He also gives you the strength to say "No!" to evil, and to avoid even the suggestion of evil.

When temptation winks at you for the first time and offers you its forbidden fruit, come to a standstill and think before yielding. Ask yourself what it could lead to and what the result would be. Do not entertain habits that can lead to your destruction. Reject them while you have the power to do so; before you are in bondage as a powerless slave. Remain faithful to God, to your true self and to your loved ones.

You are my refuge in temptation, Lord, and through Your indwelling presence I can conquer the temptation of evil. Amen.

Read: Hebrews 11:1-10

November 19

Anchor in the storm

And without faith it is impossible to please God, because anyone who comes to him must believe that he exists and that he rewards those who earnestly seek him.

— HEBREWS 11:6 —

A living faith is absolutely essential in the world today. There is a universal feeling that world events are reaching a climax. For this reason it is essential that you have an unshakable faith when everything around you is collapsing. We should firmly believe that this is still God's world and in the words of Psalm 24:1 we should fearlessly say, "The earth is the LORD's, and everything in it, the world and all who live in it."

In these chaotic days we live in, many people wonder what the future holds for humankind. Evil is rampant and nothing is done to stop it. The destructive forces make the powers of justice appear small and insignificant. But do not allow appearances to deceive you. This is still God's world!

Across the world people are longing for the knowledge that God cares and that He is in control. This longing and desire have sidetracked many people. Without faith in an omniscient God who holds the future of nations and individuals in His hand, we are lost. Jesus Christ did not come to this world to establish a new theology or to teach a new doctrine, but to bring His children new, abundant life so that they can live purposefully and victoriously, even in the most confusing circumstances.

With faith in Jesus Christ, you can meet the future with confidence and know for sure that He is your Guide and Leader in these worrying and confusing days.

Almighty God and heavenly Father, I thank You that I know through faith that I can share Your peace in the midst of the hurricane of events in this world. I know this through the power of Jesus Christ, our Redeemer. Amen.

November 20

Read: Psalm 28:1-9

Miracles through prayer

Praise be to the LORD, for he has heard my cry for mercy. The LORD is my strength and my shield; my heart trusts in him and I am helped. My heart leaps for joy and I will give thanks to him in song.
— PSALM 28:6-7 —

Despite the disbelief and cynicism of the modern age, God can still perform miracles. Every time that someone is healed in answer to prayer, God has performed a small miracle. Every time we experience peace in our hearts after a time of tension and suffering, when a young couple falls in love, when our grief becomes bearable or is converted to rejoicing gladness, then a miracle has occurred.

Many people pray to God when they experience a crisis, but when the crisis passes and their worst fears do not come true, they ignore and forget the fact that they prayed in their distress.

The evidence that God hears our prayers is overwhelming. Many Christians of our time can testify that miracles still occur in answer to faithful prayer. Lives have been reformed, the sick have been healed, destructive habits have been conquered and broken human relationships have been restored. Many people have first-hand experience that God answers prayer.

Hand your problems over to God today and wait on Him in faith. If there is something you have to do yourself, do it without delay. Do not be overwhelmed by despair in your extreme distress. At the right time and in the right way, God will answer your prayers and you will be astounded by the results.

My God and Father, I know that You are powerful and that You can do far more than I can pray for or think of, because You are the Almighty. Let this truth guide me from day to day. I pray this in the Name of Jesus and with thanksgiving. Amen.

Read: Genesis 12   November 21

The double blessing

"I will make you into a great nation and I will bless you; I will make your name great, and you will be a blessing."
– GENESIS 12:2 –

God made this special promise to Abraham when He commanded him to move to a land that Abraham did not yet know. In faith, Abraham pulled up his tent-pegs and traveled in the direction God led him.

God kept His promise. Abraham was abundantly blessed with material things, but the spiritual blessings he received for his faith cannot be measured. He could never have dreamed that the benefits from God's treasury would be so great and abundant.

Through Abraham God blessed all he came into contact with. One moment Abraham's God-given blessing as the great intercessor flowed to others; then he became the person who dug water wells in the desert where the thirsty could come freely to drink; as servant of God he blessed his environment and as priest he blessed his own family.

We may not keep God's blessing to ourselves. We do not know what others need to lead blessed lives, but the almighty God knows. Our duty is to pray that He will enable us to be the channels through which His blessing can flow to the world and so honor Him.

By revealing the nature of Jesus Christ in our lives; by appreciating and praising other people's actions, through faith in our fellow man, by encouraging others and praying for them, we can be a rich blessing to the greater glory of God in His world. That is why Paul's call in Philippians 2:5 is so important, "Your attitude should be the same as that of Christ Jesus."

Holy Father, I worship You as the Source of all true blessing. I thank You for enabling me, through Jesus Christ, to be a blessing to others. This is because Your blessing in my life is so abundant. Amen.

November 22

Read: Daniel 12:1-13

Trust God

I heard, but I did not understand. So I asked, "My Lord, what will the outcome of all this be?"

– DANIEL 12:8 –

People often find it difficult to understand God's purpose and will for their lives. They are perplexed by things that happen to them and to others around them. They try to discover a cause and reason for what happens, especially when they suffer misfortune. In their confusion they have no clear outlook on the future. As their faith diminishes, many try to place the blame on God.

The core of a strong faith is your ability to trust God completely, whatever happens. It is one thing to say that you have faith while the sun is shining and everything in your life is running smoothly. But the true test of faith comes when things turn against you; when you are tempted to question God; when you, in your despair, see no purpose or reason for your grievous circumstances.

When you study the life of Jesus Christ, you will be deeply impressed by His unshakable and unconditional trust in God. Even in the darkest moments His faith was strong enough to enable Him to carry out the will of His Father.

If you walk with God on your path of life, and if you draw your strength from Him, you will develop the ability to trust God in all circumstances. The grace of God will always be sufficient to enable you to deal with every situation in life, in the knowledge that Christ knows and cares for you and that He will do everything for your good.

Lamb of God, I look up to You to strengthen my faith through the work of Your Holy Spirit in my life. Amen.

Read: Job 5:8-27

November 23

The source of true happiness

Blessed is the man whom God corrects; so do not despise the discipline of the Almighty.

– Job 5:17 –

All of us would like to be happy, but a lot depends on what you mean by happiness. Many people think that if they had more money and could do just what they wanted they would be very happy. Facts, however, prove the contrary. The fun-seekers of this world are usually the most bored people and they are always on the lookout for new methods of satisfying their insatiable appetites for new enjoyment. Wealth and exciting, daring experiences can never guarantee permanent happiness.

The inner happiness for which most people long, arises from man's spirit. If the spirit is immoral and wants to pursue every passing fancy, you become frustrated and disillusioned. Instead of true happiness, a gray curtain of monotony descends on your life.

Happiness is a by-product of a life that is obedient to the laws of God and is led in the fellowship of the living Christ. It does not necessarily mean that your path will become easier and that you will have radiant sunshine all the way. But while you walk daily in the awareness of Christ's presence in your life, you will face the future with confidence. You know you are walking the path that He has set out for you and on which He will guide you.

On this path, you will become aware of a growing power in your life which enables you to resist temptations. You will obtain an inner balance which no evil force can destroy. Peace of mind is your rich portion, and from peace of mind happiness is born. This happiness is known only to those who love and serve God.

Merciful God, I accept with joy and thanksgiving the happiness which is the result of a committed and disciplined life. Amen.

November 24

Read: Jeremiah 1:1-12

A time to speak

Then the LORD reached out his hand and touched my mouth and said to me, "Now, I have put my words in your mouth."
— JEREMIAH 1:9 —

Some people talk far too much and are therefore tempted to say things they shouldn't. Other people however, remain quiet when they should speak and in this way they achieve the same result. How often do you battle to speak? Something must be said: an accusation must be contradicted; a wrong insinuation must be challenged; someone's character has to be defended – and you remain silent! This has happened to many people who have allowed an opportunity to say something important slip past because of fear, uncertainty or inferiority.

This type of situation so often arises when there is a debate during a meeting, especially church meetings. A few people dominate the discussion and make the others feel inferior and therefore force them into silence. In the meantime they had an important contribution to make to a meaningful debate and they should have made it.

In all your actions, whether it be in business or in pleasure, in spiritual or secular matters, you will find great comfort, encouragement and benefit by seeking the will of God, so that you can do and say the right thing. Always remain sensitive to the work of the Holy Spirit in your life. Follow His guidance without fear when you have to talk.

Christ Himself promised, "But you will receive power when the Holy Spirit comes on you; and you will be My witnesses" (Acts 1:8). By remaining in regular fellowship with Christ, you will find yourself in harmony with His will. Through His power and the guidance of the Holy Spirit, you should never fear saying how you feel.

Guide of the words that I should speak, assist me with Your Spirit to say with conviction what I believe to be right. Amen.

Read: Philippians 4:2-9

November 25

God's unique peace

Do not be anxious about anything, but in everything, by prayer and petition, with thanksgiving, present your requests to God. And the peace of God, which transcends all understanding, will guard your hearts and your minds in Christ Jesus.

— PHILIPPIANS 4:6 —

Peace *with* God will result in peace *in* God. Your debt has been paid: the Cross on Golgotha is a guarantee thereof. You should accept it and make it your own. The problem is that many people think that this is far too easy to be true. Without accepting this mercy and grace you can never have permanent peace, "Therefore, since we have been justified through faith, we have peace with God through our Lord Jesus Christ" (Rom. 5:1). Trust in God is essential for peace. Time and again, the assurance is given in the Scriptures, "God is my Savior; I trust in Him; I am no longer afraid!" And again, "You will keep in perfect peace him whose mind is steadfast, because he trusts in You" (Is. 26:3).

Peace with God is the result of an intimately personal relationship with God. Our God is not distant from us and He desires us to come into a relationship with Him. God is our peace and without knowledge of Him our search for peace is useless.

God's peace is meant for all people and not only for a select little group, "Peace to those far and near" (Is. 57:19). Without that peace, we will never rest until our dying day, "But the wicked are like the tossing sea, which cannot rest" (Is. 57:20).

It was Luther who said, "We receive in our souls, in our whole being the peace that goes beyond all understanding, the peace of reconciliation and justification, that moment when the soul says amen to everything that God did for us." I pray that you will have that peace.

Loving God of peace, help Your child to taste Your perfect peace in the midst of his struggles. Amen.

November 26

Read: Colossians 2:6-15

Spiritual maturity

So then, just as you received Christ Jesus as Lord, continue to live in him, rooted and built up in him, strengthened in the faith as you were taught, and overflowing with thankfulness.
— COLOSSIANS 2:6-7 —

One of the dark clouds threatening the church of Christ is the number of immature disciples: people who say that they love Jesus Christ, but whose love is meager and whose testimony is ineffective. They remain babies in the faith and must be fed milk at a time when they should already be living on solid food.

These people gave themselves to the Lord in great sincerity, but they have stopped growing in their spiritual lives. The Word teaches them, and all of us, that we should make an honest evaluation of our spiritual growth and development.

The point of departure for Christian growth is a personal meeting with God through the sacrifice of atonement on the cross by His Son, Jesus Christ. Through the Word, God guides us to the incarnate Word. This is done by the Holy Spirit. However, we dare not remain at this meeting. We must allow the Holy Spirit to guide us to a deeper knowledge of the risen and living Redeemer.

On the way to spiritual maturity, the Christian develops a still stronger awareness of His presence. This creates a hunger to know Him better. Thus, we come to a spiritual willingness to discipline our thoughts and to nurture them with enriching ideas from the Scriptures.

In this way our obedience to the will of the Master grows daily. It is revealed to us by the Holy Spirit.

As you grow spiritually the image of Christ is unconsciously revealed in you and your faith will enrich the lives of those around you.

Holy Spirit of God, I thank You for the sparkling new life to which You have guided me. In grace continue Your blessed work in my life. Amen.

Read: Philippians 2:1-11   November 27

Humility

Do nothing out of selfish ambition or vain conceit, but in humility consider others better than yourselves.

— PHILIPPIANS 2:3 —

There are people who are immediately on the defensive if you ask them for the reason for their actions. It is especially true if they are not very logical or if their pride is hurt. An arrogant person believes firmly and with conviction that he is always right and will even refuse to argue the point.

Unfortunately, humility is confused with weakness in our times. Many people believe that if you are humble you will be trampled on. A truly humble person will never feel hurt or offended by the ridiculous pride of an immature person. Humility has the exceptional quality of absorbing insults and disparaging remarks. Humility is able to convert bitterness to forgiveness and change hatred into love.

Christ taught us the lesson of humility through His life. His command is, "Learn from Me for I am gentle and humble in heart, and you will find rest for your souls" (Mt. 11:29). Humble people soon discover that if they walk in humility with God, they find wisdom which enables them to distinguish the essential values of life. They can display the most noble qualities of discipleship in their lives, because they follow the example of their Master.

Humility is a gift of grace that comes from God and should not be confused with making yourself a doormat. Humility gives life dignity and is always willing to listen and to understand. This virtue should be reflected in the life of every disciple of our humble Lord and Savior.

Lord my God, I pray that the nature of Jesus Christ be reflected in my daily life. Amen.

November 28

Read: Philippians 1:27-2:4

Family ties

Each of you should look not only to your own interests, but also to the interests of others.

– PHILIPPIANS 2:4 –

There are few things in life which give more satisfaction than our families. Sharing interests, joys and sorrows binds a family together so firmly, that no force on earth can break those invisible ties. Where there is a healthy, strong and noble family life, you will find that the evils of the world are absent.

In the worrisome times we live in it is important to remember that we are all part of the family of God. We were adopted into this family by Jesus Christ. As children of God we are all brothers and sisters in Christ. It is sad to say so, but we as Christians do not always behave in this way to one another.

The needs of people in the modern world are great and divergent. There are needs on the spiritual, emotional and physical levels of life. If these needs are not satisfied, you inevitably find jealousy, bitterness, despair and even hatred.

God commanded us to love our fellow man. It places the heavy obligation on us to concern ourselves with the distress of others. There is always a way in which you can help. It can be through material assistance, advice or warmhearted consolation. You would never drive off a member of your family who comes to your door looking for help. Dare you then ignore another member of the family of Christ?

The Holy Spirit teaches us to see distress and He also gives us the wisdom to know what to do in a given situation. The main thing is that true Christianity can never be selfish and that it always thinks of others with compassion.

Heavenly Father, I thank You for the family ties which bind Your children across the world to one another with love, through Jesus Christ. Amen.

Read: Matthew 16:24-28   November 29

The price of discipleship

"If anyone would come after me, he must deny himself and take up his cross and follow me."
– MATTHEW 16:24 –

In Christian circles great emphasis is placed on the special gifts which the Master gives to those who love Him and serve Him. Those who accept His sovereignty in their lives experience joy, strength, a balanced outlook on life, peace, love and many other privileges.

It is a fact that we cannot experience a deep and meaningful fellowship with the living Christ without experiencing a spiritual, moral and often physical climax as well. When Christ gives Himself to someone and is accepted in gratitude and love, that life will change radically.

What is often overlooked in the euphoria of surrender and change, is the equivalent action that Christ demands from us in return. True Christianity is neither easy nor cheap. It is not easy since you have to change the direction of your entire life and you have to place it under the guidance of the Holy Spirit. It is impossible to accept the sovereignty of Christ and still continue to live in the rut that you had lived in before meeting Him.

A change in your life pattern is possible only if you place your life in His hands to be used in His service. The price of such surrender is often higher than many people are willing to pay. It simply means placing His will above your own. Yet those who accepted the challenge and paid the price, testify that the price of complete surrender can never be measured up against the reward it brings.

Lord of my life, I give my everything to You – whatever the cost may be – because I want to remain faithful to You. Amen.

November 30

Read: Galatians 5:2-12

Faith, love and actions

The only thing that counts is faith expressing itself through love.
— GALATIANS 5:6 —

There is a form of faith that involves theological speculation and wishful thinking, and in practical, everyday life is neither here nor there. It does not lead to actions of love and is therefore not fruitful but often useless.

If my faith does not lead to a deeper experience of God, it is an illusionary faith and it will serve no permanent purpose in my life. God is the source of all true love and to have a faith that leads to action, I should have an uninterrupted connection with the Source.

Loving Jesus Christ so much that His presence is a living reality in your life is such an inspiration for your faith that your are urged by His love to do His will. A steadfast faith and trust in the glorified and living Redeemer is the foundation of all pure Christian teaching.

Faith can only be alive and meaningful if it is supported by love. Without love your faith is twisted and it will never achieve the height, depth, length or breadth of its many possibilities.

To be pleasing to God and to achieve your highest purpose, faith should be confirmed, inspired and supported by love.

If your faith finds expression in love, your beliefs become an everyday, practical reality. Then you look away from yourself and your own problems and you see the world in distress. Then you hear the Master say, "Whatever you did for one of the least of these brothers of Mine, you did for Me" (Mt. 25:40).

Then your faith is no longer only speculation and pious words, but it becomes love in action.

God of love, through our love for You we have learned to serve our fellow man in love. May we continue doing so by the grace of Your Son. Amen.

DECEMBER

December 1

Read: John 3:1-21

God's love letter

"For God so loved the world that he gave his one and only Son, that whoever believes in him shall not perish but have eternal life."
— JOHN 3:16 —

Christmas reminds us that God wrote a love letter to this world. Time and again throughout history, God has unequivocally declared His love for humankind. But the final letter in which God opened His whole heart to us, is delivered to the world's mailbox at Christmas time.

The stable in Bethlehem is God's mailbox. That is where the Child of His love was born and that Child is God's letter in which you can read just how much God loves you. God could not have said it more emphatically: He says it with His best and most precious. He says it with His only Son, Jesus Christ.

That is why Advent is so special: it is God's correspondence time. Now no one can doubt His love anymore. His love became concrete through the birth, death and resurrection of His Son.

Besides the pleasure experienced when receiving post from heaven, it also brings a great responsibility. It fills Advent with holy tension. No mother would ever give her child away; but God does! God gives away His only Son to you and to me to assure us of His boundless love.

God gives you the Child of His love, but He also asks you for your love. Faith is our answer to the love of God. God asks us to give our hearts, that is the challenge of Christmas time. That is the price which we have to pay for a blessed Christmas. We will have to reply to God's letter with Peter's words, "Lord, You know everything, You know that I love You!"

Holy God, heavenly Father, Child of Bethlehem, I profess my love for You again and beg You to purify and intensify my love during this joyous time of the year. Amen.

Read: 1 Corinthians 13:1-13

December 2

The world's need

And now these three remain: faith, hope and love. But the greatest of these is love.

— 1 Corinthians 13:13 —

The state of the world is a cause for concern. Constant strife, reports of war, terrorism and hatred amongst people is flooding the world like an ominous wave. Many plans are made to ensure people's safety. It is, however, often these very plans that are the cause of distrust and disunity.

God's solution to the problems of the world is unfortunately regarded as impractical, idealistic and simplistic. God's command is clear: you must love God above all and love your fellow man as you love yourself. There is no command from God that is more important than this.

If humankind could just learn to love, the adversity of the world would start disappearing and a solution to problems would be closer. Most people accept this truth, yet they refuse to use it in practice because it demands faith, courage and sacrifice. If contemporary Christians would live and preach the gospel, it would be the biggest single contribution to peace on earth.

Love is not only an emotional or sentimental approach to problems. To really love means to impress God's stamp on every situation where injustice, hatred, bitterness and other negative and sinful powers fester unchecked. Divine love cannot justify that which humiliates and degrades people.

Christmas is the ideal time to start flooding the world with love. Let love be your inspiration and guide and you will find yourself a co-worker of God in healing and uplifting the community where God has placed you.

God of love, through Jesus Christ I put myself under Your command as an instrument of Your love in the world. Amen.

December 3

Read: Isaiah 64:1-12

How great You are!

Since ancient times no one has heard, no ear has perceived, no eye has seen any God besides you, who acts on behalf of those who wait for him.

– Isaiah 64:4 –

Through the ages Christianity has been attacked from all sides. The reliability of our faith and even God's existence have been questioned. Thousands have experienced abuse, persecution and torture as a result of their faith, and many chose death rather than deny the Lord Jesus Christ. That is how great God's love is for His children and His children's love for their God.

If you live your life through faith in Jesus Christ, you will gradually become aware of His living presence. If you place your trust in God and surrender your life to Him unconditionally. You will become more deeply aware of the fact that He holds His hand over you and that He leads and accompanies you through the maze of life.

The more intense your relationship with the Master is, the more the Holy Spirit becomes a reality in your life. He talks with you through your thoughts and leads you in God's perfect will for your life. A life that is lived in Christ, with Christ and for Christ, is given a new dimension. You develop a feeling of self-confidence that has nothing to do with pride. You discover peace of mind – the peace that nothing else in the world can offer you.

This gift cannot be given by either man or heathen idol. It makes the words of Christ in Matthew 19:26, a living reality: "With man this is impossible, but with God all things are possible." It is this almighty God who reminds us at Christmas that He descended to us through His Son. In worship we can only rejoice, "How great You are!"

Great and Holy God, I worship You in Jesus Christ as my Father, and kneel in awe before Your greatness and kindness. Amen.

Read: Revelation 22:6-20

December 4

Jesus is coming again

"Behold, I am coming soon!"

– Revelation 22:7 –

Advent comes from the Latin word "Adventus" which means "arrival". The four weeks before Christmas when we celebrate the birth of Christ, is called Advent. The fact that the Son of God came to us in the flesh, as a person, has remained a reason for rejoicing every Christmas throughout the ages.

Christ descended from the heavenly glory to the humiliating crib and manger. This had to happen in order for Him to lift lost humanity to the heights of salvation.

Christ is the great Sower. Christmas reminds us that He sowed with tears. Psalm 126:6 applies to Him, "He who goes out weeping, carrying seed to sow, will return with songs of joy, carrying sheaves with him."

His work, which started with humiliation at His arrival on Christmas Day, will be completed when He arrives in glory to reap the harvest. It will be a triumphant arrival in majesty and glory. It will be the day of all days, the day on which the eternal fate of all people will be announced, the great Advent which is prayerfully awaited by the true congregation of Christ. Christmas proclaims time and again, "Look, I am coming soon!" Will your answer be "Yes, Lord Jesus, come!"

There are four Advent times in your life to acquire salvation of: a coming in Spirit to let you personally share in the acquired salvation; a coming in death to transfer the blessed from the sphere of the temporary into eternity; a coming in glory to end the history of humankind, followed by eternity. As such, the days before Christmas become rich in comfort. We see Christ everywhere. In our own battle and humiliation we see His crib; in our hearts we see the cross and mercy of Christ; in our hour of death His crown of victory and at any moment His second coming in glory!

Thank You, Holy Master, for the great blessing of Christmas. May my sincere prayer remain, "Yes, Lord Jesus, come!" Amen.

December 5

Read: Matthew 2:1-12

Beyond the stars

After Jesus was born ... Magi from the east came to Jerusalem.

– Matthew 2:1 –

A story was recorded somewhere about a man who bought a gold mine and in his excitement he tunnelled a kilometer into the earth in search of the precious metal. But he did not find any. His excitement changed to despair and he sold the mine for next to nothing. The new owner excavated only another three meters when he came across a fantastically rich gold vein.

We often make the same mistake as the first owner. We often lack perseverance and give up before we get to the core of a matter. The wise men from the East persevered in their search and refused to give up before they found the Gold Reef.

At first the star was their guide. God wanted to bring those who were far away, closer. That is why He searched for them on their own level and in terms that they knew – a star. They were astrologers or astronomers, learned priests of their nation. They came from Mesopotamia, the initial paradise from which Adam and Eve were driven. All the way they followed the star to worship the second Adam, Jesus Christ, the Messiah.

For these children of darkness the star was the first sign of light. The star was their guide, but not the Redeemer! And what a wonderful reward God prepared for these followers of the star! They were enchanted by the star so that they could find the Child. That is how God calls and searches: for the wise men with a star; for the shepherds with choirs of angels. In His love, God gives us stars to guide us to Jesus: "Bethlehem star, lead me to the Christ Child!"

We should not stand in awe of the star. This is only the start of our road to salvation. We have to move from the star to the Word; from nature to Scripture. This is the road to the Redeemer in His crib.

God and Father, thank You for the stars in my life; stars that lead me to You. Let me persevere on the road which will bring me to You time and again. Amen.

Read: Micah 5:1-15

December 6

A light and a lamp

But you, Bethlehem Ephrathah, though you are small among the clans of Judah, out of you will come for me one who will be ruler over Israel.

– MICAH 5:2 –

The wise men were first guided by a star; but then the Word of God lit up their way. When the star had guided them to Jerusalem, there was great agitation. Everyone was expecting a king, yet no one knew where to find Him. The Scribes got together to consider the question, "What does the Word of God say?" It was no longer only a star. For the astronomers and astrologers it must have looked like regression: away from the shining star to musty scrolls.

The wise men had their star, but no Scripture. The people of Israel had the Scripture, but were without knowledge of their King. A King who had no address. Return to the Word, for the Word speaks with irrefutable authority. That is how the particular prediction was identified in the book of Micah, the fifth chapter, the first verse: "But you, Bethlehem Ephrathah."

On to Bethlehem then, in obedience to the Word of God, towards the small town of great happenings.

The star, therefore, is subject to the Word. The golden sheen disappears, while truth and reality break through. Emotion and romance disappear and the Word of God triumphs.

The final journey to Bethlehem is always a journey on the authority of God's Word. We love the stars and reluctantly depart from them, but it is essential that we do so. We need Scripture: the pure and prophetic Word of God.

With only stars and no Scripture, we are left embarrassed by an insatiable need for eternity and with no address for our King.

The Word leads to the richest gold reef, to Bethlehem, to the stable, to the crib, to the King!

Eternal Word, prevent me from becoming so enthralled by the stars and trimmings of Christmas, that I cannot reach the incarnate Word. Amen.

December 7

Read: John 1:1-18

The Incarnate Word

The Word became flesh and made his dwelling among us. We have seen his glory.

– JOHN 1:14 –

For the three wise men their first guide was the star, but in Jerusalem they discovered the Word, and the Word led them to Bethlehem and the King. Listen to what the Word says, "For to us a Child is born, to us a Son is given, and the government will be on His shoulders. And He will be called Wonderful Counselor, Mighty God, Everlasting Father, Prince of Peace" (Is. 9:6).

Much of God is revealed in nature. However, the revelation of God in the Holy Scripture exceeds all else. It is the source of true joy during the Christmas season. The nativity scene is completed when the wise men kneel before the Child to bring homage to Him. They now understand the mystery of God in the flesh for the first time.

The enchantment of the stars is something of the past; the light of God breaks through and enters their hearts triumphantly. They understand the wonder of God becoming flesh for us. Now the Child is the most beautiful shining Morning Star.

We also have to progress from the star to the Word, from milk to solid food, and from there to worshiping in spirit and in truth. The stars all around us have to lead us to the Word, and the Word has to lead us to the crib where we can worship: offering the gold of love; the incense of prayer and the myrrh of sacrifice.

At the manger we learn what the stars could not tell us: that earth became the center of the universe on Christmas Day. Come and kneel in worship before Christ the Lord!

Once the stars disappear, the eternal day of God appears before us. God no longer speaks to us through the stars, or the Word, but He speaks to us through Jesus, Immanuel, forever and unchanging!

Loving Father, lead me past the stars and the Word to the Child in the crib: to worshiping in spirit and in truth. Amen.

Read: John 3:1-21

December 8

Gifts

"For God so loved the world that he gave his one and only Son."
– JOHN 3:16 –

Christmas is inextricably linked to gifts. Of all the gifts through the ages, God's gift remains unsurpassed. That is why we rejoice with Paul once again during this season, "Thanks be to God for His indescribable gift!" (2 Cor. 9:15).

A gift must comply with certain standards and the motive must be pure. God gave His gift out of love. We give due to a sense of duty, or because it is the fashion to do so, or with a cheating heart. Gifts of love demand a sacrifice, because if you truly want to give, you must give of yourself – of your most noble and best – as God gave. If your gift is not motivated by love, it is actually useless. "If I give all I possess to the poor and surrender my body to the flames, but have not love, I gain nothing" (1 Cor. 13:3).

The gift must have intrinsic value as well. God's gift was a "life": His only Son. That Son would through life, death and resurrection open to us the road to paradise. Therefore it was an invaluable gift. What the world wants is not so much our possessions, but ourselves: our lives, our love, our testimonies. Money cannot pay for that.

The gift must be unique. It is delightful to receive a gift which has a singular value. Nothing is as intrinsically unique as God's gift. Nothing can compare with it. We owe others the gift of a Christian disposition and testimony.

A true gift must be useful. Sometimes, on Christmas morning we wonder what to do with certain gifts. God's precious gift has been tested through the ages: in joy and in mourning; in happiness and sadness; in victory and defeat; in life and in death.

Heavenly Provider, assist me in deciding what my gifts will be. Help me not to hold back my love, but that I will give it freely. Amen.

December 9

Read: Luke 1:46-56

Rejoice in the majesty of God

"My soul glorifies the Lord and my spirit rejoices in God my Savior, for he has been mindful of the humble state of his servant."
– LUKE 1:46-48 –

Most people believe that God is great and glorious, but their fears, concerns and actions often contradict this belief. With their reasoning they accept God's greatness because they cannot imagine anything greater than the Creator. But this conviction has not penetrated their spirits or hearts. They therefore do not have the inner ability to meet the demands of life.

To appreciate the actual greatness of God, a spiritual dimension has to be added to the intellectual acceptance of the existence of a Greater Being. Professing an elevated God but leading a life of pettiness is no good. Many people live lives that are irreconcilable with a great and sacred God. It is only when your spirit comes to a realization of the greatness of God that you can start growing in your knowledge of God. You are only as big as your spirit allows you to be.

Getting to know God's true greatness, requires a genuine need to know Him. The invitation to rejoice in the greatness of the Lord must be accepted enthusiastically, especially during Christmas, by each pilgrim on the spiritual road. As your knowledge of God's true greatness increases through the teaching and guidance of the Holy Spirit, you will become more deeply aware of His living presence, and His peace and joy will become part of your life.

It is the reality of His presence, together with the awareness of His indwelling Spirit, that makes it possible for us to rejoice in the greatness of the Lord. With this in mind, let us sing our Christmas carols and hymns with renewed fervor this year.

Great and Sacred God, give me a clear understanding of Your greatness so that I can rejoice in my salvation. Amen.

Read: James 5:13-19

December 10

Time for forgiveness

Therefore confess your sins to each other and pray for each other.
– James 5:16 –

It is as if the Christmas season softens the hearts of people, and as if reconciliation during this period is not quite so difficult. No one can live without making mistakes. It is therefore extremely important to know how to deal with mistakes. Some people are overwhelmed by their mistakes and others again feel that if they ignore their mistakes they will disappear. This is no solution. You cannot live your whole life with self-reproach; you cannot erase a mistake from your memory by ignoring it, because it remains in your subconscious where it does its destructive work.

Mistakes must be dealt with in a sensible and courageous way. The first step is to confess to God the mistake you have made. He knows about it in any case and therefore it is no good trying to hide it from Him. This confession will cleanse your conscience and prepare you for the next step.

Through prayer and meditation you must find out what God's will is for you on your road to recovery. Take care that innocent people are not hurt in the process. In trying to correct a mistake, many people make confessions which cause irreparable damage and unnecessary suffering. Some confessions must be made to God only. However big the mistake might have been, His forgiveness can erase it all. When God has forgiven you, you must forgive yourself as well. It is a liberating experience.

Thank God for the fact that He is a merciful and compassionate God, and that during Christmas, He reminds us once again that He has sent His Son to cleanse us from sin. Get up and start again. Be determined not to make the same mistake again, through His power. This is your first step on the road to becoming an instrument of reconciliation in the hand of God.

Merciful God, I accept Your forgiveness with thanks. I will no longer be consumed by mistakes from the past, and with the help of Your Holy Spirit, I will not repeat them. Amen.

December 11

Read: Isaiah 40:1-11

Preparation

"In the desert prepare the way for the LORD; make straight in the wilderness a highway for our God."

– ISAIAH 40:3 –

This time of the year is characterized by preparations. Gifts must be bought, food stocks must be replenished, invitations must be sent out and Christmas cards must be mailed.

Much has to be done in preparation for the celebration; things that are specifically associated with this time of the year. There is, however, another and greater preparation to be done: the preparation of our hearts for the sake of a deeper and true meaning of Christmas.

Advent provides you with an excellent opportunity to review your spiritual life. While you are contemplating the unfathomable love of God, you must determine your attitude towards others. God gave you His Son, and you will have to decide how much of yourself you can give to God and your fellow man.

This is a time, more than any other time of the year, to heal broken relationships with love; a time to give not only tangible gifts, but especially the gift of yourself, your time and your love for the sake of your fellow man.

In these exalted and holy days preceding Christmas, we have to make a road for God in the barren desert of a loveless world. Firstly, it has to happen in your heart, by discarding everything that is ungodly and self-centered. You will then be ready to receive the Christ Child in your heart. Martin Luther said, "Even if Christ was born in Bethlehem a thousand times and not in your heart, you will still be lost!"

Holy God, help me to make room for Your Son in my life, a place of honor which will not be taken by anything or anyone else! Amen.

Read: Galatians 4:1-7   December 12

God keeps His promises

When the time had fully come, God sent his Son.
– GALATIANS 4:4 –

Never make the mistake of questioning God's promises. Despite appearances to the contrary, His complete and perfect will is still revealed in this world. As promised, He manifested Himself in the person of Jesus Christ. So the time shall come when this dispensation will come to an end. When this will happen is known to God alone. It is, however, as inevitable as the coming of His Son in the form of a man.

When you think of how God kept His promises to humankind, you may feel insignificant and unimportant, and wonder whether you have any role in the order of things. The only way in which you can test the truth of God's promises and be assured of His love for you, is to test His promises. Through the ages people have proved that God is loyal to those who put their trust in Him.

If you are inclined to be anxious and to carry the problems of the world on your insignificant shoulders, remember the Divine command to take all your anxieties to Him since He cares for you. If you suffer from acute loneliness, there are many places in the Word which assure you that God is always with you.

For each need in your life there is a promise from God that it will be satisfied. You must look for these promises in the Word as a prospector would look for a gold vein. These promises are often hidden from the eyes of the superficial reader. The Holy Spirit will reveal them to you if you pray and ask Him to.

As surely as God has kept His promise of Christmas, He will also keep His promises regarding your life.

Mentor and Master, help me to apply Your great and glorious promises to my daily life through the Holy Spirit. Amen.

December 13

Read: Isaiah 30:8-18

Break the murderous rhythm

In quietness and trust is your strength.

– Isaiah 30:15 –

At this time of the year most people are on leave, coming to a halt after hard work and a year of great demands. People are relaxing at the beach or at holiday resorts. Some discover that they rest the best in their own backyards.

It is good to come to a standstill for a while, away from the everyday rush of our lives. We must consider this another gift from God's treasury and we must utilize it fruitfully and effectively.

It is not easy to be still in this noisy, tumultuous world. That is why we have to concentrate on seeking calmness from God. The slowing down in our lives will inevitably bring about a feeling of calm, so that we will understand Isaiah's words, that our strength lies in quietness and trust. We must purposefully slow down our rushed way of life so that we can receive a vision of the vastness of time from the Lord.

In creation we find God, ourselves and our fellow human beings. Our tense nerves and muscles are soothed by the music of mountain streams or the continuous ebb and flow of the waves.

We must make time to come to a halt and see and do the things that become impossible in the race of life: a calm family conversation; observing the beauty of flowers; to see the smile in a child's eyes; to pat a stray dog's head; to spend time with the Word of the Lord.

Let us look up at the branches of tall trees and know that they grow so tall because they grow slowly. That is how God reveals His refreshing power in your life and brings you peace.

Creator God, I thank You for the peace and restoration You provide and which I experience in quiet trust in You. Amen.

Read: Psalm 127:1-5   December 14

"House" or home

Unless the LORD builds the house, its builders labor in vain.
— PSALM 127:1 —

You may possibly get the God-given chance to take stock of the priorities in your family life during this time of the year. Sometimes the world's idea of a family is so distorted that we have to redefine the basics.

What is a "home"? Is it a roof over your head to keep out the rain? Four walls to ward off the biting wind? A floor to ward off the cold from the earth? Doors to allow you admission and windows for a view? Yes, that is a house, but it is definitely not a home. A home is far more than that!

A home is a baby's smile, a mother's lullaby, children's laughter and the protective power of a father. It is the warmth of loving hearts, the light in joyful eyes, friendliness, faithfulness, camaraderie and love.

A home is the first school and the first church a child gets to know. It is here that they learn what is right, good and precious. It is here that they find a cure for every pain and comfort when they're hurt.

It is a place where joy and sadness are shared, where house mates respect and love one another and where friends are always welcome. Here the most simple meal is a meal fit for a king, because it was honestly earned and prepared with love. Money is never more important than love in a home. It is a place where the family devotions link the hearts of the family members to God.

That is what you call a home ... and that is where the Lord pours out His blessings.

Thank You, heavenly Father, that my home is already preparing me for the eternal Home of God: our home with You! Amen.

December 15   Read: John 1:1-18

Meditation for Christmas

The Word became flesh and made his dwelling among us. We have seen his glory, the glory of the One and Only, who came from the Father, full of grace and truth.

– JOHN 1:14 –

It is every Christian's calling and duty to approach Christmas with the right attitude. Prayerfully meditating on this wonder of God's mercy, we must confirm and renew our intentions: to place Christ at the center of our celebrations. To give Him the place of honor in your heart and then in your actions during this time.

Do not allow yourself to be dragged along by the commercialization of Christmas. Refuse to be a part of the mad rush and the excessive wastage that occurs close to Christmas.

Do not become so absorbed in Christmas decorations that the stable, the crib, and especially the Child, are lost. Let us pray for the simplicity of the shepherds so that we can arrive at the core of Christmas: the Christ Child.

Ensure that Christmas remains a family celebration. Do not go and search for Christmas joy in the world outside, but find it in the warmth and intimacy of the family: father, mother and children, as it was on the first night around the manger. Ensure that Christ is always welcome in your home during Christmas by avoiding superficial pleasure, worldly fun and worldly parties.

Remember that death lurks on the roads, especially at this time of the year. Christ came to bring life – let us drive responsibly like His children would.

Remember that you have a family appointment with Christ at His house on Christmas morning. Also ensure that every Christmas card you mail portrays your faith in Christ.

Do everything in your power to instill the right approach to Christmas in your children. When you are no longer here, these will be their most precious memories.

Jesus of Bethlehem, help me approach Christmas in a pure way, through the work of the Holy Spirit in my life. Amen.

Read: Matthew 5:21-26   December 16

Reconciliation

"Therefore, if you are offering your gift at the altar and there remember that your brother has something against you, leave your gift there in front of the altar. First go and be reconciled to your brother; then come and offer your gift."

— MATTHEW 5:23-24 —

Pope Paul V once said, "A love of reconciliation is neither weak nor cowardly. It requires courage, nobleness and generosity, occasionally heroism and the victory over yourself rather than over your adversary. Sometimes it may even appear as shame, but that never harms justice or the rights of the poor. In reality it is the patient, wise art of peace, love and of living with your fellow human beings in the example of Christ, with a power of heart and mind which is fashioned on His."

At this point in time we all have to start praying and working towards true Christian reconciliation. It takes two parties to ensure continuous peace, but someone has to take the first step. It is the Christian's duty even if "your brother has something against you".

Reconciliation is a person's deepest need, because the alternative is self-destruction. A person becomes most noble when he has learnt to forgive. The person who cannot or does not want to forgive others, destroys the bridge that he needs to cross himself, since we all need forgiveness.

"I forgive but I can't forget", is another way of saying "I refuse to forgive unconditionally, as Christ forgave me." There are few things that display Christ's attitude more clearly than reconciliation.

Someone who has experienced forgiveness and reconciliation in Christ and knows what it means, can forgive others. There is only one entreaty in the Lord's Prayer which is conditional, and that is the prayer for forgiveness. True followers of Christ have to be the instruments of reconciliation in His world.

God of reconciliation and forgiveness, help me to promote reconciliation in the world through Christ. I, who have been forgiven, gratefully sing my song of redemption. Amen.

December 17

Read: Psalm 42:1-11

Fulfillment in Christ

As the deer pants for streams of water, so my soul pants for you, O God. My soul thirsts for God, for the living God.

– PSALM 42:1-2 –

The same nostalgia that moved the heart of the psalmist, is still revealed today in modern man's longing for God.

People in our times have the same desires and wishes, but they hide these under psychological verbosity which they often do not understand themselves. They refuse to admit their failings and shortcomings and that's why they do not find satisfaction and happiness in their daily lives.

The consequences of this unhappy situation is a continuous search for reality along paths which their own blind hearts plan and which can never give fulfillment. The hunger for wealth becomes of primary importance; or the desire for prestige, with the social standing it gives. These things make demands on the body which it is not equipped to deal with.

Those who want self-satisfaction very seldom have time for spiritual values. These are seen as unnecessary, and he who attaches any value to them is seen as somewhat old-fashioned and out of touch with the realities of life.

If you are wise, you will realize that spiritual satisfaction and true fulfillment are the only types of satisfaction that are worthwhile. It cannot, however, be obtained along the way of materialistic thinking. A true balance between the spiritual and material is necessary. This is only possible when the living Christ takes the central position in your life.

The Master is involved in and cares for every aspect of your life. When you taste His complete provision, you will experience a rich and fruitful life.

Living Savior, in You alone do I find fulfillment and satisfaction. I praise Your name for it. Amen.

Read: Luke 2:1-20

December 18

Be faithful to your vision

"Let's go to Bethlehem and see this thing that has happened, which the Lord has told us about."

— LUKE 2:15 —

The humble shepherds received a visit from God's messengers, and they were filled with wonder. The glory of heaven, accompanied by a host of angels, was something far beyond their comprehension.

However, their reaction to this unique visit was immediate. They did not have a meeting first to discuss the event or to appoint a committee to investigate it. They did not even waste time by telling one another of the wonderful experience they had had. No, they said, "Let's go to Bethlehem." The events of that night required immediate action.

Modern disciples of the Master can experience the reality of His presence and be deeply touched by personally experiencing His love. The moment becomes almost too holy to share with others. Consequently it is hidden in the heart and eventually it becomes a vague memory without any inspiration or power.

If God has become a reality in your life in a special way, it has happened for a specific purpose. He may be so near to you that your heart may burn with a great love for Him and your fellow man. He may have a vocation for you which you must answer. The important truth is this: if you are inspired by His living presence, do not allow that vision to fade, but let it come to expression through immediate and positive action.

Christmas is a time of holy and inspired visions that call us to serve God and to become what He intended us to be. Do not let this mountain peak experience pass unused.

Lord Jesus, give me the courage and wisdom to react positively to Your inspiration in my life through Your Holy Spirit. Amen.

December 19

Read: Luke 2:8-20

God's sign – a Child

So they hurried off and found Mary and Joseph, and the baby, who was lying in the manger.

– LUKE 2:16 –

Gabe van Duinen, the Dutch theologist, tells that as a little boy he used to lie awake at night when his father was not at home. His mother was there but not his father ... But when he heard the key in the lock and his father's heavy footsteps in the passage, he was calm; then he could turn around and sleep, because father was home.

In the manger in Bethlehem the door of the world opens and God enters. God Himself, in the Person of the baby Jesus. Father is home. This is the great wealth of Christmas: the great and almighty God becomes an insignificant, weak Child, so that the weakest and smallest among us will understand.

"Christmas" is God's love in its purest form. A beckoning love which invites the lost and lapsed person to the heart of God again with the touching wave of a Child's hand reaching out from a manger filled with straw. That is why we all become children again at Christmas. Our hearts relive a timeless adventure in a world of unquestioned faith, where all things are possible immediately, and where the child of the King is the focus.

For a while we leave the foreseeable path of life and walk the path of imagination, awe and exciting joy, while we exult in the immeasurable love of God. We all become part of God's love. This inevitably touches the most monotonous life with benevolence, and allows the promise of reliving the highest peace and joy to all who have the heart of a child.

Christmas is the love of God in concrete form. God gives Himself to you in the Person of the Child of Bethlehem. He gives His Child as a sign that you can be a child of God!

I praise You, wonderful God and Father, that You became human in Christ so that I can be a child of God. Amen.

Read: Matthew 2:1-12

December 20

God works in silence

Jesus was born in Bethlehem in Judea, during the time of King Herod.

— MATTHEW 2:1 —

This historical fact would change the thinking of humankind. It would result in a re-evaluation of our values. The creatures of God's hands would live through a spiritual experience which was unknown before. The Child Jesus was the Christ who would lead man to a new, unique relationship with the eternal Father.

Apart from the miracle of Jesus' birth, it is amazing how quietly He came into the world. A few simple shepherds and a small group of star-gazers saluted His coming. This Divine humility and meekness placed a stamp on the life of His Son. As a baby He was already a refugee, and He spent the greater part of His early youth in a small town in the country.

While His ministry forced Him into the limelight, He sought the silence where He could be alone with God or with His small group of friends. Despite the fact that God worked in silence through the life of Christ, there was no other life that has had such an enormous impact on man and history. An English hymn writer wrote, "God moves in a mysterious way His wonders to perform." That principle is still true today.

While the church of Christ accepts and accommodates expressions of exuberant joy, the true church of God happens where the Spirit of God touches the spirit of man in silence. An experience with the living Christ is strictly personal and takes place in the quiet of one's spirit. It is in this silence that the unshakable assurance originates that Christ was born on earth long ago and is present with us today.

God of silences, I thank You humbly for the assurance of Your presence which I receive in silence. Amen.

December 21

Read: Luke 2:8-20

Joy to the world

"I bring you good news of great joy that will be for all the people."
– LUKE 2:10 –

There are some people who feel unworthy when they are told that they can ask Christ to come into their lives. Their idea of the greater responsibility linked to Christianity causes them to turn away from Christ in fear and trembling. They cannot accept the consequences that Christianity will have on their lives.

Things have not changed at all since the very first Christmas. As the angels spoke to the shepherds during that night and brought them "good news of great joy", so the presence of the living Christ in your life will cause the greatest joy you will ever experience.

The coming of the Savior and the gift of salvation is the great news of the Christian faith. The angels told the shepherds that their message was intended "for all people". That is why you do not have to be concerned or worried about your competence, worthiness or anything else.

Christ offers Himself in a loving way to you after you surrender your life to Him. Do not allow fear or self-reproach to deprive you of the great privilege of knowing Him as your Redeemer. In addition to this, He is also your Master and your Friend.

Allow Him into your life and experience the joy of the news which the angels announced for all people. It is a joy you dare not miss and which God also meant for you.

Redeemer and Friend, I open my heart to You in humility and gratitude. Thank You for the unparalleled joy that You give me. Amen.

Read: Luke 2:1-7

December 22

Come, Lord Jesus!

She gave birth to her firstborn, a son. She wrapped him in cloths and placed him in a manger, because there was no room for them in the inn.

– Luke 2:7 –

The wonder and mystery of Christmas has a profound influence on Christians around the world. At this time we sing wholeheartedly:

Hark, the herald angels sing
Glory to the new-born King.
Peace on earth and mercy mild
God and sinners reconciled.

For many people, however, Christmas has no spiritual meaning. The entertainment world emphasizes pleasure and superficial enjoyment so much that the deeper meaning of this sacred time is largely overshadowed. To a large percentage of people Father Christmas is of greater importance than the Christ Child.

When Jesus was born in Bethlehem, He came to a world that was similar to the world we live in today. In those days a lack of involvement, violence and injustice were rampant. People were obsessed with themselves and their own interests. There was no room in their lives for Jesus Christ.

History has shown what enormous impression Christ has made on the world and on the lives of millions of people. When you enjoy the celebrations and festivities on Christmas day, do not refuse the living Christ access to your life. Open your heart and life to Him and you will experience the fullness and joy which Christmas holds.

Not making room for Christ at this time, is to make a mockery of what God intended Christmas to be.

Child of Bethlehem, Redeemer and Savior, I open my entire life to You once again and I invite You to move into my life permanently. Amen.

December 23

Read: Luke 2:25-35

God's deed at Christmas – and mine

Moved by the Spirit, he went into the temple courts. When the parents brought in the child Jesus to do for him what the custom of the Law required, Simeon took him in his arms and praised God.

– LUKE 2:27-28 –

Christmas is for all generations and for all times. Christmas is for the invincible youth; for the dynamic adult and for the calm and mature elderly person.

Simeon was already old. The Bible testifies that he was pious and just and "moved by the Spirit". The name "Simeon" means, "the one who listens." Therefore he did not only speak to God, but he also listened.

God blessed this man richly because he attached great value to dialogue with God. The great wonder of the first Christmas took place in his life and God's grace ordained that he would take the Christ Child in his arms. He knew without a doubt that he was holding his Savior in his arms. God's mercy to His children at Christmas is indescribably great!

Like Simeon, you and I should also learn to wait on God in prayer so that this deed can take place in our lives. We must look forward to it with great excitement and accept it in faith. Faith is seeing the invisible. Then you will proclaim that Christ is a light for the nations.

So immeasurably great is God's deed on Christmas Day that He places the Child of His love in your arms. With that you receive His redemption, His blood, His body and His love; everything needed for your salvation.

On your part you must take the Child in your arms and embrace Him. Accept Him as Savior. Christmas is the coming of God to man, and the coming of man to God. This is truly Christmas!

Redeemer and Savior, I took You into my heart and life, and that is why I know that Christmas is the celebration of Christ. Amen.

Read: Micah 5:1-14

December 24

House of bread

But you, Bethlehem Ephrathah, though you are small among the clans of Judah, out of you will come for me one who will be ruler over Israel, whose origins are from of old, from ancient times.

– MICAH 5:2 –

Christ was born in Bethlehem. One has to stoop very low when you enter the Church of the Nativity in Bethlehem. Let us meet the call, "O come let us adore Him!" at this time.

"Bethlehem" means "house of bread". It is appropriate that He who became the "Bread of life" to us, was born there.

Bethlehem has a long history. Jacob buried his beloved wife, Rachel, there and erected a pillar of remembrance for their undying love. God loved the world so much that He gave His only Son. Fourteen kilometers from Bethlehem is the pillar of remembrance representing God's undying love: the cross on Golgotha.

There Ruth worked as a wanderer, married Boaz and found her true home. In Bethlehem all our wanderings, all our delusions, our dead ends and confusion end. He who was born said, "I am the way and the truth and the life" (Jn. 14:6). We, the lost children, came home and we are safe in the Father's love.

Bethlehem was the town of David's childhood, it was home. It was for the water of the well at the entrance to Bethlehem that David longed for when he fled from Saul. Here, He was born who became the "Fountain of living water" for our thirsty souls. Our hearts, filled with fear, would find relief for the "other thirst" in Him: "But whoever drinks the water that I give him will never thirst" (Jn. 4:14).

Let us bow at Bethlehem and dedicate ourselves anew to this Redeemer before we enter Christmas.

Child of Bethlehem, You are everything anyone could ever desire. I thank You that You were born in my life and became my Redeemer. Praise the Lord, O my soul, and forget not all His mercies. Amen.

December 25

Read: Matthew 1:18-25

Immanuel – God with us

"The virgin will be with child and will give birth to a son, and they will call him Immanuel – which means 'God with us.'"
— Matthew 1:23 —

Up to a century ago the disease "Marasmus" (Greek for "waste away") claimed many children's lives. Its victims were mostly children from well-to-do and wealthy homes who were treated in expensive hospitals. Scientists found that this disease was caused by need. These children did not need expensive toys or germ-free hospitals, they needed the love of their parents!

Man was wasting away in the loneliness of sin. His greatest need was for the Divine touch. Christmas declares that God, through Jesus Christ, came to take us in His arms never to let us go again. His redeeming love would fulfill man's need for love.

Immanuel: God is with us to replace fear with exuberant joy! That is why the angel said on Christmas Night, "Do not be afraid." This world has become a maze of fear. Our anxiety complex is the fruit of sin. Since Adam fearfully hid from God in paradise, man has been experiencing countless uneasy fears. God's message at Christmas is: "Do not be afraid; I am with you."

Immanuel: God is with us to drive away the darkness with radiant light. Zechariah calls the Child of Bethlehem the Rising Sun "to shine on those living in darkness and in the shadow of death" (Lk. 1:79). He comes to put and end to sin and to guide us into the wonderful light of God. Christmas gives us the right to pray, "Lead, kindly Light, amid the encircling gloom, lead Thou me on!"

Immanuel: God is with us to replace destructive hatred with self-sacrificing love. He came to teach us that hate can be conquered only by love. That love always triumphs. That if God loved us so much that He gave His Son for our sins, we too should love one another and forgive one another. This way the Jesus Child is not born in Bethlehem, but in our hearts. Not only is God with us, but we are with God!

Gloria in excelsis Deo! Praise, praise the Lord! Amen.

Read: Luke 2:8-20

December 26

Have you accepted God's gift?

Today in the town of David a Savior has been born to you; he is Christ the Lord.

− LUKE 2:11 −

Christmas prompted us once again to either face the relentless demand to accept or reject Christ as God's gift. Our choice determines our temporary and eternal well-being.

Many people are overwhelmed by the idea of giving themselves unconditionally to Christ. For some reason they are afraid to accept God's gift unconditionally.

They fear their own unworthiness or incompetence; they fear complete surrender; they are even convinced that their sins from the past make it impossible for them to accept God's gift. The good news of Christmas, declared by the angel, is that God gave His Son to be the Redeemer and Savior of humankind on the basis of God's love that encompasses and forgives all.

The angel made this announcement not to a king or to the spiritual leaders of that time, but to simple and humble shepherds. This in itself should be an indication that God's Christmas gift, His Son, is for the whole world, also for you with your particular fears and needs.

If you hesitate to become a disciple of the living Redeemer, or if you feel undeserving, incompetent and afraid, just allow God's perfect love to fill your life. Christmas has come to deliver you from all guilt and all fear. Accept Christ as your Savior − He is God's Christmas gift to you. Allow Him to guide you and to control your life.

Accept Christ as your Lord and you will experience that the good news was in fact meant for all people. Then you have not only accepted God's gift with your hands, but also with all your heart and your entire life.

Glory to God in the highest, and on earth peace to men on whom His favor rests (Lk. 2:14). Amen.

December 27

Read: Romans 8:31-39

Never the same again

The shepherds returned, glorifying and praising God for all the things they had heard and seen, which were just as they had been told.

– LUKE 2:20 –

When I was a child, I often wished I could preserve the spirit of goodwill and love that is so noticeable at Christmas the way one does with choice fruit. Then one could open a bottle of the Christmas spirit at anytime of the year and it would benefit all.

There are some experiences in life which are soon forgotten, and others which will be remembered for a long time. The events of that unforgettable night when the angel of the Lord visited them, were captured in the memories of the shepherds forever. They would undoubtedly speak about it for the rest of their lives. They were perhaps overawed because the angels chose them for such a special visit.

One wonders if they ever met the Man whom they worshiped as a child in Bethlehem. Were they among the crowds who flocked to see Him who was declared Messiah? Were any of them also at the foot of the cross on Golgotha on that dark day? We will never know. However, we can safely assume that the lives of these humble shepherds could never be the same after worshiping Him in the manger on that first Christmas night.

If you have had the enriching experience of true worship; if you have been spiritually inspired while you lifted your heart in worship and praise, it is something which will remain with you forever.

There may be dark moments of doubt and you may long to relive the glory of that worship. Once you have experienced it, however, it becomes an inextricable part of your life. It simply means identification with Christ and a renewal of your spiritual strength.

Lord Jesus, I worship You and identify with You. I thank You for the glorious new life that I have gained through Your birth, life, death and resurrection. Amen.

Read: Romans 15:1-13

December 28

Christmas in practice

May the God of hope fill you with all joy and peace as you trust in him, so that you may overflow with hope by the power of the Holy Spirit.

— ROMANS 15:13 —

Christ should not remain in the manger for the Christian. From the manger He wants to bring peace to our tempestuous hearts. From the manger He touches our cold and guilty hearts and through His salvation He fills our hearts with pure joy and peace. That is the obvious meaning of Christmas. Yet, it is a truth so great that it makes our hearts rejoice because of Christmas.

Christmas is not done yet. It is not the last word about Christmas at all. Our spiritual laziness and self-centeredness often tempt us to be content with joy and peace. We delight in what Christmas holds for us personally. The Christmas message is, however, for "all people". Christmas should teach us to be light and salt to the world.

Our hearts should become a station for transmitting God's peace and joy to the world. We may not keep it to ourselves. God does not ask the impossible of us; just do the obvious, small deed. "But you will receive power when the Holy Spirit comes on you; and you will be my witnesses" (Acts 1:8).

Give a small piece of the joy and peace of Christmas to your life partner, to your neighbors, your children, your colleagues and your employees. Let them realize that you stood at the manger, and that the joy and peace of the manger touched your heart and warmed it.

In this way your faith will grow and your joy and peace will not be limited to Christmas, but will break forth to enrich and elevate every day of the year.

Christ of every day and every night, let the peace of Christmas make the world a better place throughout the whole year. Amen.

December 29

Read: 1 Corinthians 13:1-13

Steadfast things

And now these three remain: faith, hope and love. But the greatest of these is love.

– 1 Corinthians 13:13 –

Heraclitus cynically said, "There is nothing permanent, except change." During the transition between the old and the new year, we involuntarily seek steadfastness. We are inclined to think change and decline are all around us. It may be true, but we should pray: "O God who never changes, abide by me!"

The Word of the Lord assures us that there are indeed unchangeable things in this world: faith, hope and love.

Faith is lasting, says Paul. The writer of Hebrews says it is "being sure of what we hope for and certain of what we do not see" (Heb. 11:1). "Ultimately," Thomas Merton writes, "faith is the key to the universe. The final meaning of our human existence and the answers to the questions on which our happiness depends can be found in no other way."

Faith in God the Father as Creator and Supporter, faith in Jesus Christ, our Savior and Redeemer, and faith in the Holy Spirit as our Guide and Comforter gives permanence to our existence. Faith will remain until we see Him face to face, then faith will no longer be necessary.

Hope is steadfast. What oxygen means to the lungs, hope means to life, for hope gives meaning to life. This is Christian optimism. It is the struggle of the soul to break loose from the transient: a guarantee of immortality. Not to have it brings us to the terrible alternative – despair.

Love, Paul says, remains firm. We take it with us on our journey to eternity. "Love never fails" (1 Cor. 13:8). Without love our lives would have been a graveyard. Love brings radiant, sparkling and immortal life. That is why there is no substitute for love: love is the essence of life.

Lord, You know that I love You! I thank You that faith, hope and love remain constant. Amen.

Read: Ruth 2:1-23

December 30

Time to give account

"Where did you glean today? Where did you work?"

— RUTH 2:19 —

We sit at the almost burnt-out ashes of the old year and in front of us there is the uncertain light of the new year. Involuntarily our hearts incline towards self-examination. We think of the noble resolutions which burned so brightly in our hearts at the beginning of the year, and we are filled with either self-accusation or gratitude.

Did I glean enriching ears of corn in the past year? Was it just another year of unfulfilled intentions, neglect, stagnation and superficiality? Did I make time to enrich my spirit by reading good books, listening to inspiring music, appreciating art, and trying to bring beauty where there was no beauty?

Was there growth in my spiritual life; did my relationship with God gain in depth and quality? Did my relationship with Christ, the Holy Spirit, His Word, my church and my fellow man progress?

Where did I glean the vitally important ears of life; where did I use my strength? I was possibly gathering unimportant things because I could not identify the essential things. I was at the manger in Bethlehem where I could learn humility; I was in Gethsemane where I could begin to grasp something of the struggle in prayer with God; I was at Golgotha where I could learn the meaning of sacrifice. Did I neglect doing this because I was engaged in a pursuit of pleasure, wealth, greed and status?

The Almighty places before us beautiful ears of corn: a powerful life of prayer; sailing out on the deep waters of life; committed and faithful Bible study; a Christian way of life; meditation and worship.

May our spiritual successes inspire us to growth in the new year and may our failures bring us to God and His renewing grace.

My Savior, may I hear from Your lips the undeserved encouragement of "Well done!" because I carried out Your will through Your grace. Amen.

December 31

Read: Mark 4:35-41

With Christ

"Let us go over to the other side" … they took him along.
— MARK 4:35-36 —

The deepest desire of the Christian's heart is to conclude the year before the face of God and to enter the new, unknown year holding His hand. Everywhere around us the presence of God is visible, and He speaks to our souls in a thousand voices. But God speaks clearest through His Son in His eternal Word.

In the light of His Word we look back on the road along which we came and we plead for His light on the way ahead. It is not only the transience and fragility of life that are important today. The content of the past year is of cardinal significance.

You can count your years according to number or content. A long life which is empty of faith and labor, prayer and blessing, is very short if God measures it. A short life full of faith and growth, joy and grief, love and blessing for others could be long, if God puts His measuring-tape along it. The value of our lives is not determined by the length of our years, but by what we have put into those years, as a ship is evaluated according its cargo.

If we become quiet before God, we will hear Him say, "Let us go over to the other side!" He who gave direction to our lives during the past year wants to walk with us into the future. The past is irrevocably gone. For that we are grateful, but now we have to proceed into the future. And Christ wants to be our Guide. He has promised to be with us always.

The disciples set us an inspiring example. They took Jesus with them: they took His manger to teach them humility and dependence; His cross to teach them the most profound sense of sacrifice and they took His crown to allow them to live on victorious ground. If He is with us, all is well and we can face the darkness courageously, our hands firmly clasped by His almighty hand.

Eternal God, I worship You as the Omega of the old year and the Alpha of the new. Thank You that I may travel with You on Your triumphant journey through the centuries. Amen.